#FORWARDISM

#FORWARDISM
A BOLD AND IMAGINITIVE VOYAGE TO THE FUTURE

VINCO DAVID AND ADJIEDJ BAKAS

SOEMINTRA BOOKS

VINCO DAVID foundation

TRENDS BY
Bakas

© V. David Beheer bv, July 2025

P-ISBN: 978-93-7003-163-0
E-ISBN: 978-93-7003-456-3

Title: #Forwardism: A Bold and Imaginative Voyage to the Future
Authors: Adjiedj Bakas and Vinco David[†]
Editing and translation: Peter Mulville, Matsuda Mulville, The Netherlands
Publisher: Soemintra Books, an imprint of V. David Beheer bv, Almere, The Netherlands
Cover design: Wentelwereld, Thierry Tetenburg, The Netherlands
Cover illustration: Rolffimages, New York
Authors' photo: Lace, The Netherlands

Printed in India

Contents

Part 4
Bold Choices

Part 5
Some Ideas for the Future

Foreword

In 2025, the year in which *#Forwardism* is released, major shipyards in China, Japan and the Republic of Korea are once again operating at full capacity, with orders for new ships increasing at a rate not seen since before the 2008 financial crisis. This is great news—world trade is on the rise again.

Yet China, the workshop of the world, is ageing so rapidly that the Netherlands must look for other trading partners as a partial replacement. The Scientific Council for Government Policy (WRR) has concluded that India is the most logical alternative.

In its analysis *From Made in China to Made in India?*, the WRR notes that while concerns over excessive dependence on China are top of the political agenda, the country's demographic developments receive little attention. 'The question is whether China will still be able to produce the goods that are imported in large numbers by the Netherlands in the coming decades, or whether it will give priority to it.' China's ageing population means it will have approximately 220 million fewer workers by 2050—a shrinkage of 20 per cent. 'The size of this decline is equal to the total working population of the European Union in 2023.'

For decades, China's surplus labour force in the countryside enabled it to produce goods cheaply. That surplus is now dwindling, urban migration is decreasing and wages are rising faster than ever before. Chinese companies, increasingly making high-quality products, can afford to pay higher wages, but there will come a time when they can no longer sustain this. 'To put it bluntly, China has fewer and fewer people available for production work to fill the Western, and therefore also Dutch, store shelves,' writes the WRR.

Furthermore, as the Chinese middle class grows, domestic consumption increases, leaving less room for exports. Of course, the Chinese government can turn all kinds of buttons to maintain the export success for as long as possible. Think of encouraging larger families, raising the retirement age and further increasing labour productivity, which remains lower than in the Netherlands or the US.

But assuming the Netherlands wants to maintain its position as a global hub and continue filling its store shelves with cheap products, it is necessary to focus on new production countries. According to the WRR, Indonesia, Vietnam, the Philippines and Malaysia can boast a growing working population 'certainly until 2050', but in terms of size they are not the ideal successor to China. The greatest 'demographic potential' lies in India, which overtook China as the world's most populous country in 2023 and is set to continue growing until 2070.

Compared to its larger neighbour, India's manufacturing industry is still relatively small, although the government is striving to expand it. One downside is India's protectionist policy. High import tariffs make imported semi-finished products expensive, which in turn raises the cost of final production.

The WRR concludes that to become the 'new factory of the world', India has a long way to go, including in terms of bureaucracy. The same applies to Sub-Saharan Africa, which is currently dealing with 'greening': an increasing number of younger people in society. The combination of enormous population growth and abundant cheap labour sounds ideal, but the WRR is sceptical. 'Demographic momentum or dividend in Sub-Saharan Africa alone is probably not enough to attract a substantial share of global production.' The WRR advises the Dutch government to strengthen trade and investment relations with multiple countries and regions that are not facing an ageing population crisis. Betting on one horse seems unwise. Given the large-scale investments in infrastructure and the well-integrated production chains, Chinese production is 'difficult to replace'.

Visionaries Adjiedj Bakas and Vinco David anticipated this shift years ago when they began writing *#Forwardism*. In this inspirational book, they examine the economic megatrends reshaping the world, particularly in nations with a demographic dividend of many young people. These new generations aspire to progress quickly—starting with Generation Z, people born between 1997 and 2012, following the Millennials. The oldest members of Generation Z reached their late 20s in 2024, with many completing college, getting married and starting families, while the youngest will be aged around 12. Generation Alpha, individuals born between 2010 and 2024, will be succeeded by Generation Beta, encompassing those born between 2025 and 2039.

India boasts so many ambitious young people that it could truly become the second workshop of the world. And for the Netherlands, strengthening economic ties with India is therefore extremely important.

Here at the Dutch embassy, we applaud #*Forwardism*, in which the authors focus on what is possible instead of what is not. Their approach is pragmatic and practical, yet also creative. Their out-of-the-box thinking resonates with us, as does their advocacy for *Karma Capitalism* and *Happynomy*—the Economy of Happiness.

I do hope that you will enjoy this insightful book as much as I did.

—Bernd Scholtz
Head of the Economic Department,
Embassy of the Kingdom of the Netherlands, India

Embassy of the
Kingdom of the Netherlands

Authors' Note

Dear readers,

This book is a bold voyage into the future. We, the authors, are your tour guides. We share our rich knowledge with you. It was an immense pleasure to write this book, which is filled with hope, opportunities, positivity and optimism. This book is for everybody—whether you live in a city or a rural area. Everyone needs hope and optimism in life.

Despite that, many people lack knowledge about the big shift that is now taking place in the world. With this book, we want to enrich and inspire you. We want you to embrace all the opportunities you have. You can then choose the right path, the right education, learn the right skills and make the best decisions to live a good life. We hope that our enthusiasm ignites yours.

Due to AI-driven teaching, every child—even one living in the most remote village—will soon have Einstein as their teacher, despite the shortage of 'human' teachers. However, you don't have to wait for this to happen. This book opens up your mind, reshapes your mindset and offers you plenty of interesting ideas. With self-help, self-empowerment and self-organization, you can turn these ideas into reality.

Let's take an example. Due to an ageing population in Europe, job opportunities for young Indians are plenty. Portugal already offers visas to youngsters from India and Nepal to work in tourism and healthcare there. Europe is also one big Disneyland for tourists from all over the world. Within five years of working in these countries, you would have saved enough money to buy your own house in India. Your youth is a valuable asset! In depopulated rural areas in Portugal, Spain, France and Italy, you can buy a whole empty village for just $1. Of course, you have to renovate these houses, which have been uninhabited for years. But if you are handy and teach yourselves (via YouTube) timbering, laying bricks, plastering, painting, renewing electricity and plumbing, you can do it yourself. With a group of friends, you can start your own community, make good money and grow your savings while learning new languages and cultures. Isn't it nice to try this out for a while? You don't have to, but we interviewed many young Indians and Nepalese who chose such a lifestyle happily for a shorter or longer period of time.

We are both born optimists—a glass is always half full for us. Although we both graduated from renowned Dutch universities, we are no scientists and hence have decided not to write academic books. We are strictly storytellers. So you will not find one single footnote in this story. If we quote someone, we name our source, and if you want to know more about their works, Google, ChatGPT or DeepSeek will help you out. We thus invite you to just open up your mind, enjoy the story, let all the knowledge that we share with you sink in and let loose the emotions that this story invokes in you. Just enjoy! Feel the hope, feel the opportunities, get energized and embrace the brave new world this book describes.

Dear readers, the authors of this travelogue into the future are from the Global North—the rich, Western part of the world—which is now ageing fast. We have authored 42 books previously, which were only written for our regular audience in the Global North. One of our books was translated into Chinese and two others were translated into Brazilian-Portuguese, but those were translations of a purely 'Western' book. Now, for the first time, we have penned a book that is targeted specifically to the youth in the Global South.

With this book, we want to change your mindset. Indians typically are not known for rocking the boat. They don't have the mindset to get up and change radically, like the Chinese do. Probably this mindset is a remnant of the caste system that kept people in place for millennia. In combination with the shackles of the infamous Indian bureaucracy, this mindset prevents Indians from shifting into the superpower mode that is the need of the hour. We aim to stir up this risk-abiding mindset of passivity. So, dear readers, please arise and transform yourselves!

We started the research for this book back in 2010. In our lives, we have travelled extensively all over the world, both in the Global North and in the Global South. We are happy that so many people in the Global South have achieved so much in the past 50 years (yes, we are old men).

However, we believe that even more Indians can earn higher incomes if they make use of the knowledge that we share with them here. As mentioned before, you should view this book as a source of knowledge and inspiration. In the Netherlands, a book like this is considered a part of the popular-scientific genre, as it combines (scientific) information with entertainment. It can also be referred to as 'infotainment'. Think of it as a film script of a futuristic Bollywood movie—without the songs and dance. Fantasize the song and dance while reading it, if you wish.

Are you afraid that you don't have enough talent to make good use of all that this book teaches you? The fact that jellyfish have survived for 650 million years without brains gives hope to many people. So, don't worry.

Are you gay or lesbian and are afraid that you cannot take advantage of all the opportunities that we discuss in this book? Don't worry either. We have been a happily married gay couple for 25 years and have built a successful international career. Despite our openly gay lifestyle, nobody has ever dared to discriminate against us. Ever.

The future is not for people who are afraid. The future belongs to those who dare. And with this book, we dare you to dare!

Amsterdam–Almere, New Delhi,
Mumbai, summer 2025.
Adjiedj Bakas
Vinco David[†]

[†]Deceased in 2023

Introduction: Welcome to the Age of #Forwardism

Sharda is dozing in her beach chair in Cornwall. She is 54 and leads a busy yet happy life. She is reading a novel while her heart surgery takes place. A minuscule robot has been implanted via her veins into her body, and it's currently walking in and around her heart, repairing everything that's in need of repair. The whole cardiac area, including the endocardium and pericardium, will be as good as new by the end of the afternoon. Without surgery. Without any pain. The only thing that bothers her is that, while this operation takes place, she is not allowed to use any computer, mobile phone or any other electronic equipment, as it may disrupt the mini-robot working on her heart. So she is stuck with old-fashioned magazines and books again: nostalgia meets modernity. She shrugs. Next week, she will get a new ear. She had a car accident several weeks ago, and since then, her left ear has not been functioning well. The insurance company decided that repairing it would prove too expensive. A new human ear is currently being grown on a mouse in the hospital, tailor-made and designed just for her. It will be ready next week, and then her old ear will be removed and replaced by the brand new one. After she recovers, she will get a new kidney, collected from Miss Piggy 77—a sweet pig that will donate one of her kidneys to Sharda. Nowadays, pig parts fit very well into human bodies, so pigs are used more for medical purposes than culinary ones. The Party of the Animals in the European Parliament wants to stop this practice, but this predominantly Dutch-British party is hardly taken seriously in Europe. That's why they stick to terrorism. The clinic warned Sharda to be discreet about her pig's kidney, to avoid attracting too much unwanted attention to the clinic.

We no longer live in times of change but in a change of times. The world order is shifting from unipolar to multipolar; demographics and power structures are evolving at an incredible rate. Unlike anything we've seen before, a revolution in innovation and technology is accelerating human progress.

The Age of Chaos has begun. In early Greek cosmology, chaos was a mythological abyss—an emptiness that existed before the universe and everything in it were created. History tells us that all momentous change is preceded by chaos.

The 15th century was an Age of Chaos too. Mankind faced extreme weather, torrential rain, raging rivers, rising seas and other natural disasters. Yet, as terrible as they were, these adversities triggered innovation. The Dutch built dykes to protect their land from floods; Florence lost a third of its population to the plague but emerged as one of the world's major centres of invention, art and architecture; Germany lost one-third of its population in a civil war between Catholics and Protestants but almost simultaneously gifted the world the printing press.

India, too, suffered its own Age of Chaos. In 1526, after a lengthy period of restlessness and violence, the Mughal Empire united India's separate kingdoms under the rule of Emperor Babur, a descendant of the famed Uzbek king Timur. This new and powerful empire remained largely peaceful during much of the 17th century—a factor in India's economic expansion—thanks to the efficient, centralized and standardized way in which it was ruled.

At that time, the areas we now call China and India accounted for 80 per cent of the world's gross domestic product (GDP), while Europe, Africa, the Americas and Australia collectively made up only 20 per cent. The Taj Mahal stands as a proud testament to that great era. Mughal administration records refer to the empire as the 'dominion of Hindustan' or the 'country of Hind', though it became widely known as Hindustan. The empire's decline began in 1707 and ended with British colonization.

According to renowned economist Utsa Patnaik, Britain drained India of nearly $45 trillion during colonial rule. To put this staggering sum into perspective, $45 trillion is 17 times the total annual GDP of the UK today. So, India seemingly financed Britain's Industrial Revolution. From the 15th century onwards, geopolitical and economic power shifted from East to West—the former declining while the latter transformed into a global powerhouse. But now, in the 21st century, the pendulum is swinging back. The times are always changing, and we are changing with them.

Economic Growth; Changing Business

The Chinese word for 'crisis' comprises two elements: danger and opportunity. Both prove true in an Age of Chaos. Over the past few years, central banks around the world have lowered their interest rates and are now laying the groundwork for a transition to life with less stimulus. And during this chaotic transition, capital will flow from low-interest to high-interest regions.

Matterhorn Asset Management's Matthew Piepenburg claims a fundamental change during Alan Greenspan's time as Chairman of the Federal Reserve (the Fed) turned Wall Street into 'a circus'; he asserts that current policies—and their harmful solutions—would have been unthinkable in the past. Piepenburg believes that things will end badly for the US due to Wall Street's toxic relationship with the Fed, a declining currency, artificial markets, rising inflation and a weakening reserve currency.

Many of today's financial problems are blamed on COVID-19, a crisis that justified extraordinary levels of government spending. And yet, markets continue to believe in the narrative of a transitory solution. Higher inflation—accompanied by social and political unrest on a global scale—is the only politically viable way to address debt. Because preserving purchasing power matters more than price stability, Piepenburg says gold (insurance for currency) will surge when faith in markets is lost.

Men Love War, Women Love Soldiers

Major conflicts often emerge in an Age of Chaos. The turbulent 1950s-1960s saw the Vietnam War, the Korean War and the Indo-Pakistani War of 1965. Today, we are witnessing conflicts in Ukraine and Gaza. Despite all human innovation, one trend remains: men love war and women love soldiers.

Some thinkers argue that the industrialized military might of the West wants wars to continue indefinitely—to maintain US-led world order and prevent the rise of a new multipolar world order. Whether they are correct or not is debatable, but one thing is certain: the West cannot fight multiple wars on different fronts simultaneously. So a third war in Asia (over Taiwan, perhaps) is unlikely.

However, tensions persist in Asia and must be addressed. Animosity between China and countries in the South China Sea, such as the Philippines, remains a major issue. And social unrest in India's neighbours—Sri Lanka, Bangladesh and Myanmar—adds to the region's volatility.

The Taiwanization of China

Following the financial crisis of 2008, China positioned itself as an economic locomotive, pulling the world towards recovery. However, its real-estate investments—an important part of that locomotive—not only expanded too quickly but also were based on terms deemed too risky. The Chinese real-estate boom ground to a halt in 2020 when the government bailed out property-development giant Evergrande. While China will certainly avoid a deep recession or even depression, it may not be able to avert a prolonged, grinding semi-slump that profoundly reshapes global perceptions of the country.

Meanwhile, AUKUS—a trilateral strategic defence alliance between Australia, the UK and the US—was formed in 2021. Initially focusing on developing a new generation of nuclear-powered submarines, AUKUS has since broadened its mission to include advanced technologies and increased cooperation in the Indo-Pacific region, where China's rise is seen as a growing threat. This evolution suggests that China may need to adopt a less assertive stance, both economically and militarily.

Tensions between India and China over their disputed border in Kashmir also require a quick and peaceful resolution. Similarly, the wars in Ukraine and Gaza must end at the negotiating table soon.

Israel is an AI and hi-tech powerhouse—the world's second largest Silicon Valley—from where most of the hardware or software for our computers and smartphones originates. India and Israel share a strong partnership in various sectors.

Taiwan, seeking neither to be a puppet of the US nor to lie in ruins like Ukraine, may ultimately rejoin China voluntarily to avoid destruction. Should this happen, it will lead to the Taiwanization of China, where many citizens, unhappy with Xi's regime, view Taiwan as a better and happier version of their country. The US will step back because warmongering over Taiwan will not pay off.

An Energy Revolution

The war in Ukraine has led to western sanctions against Russia, a superpower, which in turn shifted its focus from West to East. Asian countries now buy more oil, liquefied natural gas (LNG) and natural gas from Russia than ever before. India, in turn, re-exports some of this energy back to Europe, bypassing sanctions—a big win for India because Europe cannot function without Russian energy.

There is more than enough oil, LNG and natural gas to meet global energy demands for decades to come. However, because some energy sources are either politically restricted (nuclear, coal, oil) or unable to meet the increased demand (renewables), more energy sources are needed to sustain a 21st-century global economy.

UN: World 700 per cent Richer by the Year 2099

With the global population now at 8 billion and expected to reach 11 billion by the end of the 21st century, economic growth will continue. The United Nations (UN) expects global GDP to be seven times higher by 2099, making humanity 700 per cent richer. If we therefore distribute our increasing wealth in the right way, we can eradicate poverty. Humanity will also benefit if we heed the UN's advice and spend 2 per cent of our growing GDP annually on adapting to climate change and extreme weather. The recent droughts in Delhi (North India) and floods in Kerala (South India) prove we must adapt, but adaptation is expensive.

Abiotic Oil and Gas

While some people argue that we must stop using fossil fuels, the 'abiogenic hypothesis' suggests the Earth will forever produce oil and gas for humanity's use. First proposed by German mineralogist Georgius Agricola in the 16th century, the hypothesis is that oil and gas do not originate from fossil deposits. Instead, they are formed from deep carbon deposits (known as abiotic oil) that have existed since our planet was formed, meaning that, theoretically, the planet will continue to generate oil and gas indefinitely. If this hypothesis is correct, Peak Oil and Peak Gas will never occur.

Although more and more people are choosing hybrid or electric cars nowadays, most drivers still prefer petrol or diesel engines. There is also more than enough uranium and thorium for humanity to fuel nuclear power stations for centuries. So with an abundance of energy and newly found natural resources, we can turn the 21st century into a new Golden Age.

The Age of Plenty

Meanwhile, the cost of generating green hydrogen gas through electrolysis is coming down. When burnt in a fuel cell alongside oxygen, hydrogen produces heat (with water as a by-product). Most importantly, the process is clean, with no carbon emissions or other forms of pollution. In fact, hydrogen energy can generate the heat necessary for some industrial processes—something that cannot be produced in a cost-effective way by using renewable sources of energy like wind or the sun.

Traditionally, extracting hydrogen from methane or water has been an inefficient process, requiring vast amounts of electricity. Due to the excessive cost of production, hydrogen failed to compete with other energy sources. Moreover, hydrogen is not only highly combustible but also uneconomical to transport over long distances (hydrogen tanks would be prohibitively large). However, in much the same way as natural gas is converted into LNG for portability where pipelines are unavailable or inadequate (across oceans, for example), recent research suggests hydrogen could be turned into ammonia. With an energy density three times higher than hydrogen, ammonia is far less flammable, potentially avoiding disasters such as the Hindenburg fire. Furthermore, infrastructure for the large-scale production and distribution of ammonia is already in place, thanks to its important commercial role in the petrochemical and agricultural industries.

Although some people or nations have written off using nuclear power for electricity and transportation, the same cannot be said on a global scale. Companies such as Rolls-Royce are developing small modular reactors (SMRs), as will be discussed later. We will also see more uranium- and thorium-powered nuclear power stations in the future.

The 21st century will be defined by its energy resources. While many Western youngsters believe humanity will go extinct because of climate change, the reality is different. The UN expects an average person to earn 450 per cent of today's income by 2100, but climate change is expected to reduce that to 434 per cent. The authors believe that climate change is certainly a problem, but it is not an apocalyptic threat. So move on, enjoy life and don't worry too much, folks.

AI and Robotics on the Rise

Humanity will benefit from revolutionary innovation happening around our hyper-connected world. A fine example is the robot from China that not only carries luggage but also does the shopping. Or the Republic of Korea's idea to ship people's airport purchases through underground tubes to their departure aircraft, or even directly to their homes. The country's shipbuilder Hyundai is also building autonomous, self-steering tankers and cargo ships that no longer require sailors to spend long, lonely periods at sea.

Beijing's Daxing Airport shows us what future airports and airport cities will look like. Artificial Intelligence and Facial Recognition (AI+FR) will make logistics, the entire boarding process, shopping and entertainment options less bureaucratic and more customer-friendly. This hi-tech combination of AI+FR will advance further, making most administrative jobs redundant, and healthcare, banking and many other industries more efficient. The boring and mundane will be more fun.

Hi-tech innovation also enables cybercriminals to operate. Digital crime is causing enormous damage to businesses and governments everywhere. The Italian government recently announced it will invest more than €11 billion to fight ransomware and other forms of online criminality. More governments and businesses are expected to follow a similar approach. Ongoing digitization has other setbacks too. In 2024, many Windows-based systems around the world stopped working simultaneously because of a security issue. Although resolved within days, the financial and commercial damage was enormous. We must prepare ourselves for more digital crises in the future.

In 1970, China was poorer than Somalia, but today it is a superpower. A few errors made during its rapid development are now having visible effects. Overusing groundwater has led to the sinking of coastal Chinese cities and their heavy skyscrapers. Hence, it is necessary to implement desalination technology and seawater distribution to reduce groundwater use for agriculture and public consumption, preventing further sinking. Surrounded by water, India can utilize Israeli desalination technology to mass-produce water, distributing it everywhere to make the countryside greener. There is also a need for better preservation of rainwater for reuse during the dry season, as currently demonstrated by technology in Thailand.

Much like the competition between VHS and Betamax videotape formats in earlier decades, the 21st century's Digitization and Industry 4.0 revolution has two standards— the Western and the Chinese. However, successful companies worldwide must be able to work with both standards. Through its Belt and Road Initiative (BRI)—sometimes referred to as the New Silk Road—China will develop routes to ship both goods and money, making the yuan the most important currency unit in every country connected via these routes. Information technology (IT) will flow along these routes too, with exported Chinese technology reaching all destinations throughout the Global South.

BRICS and the Global South: A Geopolitical Shift

The most important power bloc on the rise today is BRICS. The name is an acronym, formed from the initials of its founder members: Brazil, Russia, India, China and South Africa. While BRICS members Russia and China have an ageing population, many others—populous Indonesia or Nigeria, for example—have a demographic dividend in the form of young people. The organization exercises influence on the Global South countries that have, since the end of World War II, been traditionally influenced by the US. Significant consequences of this power shift include the de-dollarization of international trade and the Sinicization of hi-tech in countries where Huawei has replaced the authority of Apple and Microsoft. The dominance of Chinese AI will increase further to compete with the US AI. The Indian IT industry, which until now has been US-oriented, will need to adapt to this crucial change. Students at over 2,000 Indian IT universities must learn how to operate Chinese software and hardware. Nonetheless, India (an AI superpower) has the advantage of operating independently in both markets.

Aerohaptic Holograms Are on their Way

The popular *Star Trek* TV franchise has introduced millions of viewers to the idea of a 'holodeck'—an immersive, realistic 3D holographic projection of a complete environment in which participants can interact with, and even touch, their surroundings.

In the 21st century, holograms already have a variety of applications, such as medical, education, art, security and defence. Scientists are also developing new ways to use lasers, modern digital processors and motion-sensing technologies to create innovative holograms that could change how we interact. Researchers in Glasgow have developed a hologram that allows you to reach out and feel it—much like what the holodeck participants experience on *Star Trek*. According to Ravinder Dahiya, a researcher who worked on the Glasgow project, this hologram system uses jets of air known as 'aerohaptics' to replicate the sensation of touch. Aerohaptics allow users to feel others' fingers, hands and wrists. This technology could, in time, enable us to virtually meet colleagues on the other side of the world 'and really feel their handshake'.

Like previous touch-sensory holograms, the aerohaptic system doesn't require a handheld controller or smart gloves. Instead, a nozzle, responding to the movements of our hand, blows air with an appropriate amount of force. Dahiya and his team have evaluated this with an interactive projection of a basketball. Using aerohaptics, subjects can feel the virtual surface of the ball as they roll it around, throw it and catch it.

Aerohaptics could even be the beginning of something like a holodeck. While we don't expect scientists to be delivering the full *Star Trek* experience soon, they are boldly going in new directions to add exciting functionality to the existing systems. We can soon expect hologram users to feel hot or cold surfaces if the airflow temperature is modified. Scientists are also exploring the possibility of adding airflow scents, increasing the interactive experience of virtual objects by allowing users to smell them as well. So if we lived far away from our loved ones, we could still touch, smell and feel their holograms. It could also help clinicians to collaborate on treatments and patients to feel more involved and informed. Doctors could view and discuss tumour cells, or show patients what happens during a medical procedure in detail. This Age of Chaos is leading us to a great new order.

Demographics Are Radically Changing

By 2050, the expected world population (around 10 billion) will be an ageing population, meaning companies must be prepared to engage with more elderly or disabled customers and foreign visitors.

The combined middle-class people in India and China, numbering more than 800 million, love to travel. While Europe, with a current population of 744 million, remains the wealthiest, most compact and most diverse continent, it will gradually change into a Pleasure Empire or Leisure Empire—one large open-air Disneyland for tourists from all over the world. From an economic perspective, that is not necessarily a terrible outcome.

From 2050 onwards, demographics will change radically, slowing down population growth. From 10 billion in 2050, the world population is expected to reach only 11 billion by 2099. Industries must, therefore, not only adapt to more consumers over the next 25–30 years but also be prepared to stabilize in line with population growth thereafter. Companies must be organized in ways that allow them to survive the post-2100 stagnation easily and in a sustainable manner.

The population of China, for example, is expected to decline by 50 per cent this century. The world population will stagnate for several reasons. Most of today's elderly baby boomers will die within the next 20 years, which means ageing will peak in 2040 because Millennials and Generation Z, especially well-educated women in these generations, want fewer children. Men are also facing increasing fertility issues (male infertility is partly due to microplastics in our bodies). Furthermore, from 2050 onwards, many people are expected to prefer the Emotional Machine—a robotic copy of themselves, perfectly capable of expressing emotions. Imagine if we could buy a flawless replica of ourselves, without having to change its dirty nappies!

It is needless to say that a stagnating world population after the year 2100 is also good for the environment.

Gender and Minorities

Running the household was a full-time job during our grandmothers' time. Now, thanks to innovative modern appliances like washing machines, vacuum cleaners, fridges and freezers, household chores take a fraction of the time, empowering women to enter the job market en masse. As modern society benefits from female brainpower and talent much more than in earlier centuries, it could be said that the Industrial Revolution paved the way for women's liberation.

Minorities exist in every country, facing difficulties and discrimination in most of them. It takes a long time for the true value of minorities to be recognized. A recent genetic study in Spain suggests Christopher Columbus was Jewish and Spanish, rather than Italian. So, while Spain violently discriminated against its Jewish population, Columbus discovered the Americas in the name of the Spanish king, delivering home enormous riches. The Allied victory in World War II was partly owed to the endeavours of Alan Turing, a brilliant mathematician and gay man. Born in London in 1912, he studied at both Cambridge and Princeton universities before cracking the Nazi Enigma code, intercepting their secret communications and winning the war. Yet he faced rampant discrimination. Prosecuted for homosexuality, he chose chemical castration instead of a prison sentence, and within a couple of years, committed suicide by eating a poisoned apple. Sixty years later, in 2013, Queen Elizabeth II granted the late Turing a rare 'mercy pardon'.

In present-day BRICS member states and Global South countries, according to the World Pride Organization around 5–10 per cent of the population is gay or bisexual. Their lives are often difficult, but many countries allow them to live freely to benefit from the talents of their own 'Alan

Turings' so that the populations can develop and progress.

Medieval Italy benefitted enormously from the talents of great artists like Michelangelo, Botticelli and Leonardo da Vinci, all of whom might have been gay or bisexual. Their renowned artworks, such as Michelangelo's painting of the Sistine Chapel ceiling in Vatican City, attract millions of visitors annually and contribute to the global image of Italy as a country rich in art and culture. Some historical evidence suggests the Macedonian king Alexander the Great was openly gay or bisexual, as was Mughal emperor Babur.

Many Chinese emperors were publicly gay or bisexual too, and successfully led their country to become a superpower. Ancient China accepted sexual and gender diversity; gay men were known as 'men of the cut sleeve'—a phrase dating back to the Han dynasty. The historical tale follows a gay Chinese emperor lying on a bed with his lover, whose head rested on the silk sleeve of the emperor's gown. The emperor had to leave but did not want to disturb his lover's sleep. So he took a pair of scissors and cut off his silk sleeve instead.

Taiwan, Nepal and Thailand are so far the only Asian countries to recognize same-sex marriage. Gay marriage has been legal in Brazil since 2013 and in South Africa since 2006. In Russia, homosexuality remains a stigma, although many gay men and lesbian women have contributed to Russia's rise to greatness.

What authorities in India and China—and many other countries—forget is that homosexuality is simply a part of being human, as it is amongst mammals.

More Men than Women

According to Human Rights Watch's Brian Stauffer, *Newsweek*, around 30–40 years ago, informed its female readers aged over 40 that they were more likely to be killed by terrorists than find a husband. Women are considered the victims facing the horrible fate of remaining single for being too many in numbers. The World Health Organization (WHO) suggested a ratio of 105 male births to every 100 female births, in keeping with men's lower life expectancy. For decades, the boy-to-girl birth ratio in China has sometimes exceeded 120 boys for every 100 girls, while it is significantly more than 105 boys for every 100 girls in India. There are an estimated 80 million extra men in these two countries alone.

Stauffer describes an Indian law that makes it illegal to screen the sex of foetuses for the purpose of sex-selective abortions (in favour of boys). China's one-child policy, implemented between 1979 and 2015, followed similar aims, encouraging many parents to prefer a boy as their only child. Whether it's garden-variety sexism or parents' genuine belief that a son is needed to care for them financially and provide grandchildren, such a perspective stems from gender discrimination. It leads to a shortage of brides and harmful human consequences in areas where bride traffickers prey on the vulnerable. Women and girls in countries bordering China could find themselves 'sold' for around $3,000–$13,000 to Chinese parents struggling to find brides for their sons. Often locked in rooms and repeatedly raped until pregnant, these unfortunate women are sometimes permitted to 'escape' after childbirth, but without their children.

According to Stauffer, the trafficking of brides and young women is already a problem in Cambodia, North Korea and Vietnam, and may soon become more widespread. The situation has escalated with no solution in hand, leading to social instability, workforce distortions, economic shifts and increasing violence against women. A shortage of women has harmful consequences for everyone on the planet. While sex-selective abortion is outlawed in India and China's one-child policy was replaced by a two-child and later a three-child policy, these 'prohibitions are often both ineffective and a threat to women's rights'. Urgent action is needed across the world to combat violence against women, gender discrimination, trafficking and a preference for male children.

A surplus of boys could lead to bigger issues like violence, terrorism and conflict on both a local and global scale. As will be discussed later, a huge surplus of young men could lead to civil war in countries such as India, a risk Indo-Caribbean author V.S. Naipaul writes about in his book *India: A Million Mutinies Now*. India, therefore, delivers many of its male soldiers to the UN Peacekeeping forces and sends many more young men to work in the Middle East. Only time will tell if these policies are effective enough. For now, the authors advise India, where violent crimes against women are common, to quickly introduce gay marriage legislation, as a shortage of women (or a surplus of men) leads to sexual frustration, rape and more heinous acts.

In many societies, it remains culturally or legally unacceptable that men have sex with one another, let alone form a marital relationship. For example, Pakistani men watch gay porn on Pornhub more than any other country, despite Pakistan having (officially and unofficially), a homophobic society.

The End of Poverty?

Global poverty has decreased immensely since 1990. India and China now have a large middle class of hundreds of millions of people, something that did not exist in the

1970s. It is the same story in countries across the Global South, where the number of middle-class citizens increases as poverty decreases. However, the World Bank says the trend is slowing down after COVID-19.

Writing for the daily Dutch newspaper *Het Financieele Dagblad*, Marcel de Boer and Marijn Jongsma report that 8.5 per cent of the global population (690 million people) live in extreme poverty, which is significantly less than in 1990. By 2030, 80 per cent of global poverty is expected to be concentrated in sub-Saharan countries where inequality is high and economic growth is low. Blighted by debt, financial mismanagement and conflict, some countries in Africa are among the world's poorest, gaining little from globalization trends happening elsewhere. African populations are vulnerable to the effects of climate change and extreme weather, unlike in Asia, where people are more susceptible but suffer less. According to the World Bank, loss from natural disasters in the poorest countries between 2011 and 2023 was five times higher than the average in slightly wealthier countries—the cost of adapting to climate change in poorer countries is five times higher too. The problems of climate change are compounded by less international aid flowing into Africa nowadays, leading to expensive financing for the poorest countries. Furthermore, poorer populations suffer from multiple deprivations simultaneously. Whether it is the effects of an unhealthy diet (exacerbated by fluctuating food prices combined with a derisory income), lack of local educational and healthcare facilities, or the impact of regional conflict, their basic needs are not being met.

New Aircraft Changes Travelling

The next generation of aircraft is multipurpose, more fuel-efficient and more sustainable. A successor to the once popular Concorde is already in development. The new model is likely to be a hypersonic aircraft, enabling us to fly from New Delhi to London in just two hours. Nuclear-powered flying resorts are also being developed, offering enormous hotel rooms, sports facilities, restaurants, conference facilities and much more. Before long, airships capable of landing in the impenetrable jungles of Africa and elsewhere will take to the skies, transporting materials and people in the quest for natural resources. Huge amounts of gold deposits have been discovered recently under the dense jungles of Uganda, which is currently a poor country.

At the opposite end of the air-travel spectrum, small electric aircraft with a dozen or so passengers will soon be operating in remote areas, increasing human mobility and enabling commuters to live further from their place of work. These 'flying buses' don't even need an airport; a 300-metre airstrip on a closed section of the highway, on a piece of farmland or on the roof of a conference centre will suffice. By adding a third dimension of airborne commuter traffic, pressure on the road and rail networks will decrease. Another advantage of electric aircraft is their lower CO_2 emissions.

Space tourism, already an affordable luxury for the ultra-rich, will be a possibility for many more intrepid travellers in the near future. This sector requires additional 'spaceports'—the facilities and infrastructure for spacecraft to depart from and return to Earth.

The United Arab Emirates (UAE) is embarking on a bold journey. In 2024, it unveiled plans for a 1,200-mile underwater high-speed railway from Dubai to Mumbai, two megacities with many existing business connections. Elon Musk has also proposed a fast underwater bullet train connection under the Atlantic Ocean, connecting the megacities of London and New York. This initiative isn't just about getting from place A to place B—it's about creating an immersive, awe-inspiring travel experience that promises breathtaking views beneath the ocean surface. These types of ambitious leaps in transportation could soon redefine how we crisscross the world.

While the future of travel offers exciting possibilities, moving around the globe also presents some worrying challenges, such as human trafficking.

Travel Infrastructure as a Weapon of Mass Migration

Many rogue states allow (or use) weapons of mass migration, a term coined by author Kelly M. Greenhill, to be used against their neighbours or against other wealthier countries. A weapon of mass migration is a way to blackmail. In *Weapons of Mass Migration*, Greenhill argues that North Korea blackmails China. If China does not give in to North Korea's demands, this country threatens to send disruptive waves of Korean migrants to China. There is an extensive network of human traffickers in Africa, Asia, Latin America, Europe and North America. The Nigerian Mafia, for instance, earns more through trafficking humans to Europe than through trafficking drugs, according to the Chartered Institute of Bankers of Nigeria (CIBN). The same is true for the Italian Mafia, according to Europol, the European Police Organization.

Whenever rich countries or regions fail to meet the demands of rogue states or human traffickers (or the NGOs who legitimize their activities through collaboration), the floodgates are opened and illegal immigrants flow across the borders towards better economic opportunities. Denmark and Sweden are the first northern European countries to recognize this as a geopolitical weapon and have accordingly introduced strict measures to curb illegal migration. This problem, however, is not particular to Europe. Walls, fences and barriers are being built by wealthy countries across the world to prevent poor immigrants from illegally pouring into their land. As South Africa and Brazil are building walls along their borders, European countries are following suit. A high border fence has already been erected along the Greece–Turkey border. Hungary and other eastern European countries have built fences and walls to stop an influx of immigrants from Syria, Afghanistan and Africa. Lithuania is also building a wall along its border with Belarus.

The fortification of Europe has consequences for tourism. As borders and border controls return, the free movement of people is curtailed. We can expect border walls to be built in Asia too.

Al-Qaeda and Islamic State (IS) are invigorated and already active in populous regions of Africa and Europe. They have recruited Syrian and Afghan refugees who entered Europe when civil war erupted in their homelands. Meanwhile, ever since the Taliban took over in Afghanistan, the supposedly dead son of Osama bin Laden has started training a new generation of terrorists in the revived training camps there.

Higher Taxes and Climatism's Influence on Flying

Having spent billions during the COVID-19 pandemic, many governments in the world require substantial finance. Consequently, we can expect to pay more tax. Treasury departments will introduce new taxation in areas that impact climate change, and lawmakers will legislate against tax evasion, curtailing tax dodges. Higher taxation for working citizens leaves them with less disposable income for activities such as travel. While we need to adapt to extreme weather and climate change, will less flying benefit humanity? The authors don't believe so.

Although more new aircraft than ever before are being purchased by low-cost airlines in Asia, such as IndiGo in India, climate and its policies have an impact on much more than flying and travel.

Adapting to Extreme Weather and Climate Change

Young people in the West are terrified of climate change, but humanity has defeated greater threats over the past century. While climate change is a major problem, rather than allowing young people to be fearful of it, we should encourage them to be innovative. That is all the more reason why the authors want to discuss weather, climate and innovation in this book.

We are living in the age of climate panic. Climate change is seen as an existential threat to humanity and the planet, yet the number of deaths resulting from a natural disaster has fallen by 99 per cent over the past 100 years. Activists, however, have used this panic to cultivate a belief, a religion, a cult—something the authors call the 'Climate Church'.

Two significant critics of the apostles of our Climate Church are former Greenpeace members Bjorn Lomborg from Denmark and Patrick Moore from Canada. Lomborg, who authored the book *False Alarm: How Climate Change Panic Costs Us Trillions, Hurts the Poor, and Fails to Fix the Planet* and is one of *Time* magazine's 100 most influential people, says the world is a better place today because we have fixed many of its biggest problems. While the problems of extreme weather and climate change are increasing, they are 'actually smaller than most of the problems we've fixed'. The authors agree with Lomborg and Moore. In our opinion, the Climate Church preachers are exaggerating climate change and spreading doom-laden fantasies, much as some religious leaders did in the past. They enjoy scaremongering with their climate porn. While the doomsayers create climate depression amongst many western youngsters, the high priests of the Climate Church live in opulence. They include the first US Special Presidential Envoy for Climate John Kerry, former US Vice President Al Gore (a founder member of our church), former European Commissioner for Climate Action Frans Timmermans and actor Leonardo DiCaprio. They fly around in private or government-sponsored jets, simultaneously advocating that people should be subject to flight-shame, fat-shame, meat-shame, luxury-shame, chocolate-shame, energy-shame and capitalism-shame. In short, their sermons advocate consuming less and living a miserable life, as if it were the early 1800s again.

Coincidentally, the Italian Mafia, mentioned earlier in the context of human trafficking, also benefits from the Climate Church. They set forests ablaze, and then claim the deforested land for EU-subsidized solar panels. Even the Mafia goes green!

Climate Change is a Consequence of the Industrial Revolution

Climate change is real, and it is due, in part, to human activities since the beginning of the Industrial Revolution in the 19th century. Before 1850, 99 per cent of the world's population (1.3 billion) was poor. Only the landed nobility and successful merchants were rich; the middle class hardly existed and the poor did not produce significant CO_2 emissions. Thanks to the Industrial Revolution, we became richer, a sizeable middle class emerged, the global economy expanded, consumerism developed and, within 100 years from 1850, the global population doubled to 2.5 billion (it has since tripled to 8 billion). Before 1800, the world population grew at a much slower pace and took many centuries to double. The Industrial Revolution launched a wave of health, sanitary and other innovations that allowed us not only to feed and grow the population at a much faster rate but also to travel and migrate more easily than before.

According to Airbus, most flights are taken for visiting family and friends, followed by tourism, and finally business. Some climate activists may be sincere, but most exploit this theme to advocate a sort of neo-communism whereby everyone, except the green-earth apparatchiks, is deprived of material luxury and the freedom to make personal life choices. At least there is equality among the masses today, albeit medieval; what the Climate Church advocates is equality in which 99 per cent of the population is poor again.

Geoengineering Might Save Us from Climate Disasters

It does not need to get to that point. A century ago, scientists had already discovered that the Industrial Revolution caused climate change, and it was widely reported in newspapers at the time.

Brilliant German engineers like Anton Flettner developed ideas about how to adapt to climate change and still enjoy the fruits of the Industrial Revolution. Unfortunately, World War II prevented such ideas from materializing—and climate change was then pushed off the agenda. However, a futuristic fleet of 'cloudseeders', based on the 1920s Flettner rotor design, could create protective clouds using seawater if the Earth becomes too hot. Designed by Nobel prize-winning UK scientists John Latham and Stephen Salter, this fleet would pump fine particles of seawater into the clouds, thickening them to deflect incoming sunlight. The fleet's electric propulsion and spraying power would be generated by the Flettner rotors and accompanying turbines.

This radical idea may help save us from disastrous climate change, but we must implement it well. Cloud seeding in Dubai has led to heavy rainfall and uncontrollable floods. There are many more highly effective solutions to limit climate change or adapt to it, without needing to change our lifestyle. Let's hope the Climate Church does not sabotage or ignore these ideas just because they don't fit with its communist narrative. It already lobbies against innovation, nuclear energy, natural gas and LNG.

In many parts of the world today, factories, smart cities, offices and homes are shifting to natural gas and LNG as their source of power, and as mentioned earlier, there is enough gas to last for centuries. Even if we put aside the abiotic hypothesis, gas is the cleanest source of fossil fuel energy (if it is indeed a fossil fuel). Furthermore, nuclear power is making a comeback. The Rolls-Royce SMR promises to provide every village with cheap, clean emission-free energy. It is also evident that SMRs can power ships and aircraft. South Korean, Danish and American companies are building SMRs; the Danish ones are built on ships and can sail to wherever they are needed. Nuclear power, therefore, could soon contribute to emission-free travel worldwide. Nuclear-fusion technology is also developing fast—the Russians already have floating nuclear power stations.

Lomborg writes that what climate activists want 'will cost the world US$ 2,000 billion annually, in order to achieve 0.05 centigrade of cooling'—a change no human being or animal will notice. Meanwhile, the Climate Church's high priests get wealthy by building wind farms everywhere (the minarets of this new religion) and burning valuable forests in biomass plants. This religious fervour makes the environment uglier and less attractive for citizens or tourists, while also weakening government and private finances. We can only spend a rupee or dollar once. It's up to us to decide whether we should spend it on the Climate Church's wasteful approach or on what is necessary to save us from disaster.

Expectations

Will the middle class, whether living in the West, in Asia or in the Global South, accept deprivation as preached by the Climate Church? The authors do not believe so.

The global elites will soon face the geopolitical reality of increasingly self-aware populations who are developing a global consciousness. It will then be difficult for these elites to maintain their dominance. However, they can expand their power by using technologies such as AI+FR to control these populations. This is happening in China, where the Communist Party has implemented a hi-tech surveillance state. China has also sold its mass surveillance technology to other countries in the Global South, such as Iran and Venezuela, where dictators use it to quell public protests against their regimes. Venezuela was once South America's richest country, but the communist regime there has ruined it. The Iranians are wonderful people, boasting a millennia-old culture, but the Islamist dictatorship has brought only misery to the country, using income from oil to export Islamism around the world. In this scenario, curbing the influence of dictators and rogue states in future will be a major challenge.

Neither have global power structures posed such a monumental threat to humankind, nor has humankind been such an immense threat to institutionalized power. Every action prompts an equally powerful and opposite reaction, so even if the elites think they truly run the world, human nature has a way of exposing flaws in that assumption. Humans are not meant to be 'controlled'; they are destined to be nurtured instead. It is important to note that the *E* of Economy is also the *E* of Emotion. As Mickey Huibregtsen, former senior partner at research organization McKinsey & Company, predicted in his book *Management Made Simple: Ideas of a former McKinsey Partner*, an 'Emotional Revolution' will occur as well.

In the following paragraphs, the authors take an in-depth look at the impact of a global political awakening and modern technology on the world.

How the West Is Getting Lost

The era of global domination by the West, which has lasted for 500 years, will end in the 21st century. The Western-dominated world order will be replaced by the rise of a new multipolar world order. Like every great empire, the West is declining from within due to overstretch, corruption, power abuse, nepotism, poor leadership and unhappy citizens.

Leftists hoping for the downfall of the West followed a brilliant conquest strategy in the US. They infiltrated universities, Hollywood and the mainstream media with their ideas. After conquering these three important pillars of US society, they put their agents to work across the rest of society. The whole operation was financed by billionaires with their own reasons for weakening the very West that had made them rich. They had not expected the rapid rise of social media, so now we see they have made inroads into

Silicon Valley too. Today's major stakeholders on social media are following the same leftist agenda, erasing the last vestiges of freedom of expression.

Coined by Zbigniew Brzezinski (former National Security Advisor to US President Jimmy Carter) in *Between Two Ages: America's Role in the Technetronic Era*, the phrase 'global political awakening' refers to a unique time in human history when everyone on the planet becomes activated by political consciousness. Andrew Gavin Marshall says this 'new and unique development' is 'unprecedented in reach and volume', identifying it as the greatest threat to power structures around the world. This surge of support for cultural respect and economic opportunities is being shown 'in a world scarred by memories of colonial or imperial domination'. This awakening presents a grave challenge to globalization and the political economy; it affects organized powers like countries, multinationals, banks, central banks, international bodies, militaries, intelligence agencies, the media and academia.

For the first time in history, we have a transnational capitalist class, or 'superclass', as David Rothkopf calls them in his book *Superclass: The Global Power Elite and the World They Are Making, comprising* a truly global, heavily integrated elite. However, as they have globalized their power to construct a new world order of governance and global government, they have simultaneously globalized populations.

The 'Technetronic Revolution' is a technological revolution that involves two major geopolitical developments. Firstly, the capability for mass communication has rapidly accelerates as technology advances, enabling instant global interaction. Immediate access to information from around the world has the makings of a fundamental stimulus for

Brzezinski's global political awakening on a massive scale. Secondly, this revolution simultaneously enables elites to redirect and control society in ways previously unimaginable, culminating in the global scientific dictatorship that we have been warned about since the early decades of the 20th century. As science unleashes the powers of genetics, biometrics, surveillance and new forms of modern eugenics, the potential for a scientific elite to control the masses with psychosocial tools (psychological systems of control) has never been greater.

What Is the Global Political Awakening?

A central challenge to global geopolitics—the worldwide yearning for human dignity—contrasts with the Global North's notion of what people want: access to democracy, open markets and free-trade wealth. Brzezinski notes that the global political awakening, which is interpreted in radically different forms across the Global South, has its origins in the French Revolution's powerful national consciousness. Since the 1789 revolution, nationalist movements have reflected the sentiment of 'populist passions and growing mass commitment', as seen in the successful rise of Bolshevism and Fascism, civil conflict in China, India's resistance against colonialism and the revolution in Mexico, to name a few. Moreover, Europe's empires crumbled after World War II because of political stirrings. This implies that populations are developing political, social and economic consciousness, subsequently partaking in actions aimed at generating a major shift, change or revolution in these areas. This is central to the concept of political awakening and happens regardless of any outcome seen in previous awakenings. No social transformation thus presents a greater or more direct challenge to entrenched and centralized power structures, whether political, social or economic in nature.

At present, communication advancements and immediate access to global information enable a 'community of shared perceptions and envy [...] galvanized and channelled by demagogic political or religious passions'. This energy challenges individual countries as well as the US-led global hierarchy; borders are no obstacles to seething unrest seen across the developing world. United in a desire to resist the perceived negative influence the outside world has on national populations, susceptible people across the Global South (and increasingly Europe) are gearing up against the external powers they envy, but which maintain the disliked status quo. This 'demographic revolution', in Brzezinski's words, embodies a 'political time-bomb' and is most notable in the Third World's restless, resentful youth aged under 25. Students who are dissatisfied and impatient, for instance, are already congregating, awaiting a trigger—a cause, a faith, a hatred—to join in the protests. In a world filled with economic, racial and ethnic inequities, the politically awakened, underprivileged masses demand democracy, social rights, human rights and self-determination (ethnic, religious and national). Supranational self-determination, however, does not mean having a 'world government'—mankind is not 'remotely ready for world government'.

Power Structures Threatened

The baby boomers, defined as people born between 1946 and 1964, are followed by Generation X (1965–1980), Generation Y or Millennials (1981–1996), Generation Z or Zoomers (1997–2012), Generation Alpha (2010–2024) and Generation Beta (2025–2039). Each generation has its own characteristics.

Ageing will peak in 2040, when most baby boomers, who currently rule the world, will be dead, and untold wealth will be transferred between generations. Although Generation X is now at its mightiest, this cohort is starting to retire, which means Millennials will take over leadership in the coming decade. While many countries are gerontocracies (societies governed by the elderly) to date, the eager and restless youth of Generation Z are not willing to wait for their opportunity. The CIA, therefore, has warned us about Z-Bellion—a Generation Z rebellion against previous generations, governments, current leaders and institutions.

In 2024, Generation Z revolted against the government in Kenya and Nigeria. This will happen in more countries in the Global South. Thus, to understand the global political awakening, it is imperative to understand and analyse the global power structure it threatens.

Elites have always sought to satisfy their own desire for power by controlling populations and individuals. Irrespective of whether the political system is fascist, communist, socialist or democratic, elites who seek power and control are inherent to governance. In 1928, Edward Bernays, nephew of psychoanalyst Sigmund Freud, wrote one of his most influential works *Propaganda*. He also wrote *Public Relations, but outside the field of public relations, of which he is known as the 'father',* few people have heard of Bernays. His views and impact on elites and social control, however, have been profound and extensive.

By understanding the 'mechanisms and motives of the group mind' in a modern democracy, it is possible to covertly control the masses through deliberate manipulation of their habits and opinions. The manipulators are, according to Bernays, an 'invisible government' or the true ruling power. This hidden authority—experts in 'mental processes and social patterns'—is a handful of people who steer the national mindset in all spheres of life.

In the years following World War II, the US became a global hegemon whose imperial impetus was the strategic concept of 'containment'—containing the spread of communism. Thus, the imperial adventures of the US in Korea, the Middle East, Africa, Asia and South America defined a desire to 'roll back' Soviet and communist influence. Furthermore, the US was given the responsibility to oversee and manage the international monetary system and global political economy, a role it took on through agreements and the creation of institutions such as the World Bank, the International Monetary Fund (IMF), NATO, the UN and GATT (later replaced by the World Trade Organization). One central institution that proved significant in establishing a consensus among Western elites and providing a forum for expanding Western hegemony was the Bilderberg Group, founded in 1954 as an international think tank.

This status quo has already changed because of the increasing global influence of China and, starting in the first Trump era, a less interventionist attitude of the US.

Technocracy Blends Democracy and Autocracy: Welcome to Generation T

Brzezinski suggests industry is no longer the main determinant of social change. A revolution in technology and electronics has shaped the 'technetronic society', not only economically but also culturally and psychologically. Experiments in social manipulation also prove that 'environmental and biochemical manipulation of the brain' controls human behaviour and intellect.

It is not only China that is moving towards greater surveillance of its population. Democracies in the West are also evolving into surveillance states, allowing fewer freedoms. The very freedom of expression that made the West so progressive in the past is now being curbed.

In recent decades, our working ways have changed. Accelerated by the COVID-19 pandemic, the use of modern technology is having a significant impact. Technology and globalization have created a workplace that is no longer bound to a specific geographical location. Instead, digital collaboration is becoming the new standard, which could create a disconnect between the worker and their workplace if not carefully managed. Hence, to foster creativity and innovation, we must reintroduce the human factor into work.

Globalism vs Nativism Leads to Slowbalization

According to Brzezinski, the emerging 'transnational elites' (businessmen, scholars, professionals, public officials), who are not bound by international borders and national traditions, have a staunch globalist outlook and put their own interests ahead of those of the politically active masses. This dangerous attitude distances the cosmopolitan elites from the people, whose 'nativism' is consequently exploited by nationalist politics. However, in the technetronic revolution, a more controlled and guided society will emerge in the Global South, dominated by an elite power with a scientifically superior intellect, digital expertise and fewer liberal values. These highly controlled societies will become the norm in Global North democracies too, as a result of the West's fascination with technical efficiency. Consequently, human individuality will be lost in future surveillance states.

Political scientist Samuel Huntington writes that 'the primacy of equality' was a social, economic and political goal in the 1960s, as democracy and citizen participation surged in the US. An awareness of empire and exploitation directly challenged the 'systems of authority', with fewer citizens recognizing the superiority of age, rank, status or ability. The decade's social, racial and military concerns put hierarchy and expertise 'under heavy attack'. An educated, mobilized, involved society needs more balance; the continuous expansion of political democracy needs 'desirable limits'. Too much democracy can lead to a vulnerable democracy in crisis, so the solution must be greater authority.

Rothkopf claims individual nation-states with local or national power structures and a cultural concept of sovereignty cannot act alone to fulfil their 'portion of the social contract' in a globalized world, where national borders are no barrier to movement and threats. A global governance mechanism that offers temporary, creative solutions can be achieved but is effective 'only when it is anti-democratic'. The authors only partly agree with Rothkopf. While modern China is part of the global 'superclass' it follows its own national agenda 'China First', an approach many other countries will adopt.

Global sociopolitical and economic conditions are related to the emergence and expansion of the global political awakening, which, according to Brzezinski, is currently one of the primary global geopolitical challenges. Up until now, this awakening has been confined to developing countries across the Global South—the so-called Third World, including the Middle East, Central and Southeast Asia, Africa and Latin America. In recent decades, however, developments in Venezuela, Bolivia and Iran have started to exemplify the nationalist orientation of this awakening, which is happening in a world increasingly moving towards global governance and global institutions.

A political awakening of the masses in India, for example, led to the fall of the Nehru-Gandhi dynastic rule of the Congress party.

Dealing with Poverty

We must look at the causes of and potential solutions for the majority of the world's population living in poverty and social dislocation. Poverty is related to the historic and ongoing construction of a globalized world order in which wages and incomes are kept low by employers who seek the cheapest employees. Furthermore, industries always try to acquire raw materials from the countries that supply them at the lowest cost, thus controlling the market and the only source of income for rural communities. Competition for the supply of the cheapest labour or commodities in a globalized world is fierce because retail consumers in wealthier countries expect to pay bargain prices. This generally hurts poor countries as well as the underpaid workers in wealthier ones. Notably, real wages for workers in the bottom half of the income scale in developed countries have hardly risen in 30 years, while profits and earnings have risen for investors and workers in the top half.

Thanks to the internet and digitization, globalization not only impacts labour and prices but also the flow of information. The same infrastructure that is being further institutionalized by the global elite is also providing ordinary people with much better access to information. Workers and populations, therefore, discover that their own political or economic situations need not be taken as given; things can be (and often are) different and much better elsewhere in the world, or even within their own countries. This awareness of their own poverty pushes them towards an awakening like never before.

Societies are judged on how they treat their weakest members—the poor and socially displaced—something the elites, who have lost touch with reality, vastly underestimate. Poverty forces people to look at the world differently when they see the harsh restraints society has imposed upon the human spirit. There must be more to life than a daily struggle to secure water, shelter and food.

Why should we exploit humanity by subjecting it to poverty? Imagine if all human beings were allowed to flourish, both individually and collectively, how different, or even better, the world would be today. Think of all the lost ideas, art, expression, intellect and beauty from those people who had the potential but never had a voice. Until we address this fundamental issue, any notion of humanity being 'civilized' is nothing but a cynical joke. Although we haven't completely figured out human civilization yet and don't have a proper definition of 'civilized', we do need to make it humane.

However, we must not expect this change to come from the global elites. Change is needed from the bottom up, and it starts with a push for fair wages, a fair price for commodities such as agricultural goods, and a fair distribution of income and wealth. We may see more unrest in (and between) countries where a large income disparity exists.

Fighting Ransomware and Terrorism

As discussed earlier, digitization is moving fast. We are accelerating towards a world with two competing IT standards: a US one and a Chinese one. With 6G as the successor to the present 5G, a Virtual Reality (VR) world will become an actual reality within 10 years. Then we could, for instance, experience travel from the safety of our own homes—safe from viruses, pandemics, terrorism and criminality.

The world is better connected in other ways too. For example, communicating in different languages on the spot is already possible. A traveller from Japan could speak Japanese to someone selling chocolates or cosmetics in Norway, and the salesperson would understand and respond in Norwegian. The Japanese customer, in turn, would grasp the response. Hence, no multilingual salespeople are needed any more.

On the other hand, ongoing digitization also brings new risks and dangers, of which ransomware is one. In North America and Europe, hackers have attacked several hospitals, power stations, dams and government institutions, demanding large sums to unblock the affected systems. Terrorists with a computer on the ground can hijack an aircraft in flight—they don't need to be aboard to cause havoc and bloodshed. Most reports on digital terrorism come today from rogue states, such as Belarus, North Korea and Iran.

Young Iranians, deeply unhappy with their Islamist dictatorship, are refusing to have babies who might be trained by the regime as future terrorists. This revolt is leading to a rapidly ageing population. The Iranian government, therefore, is turning to populous regions with countless young men, such as Gaza, Lebanon, Iraq, Mali and Nigeria. Boko Haram, for example, is an Iran-sponsored Islamist jihadist group in Nigeria, which is waging civil wars across West and Central Africa.

Before the 9/11 attack on the US in 2001, flying was seamless. Since then, security measures have made flying less easy. Although the Islamist terrorist organizations like Al-Qaeda, IS and the Taliban are currently occupied elsewhere (primarily in Africa), they will soon enough turn to the West and Asia again, targeting airports, aircraft and tourist destinations. The cost of fighting and curbing Islamic terrorism in Europe will be excessive. As former Turkish Foreign Minister Mevlüt Çavuşoğlu predicted, 'Europe will soon be the site of religious wars' between indigenous Christian Europeans and Islamic immigrants. The authors hope this will not happen, but some trends are perpetual.

Rise of Wokeism

One such trend is 'men love wars, women love soldiers', which was discussed earlier. Today's European youth is agitated because there has not been a major war in the continent since 1945. They find peace boring and are attracted to a new fascism imported from the US: Wokeism. The Woke generation ignores the fact that Wokeism, which calls itself 'anti-fascist', was developed to undermine the West from within. Preaching guilt and spreading panic about the end of the world, both Woke identity politics and the Climate Church are anti-capitalism, anti-consumerism and anti-everything that is fun. However, many Indians and Chinese still believe in the so-called 'American dream' and continue to migrate (legally or illegally) to the US or the UK.

The West is indeed deteriorating due to Wokeism, Climatism, self-hatred, imperial overstretch, mismanagement and poor leadership. But all is not lost yet. As John Stuart Mill observed, a widely admired sage is 'not the man who hopes when others despair, but the man who despairs when others hope'. Unfortunately, the preachings of the Climate Church and Woke doomsayers have manipulated the West into believing that it must despair over the current state of affairs. This book, therefore, intends to be both optimistic and realistic, in the hope that it lifts the masses from their gloomy emotions. The authors also hope it inspires young people around the world to benefit from the megatrends in this Age of Chaos.

More About Woke Identity Politics

In his books *The Strange Death of Europe: Immigration, Identity, Islam* and *The Madness of Crowds: Gender, Race and Identity*, the UK thinker Douglas Murray describes how the West deals with identity politics, mass migration, the movement of 'Black Lives Matter' and radical Islam. By submitting to the demands of these groups, the West is relinquishing its values, such as freedom of expression. While Eastern Europe was moving to the far right after communist rule, Western Europe and North America were moving to the far left—both extremes are a loss for them. One of the authors of this book is brown-skinned, gay and disabled, yet he opposes Woke identity politics, which ignores the complexities of one's complete identity by overly focusing on a single aspect of it. It separates the various groups that a society is composed of, instead of bringing them together. Wokeism doesn't take account of the integrative role of politics and destroys the fabric of society.

The authors believe the 1773 quote—'Make yourselves sheep and the wolves will eat you'—by Benjamin Franklin, one of the Founding Fathers of the US, still holds true. They refuse to be sheep at a time when so many wolves are on the prowl. Across their beloved continent of Europe, many flocks of sheep can be found in the US and Canada, who have already abandoned Western values and the Judeo-Christian cultural heritage, both of which advanced the world and created more freedom for the masses than humanity has ever seen.

As Dan Hitchens argues, grand narratives have collapsed in Western countries that once looked to God for leadership but now 'gaze round helplessly: won't somebody lead us, please?' Today, the only purpose of life is advocating for social justice, intersectionality and identity politics—a mysterious, frightening shapeshifter that occasionally destroys reputations, careers and lives. Its punishment transcends generations, as exemplified by the racing driver stripped of a sponsorship deal because of what happened before he was born (his father had used 'an offensive racial epithet' on the radio). The West is going through an identity crisis, ignorant of a past that shapes its choices; the West is 'tearing itself apart' with crazy contemporary ideologies.

Young people today in BRICS and Global South countries combine the ideals of liberalism and ancient spirituality with a thirst for knowledge to learn and achieve more—to move quickly towards #Forwardism. Instead of falling into the Wokeism trap, these countries must invest in their identities and economic progress.

Adapting to Pandemics

According to the UK newspaper *The Telegraph*, the COVID-19 virus originated in the Chinese city of Wuhan, in a military lab funded by the Chinese, the European Union (EU) and the US. Leaked grant proposals dating from 2018 show that Wuhan scientists were planning to release enhanced coronaviruses into Chinese bat populations to inoculate them against diseases that could spread to humans. The rest is history.

The WHO has warned that more pandemics are expected. The government of Singapore has told its citizens they must learn to live with COVID-19 in all its current known and future unknown variants. Singapore's Changi Airport is one of the major aviation hubs in the world, and it's not only humans who travel from here—viruses accompany them. With comets plunging to Earth and space tourism emerging, even viruses from space could arrive at our doorstep soon.

Many viruses dwell in the forests we have destroyed, so they migrate to our homes because they have lost theirs. The only solution is to plant more trees—to give the viruses somewhere to live. China plants more trees annually than the rest of the world combined, so we should follow its example if we want to curb pandemics and prevent new lockdowns or travel restrictions.

We also know that as populations become immune, viruses tend to be less virulent over time.

Part 1

The Perfect Storm for a New Renaissance

1

The Perfect Storm

Yao Ming and his family are making a trip to the sea in his new electric car. He loves the car as it does not make any noise while driving and can be recharged in three hours. He bought the car last month and is very proud to be the first in his neighbourhood to own a car that no longer needs oil. His neighbours have hybrid cars, which still run partly on oil. Yao Ming found his car on the internet while looking for the latest technology in automobile manufacturing. Chinese car maker Wong Electric Industries promoted the car as the latest model in car technology that outsmarted existing hybrid cars. Being sensitive to emerging technology and having a green heart, Yao Ming decided to buy the car. As a professor of Renewable Energy at the Shanghai Green Project University, Yao Ming feels obligated to set a green example for his students and neighbours. The car was rather expensive, which meant that the family had to skip their planned summer trip to Europe this year. They were to fly with Sunair China—the first airline in China powered entirely by solar cells. His children did not like the idea, but Yao Ming explained that he had to make a choice, and the car was the greenest option. He promised them they would make several trips to the sea in summer in their new car.

After the fall of the Roman Empire, Europe and the rest of the Western world during the early Middle Ages were so insignificant that the Chinese emperor refused to receive Europeans at his court. Later in the 15th century, a new age dawned in Europe. Increased trading activities created wealth that enabled arts, sciences and literature to flourish. There was a renewed interest in the traditions and beliefs of the ancient Greeks and Romans, which were rediscovered and adopted with such enthusiasm that future historians saw this period as a rebirth or 'Renaissance' of the classical world. This era witnessed a loosening of the strict social bonds that had been necessary for survival during the Middle Ages, and the 'individual' consequently emerged from an anonymous crowd to discover the beauty of the world. This was the age in which explorers embarked on voyages of discovery, leading to the subjugation of a greater part of the world in the name of European colonialism. The Renaissance contained the seeds of the Enlightenment, an intellectual movement in Europe in the 17th and 18th centuries, which became the basis of modern societies. The Renaissance marks the moment humanity picked up the threads of development and progress after spending 1,000 years in darkness and stagnation following the fall of the Roman Empire.

The era was an exclusive period that was destined to benefit the town-dwelling elites. Change was more elusive for those millions of Europeans trying to secure a living in the countryside before the advent of numerous religious wars (another characteristic of the period).

While Europeans were lost in centuries of darkness before the Renaissance, there were others elsewhere who experienced progress and great riches. Take China, for instance, which blossomed during the Tang dynasty.

Between the seventh and ninth centuries, China was far more advanced than any country in the West, and its capital Xian had two million inhabitants, making it the biggest city in the world at the time. India also enjoyed fabulous fortune in the Middle Ages—something that would have been inconceivable in the West. The Mughal emperor Babur noted in his memoirs that 'bad times create strong men; strong men create good times; good times create weak men; weak men create bad times'. While accurately predicting the trajectory of his own dynasty—his last remaining heir was defeated by the British in the 19th century—Babur highlighted that progress is not inevitable.

The Iron Era

History is the sum of human lives, and just as those lives are characterized by highs and lows, history is also a series of peaks and downfalls. History has proven time and again that nothing is constant: wealth comes and goes; good times are replaced by bad ones; stability is punctuated by moments when we must start over. In Hinduism, time is divided into four ages or 'yugas' that follow one another: *Satya Yuga* (the Golden Era), *Treta Yuga* (the Silver Era), *Dvapara Yuga* (the Copper Era) and *Kali Yuga* (the Iron Era). The *Satya Yuga* is characterized by *Veda* or 'pure knowledge and a higher principle', representing a time when people are happy and live in harmony. A gradual decline follows *Satya Yuga*, during which people fall deeper into darkness until they hit rock bottom in the *Kali Yuga*. At this lowest point, humanity must drag itself from the depths of sin and corruption, and start the cycle anew. This Hindu philosophy inspired the writings of Babur, a Muslim ruler. The signs set down by Hindu sages millennia ago are glaring at us today: (1) we are driven by selfishness and instant gratification; (2)

we barely notice those around us; (3) we satisfy every sexual lust to the point of depravity; (4) millions of us have fled from conflict or violence; (5) we no longer hold truth dear, distorting facts to suit our own selves; (6) we are ruled by elites, politicians and elite-politicians so preoccupied with garnering riches for themselves that they can no longer be trusted to safeguard the well-being of their communities. During *Kali Yuga,* basic emotions and selfishness triumph over intelligence and reason.

Feelings Are Running High

French political commentator Dominique Moïsi expounds the view that a globalized world is ruled by emotions. In the 20th century, 'the age of ideology' gave way to 'the age of identity', precipitated by the end of the Cold War. He argues that in a world where everything and everyone are linked, it is most important to know who you are in order to assert your own identity. We are distinguished by our personal identity and self-confidence—facets that inspire others to respect us—rather than our political beliefs. According to Moïsi, geopolitical relationships are also influenced by emotions. For instance, Western countries view world politics with a sense of superiority, believing their values are universal and should be the norm for international relations. Russia and many Asian countries (particularly India and China), on the other hand, are more pragmatic, displaying less interest in the worldview and more in their global role. The US and Western Europe are still influenced by Cold War-era thinking that polarizes good and evil. In a globalized world, however, universal values play a lesser role, Western authority dwindles and its economic supremacy falters in the face of increased competition. As a result, Asian countries see opportunities for advancement while the West reacts to global events with fear and bitterness.

Populations in Asia can attain Western living standards without sacrificing their own identities, leading Moïsi to juxtapose a Western culture of fear with an Eastern culture of hope. He further identifies a third group of countries in Latin America and the Baltic, but mainly in the Middle East, which struggle with issues both predating and exacerbated by globalization. Left trailing behind by the front runners in the race for progress, their losing position translates into a culture of humiliation, anger and even hate. With the proliferation of mass media, advanced communication and human mobility under globalization, this hate culture is spreading throughout the world. This is exemplified by the Arab influence on Islam in Asia and the Balkans, and by the Muslim diaspora in Western Europe, where Islamic terrorism, aggravated by the West's culture of fear, is the most extreme manifestation of an exported hate culture. Conversely, the Asian culture of hope is being exported too. For instance, the United Arab Emirates has emotionally and psychologically aligned itself with Asia by attempting to adopt Singapore's model of economic growth.

The Chinese Dream

In the axis of hope, China is the brightest example. Without abandoning its Marxist identity, Chinese leaders have successfully embraced market-led capitalism, learning from their comrades' mistakes in the Soviet Union. Combining economic and political renewal was a Soviet blunder that saw the economy collapse, followed by the disbandment of the federal union. Party officials in Beijing understood that reform was inevitable, but knew it could never lead to democratization. So they chose to preserve the one-party state while simultaneously introducing elements of market-led capitalism. By 2019, with the Chinese Communist Party having consolidated its firm grip on the reins, China boasted more homeowners, more postgraduates and more internet users than any other country.

Forty years ago, China was poor and underdeveloped, but the lives of today's 800 million inhabitants have dramatically improved since then, with less than 1 per cent of the population living in extreme poverty (although the World Bank claims 500 million Chinese still live on less than US$5.50 per day). Zhang Jun at Fudan University suggests China could further improve this economic picture by opening the huge market potential in telecoms, healthcare, education, entertainment and finance. This would increase consumption and reduce savings, giving China a more balanced development model. Polls show that Chinese citizens are among the most optimistic people on Earth; the population is enthusiastic, driven and entrepreneurial. Unlike in the Western world, where the middle class feels the strain and children are no longer guaranteed to be wealthier than their parents (as discussed later), China has a growing middle class, whose youth are secure in the knowledge that they will be more affluent than their parents' generation.

This new Chinese élan is coupled with enormous self-confidence and the desire to occupy a central position on the global stage. China is working hard to realize its ambition of becoming an economic, political and military superpower. Its ambitious crowning glory is the BRI project, which, when completed in 2049, will link 68 countries across Asia, South America, Oceania, Africa and Europe, serving about 65 per cent of people on the planet. Top party officials in China call it a 'Community of Common Destiny'.

To make BRI a reality, China is engaged at the international level, building 41 gas and oil pipelines; 203 bridges, roads, railways and harbours; and 199 power centres, to be fuelled by a combination of gas, oil, nuclear and alternative energies. Parag Khanna, author of *The Future Is Asian: Commerce, Conflict, and Culture in the 21st Century,* calls BRI the 'most significant diplomatic project of the 21st century'. It's like the founding of the UN, the World Bank and the Marshall Plan rolled into one, but with a crucial difference—BRI was conceived in Asia, launched in Asia and will be led by Asians. There are, however, several significant difficulties challenging BRI. Enthusiasm is waning in countries along the New Silk Road, countries that are struggling to pay the expenses, or that risk losing harbours and other properties to China. The West is also watching Chinese ambitions with consternation, fearing an attempt to undermine the established economic and political world order. The US has already launched a trade war to curb China's enthusiasm, and a US–Australia–Japan investment initiative aims to strengthen infrastructure in the region. A primary goal for this joint effort is to supply Papua New Guinea with electricity, allowing one of the world's poorest countries to be an early beneficiary of shifting power relationships among the richest.

It is proven that China's rivals are suspicious. Investigations into China's BRI activity show that the largest investments are made in regions with strategic military importance, whereas work is at a standstill where there is little strategic advantage to be gained. The same research suggests that China's long-term BRI investments may not be economically worthwhile.

Political and economic powers often shift over the centuries. Genoa and Venice in the 16th century lost their economic hegemony to Amsterdam, which in turn passed the baton to London, only to lose it to New York after World War I. At present, it is Beijing's turn, along with Delhi, Jakarta and Mumbai. It is possible in a globalized world to have multiple centres of power operating simultaneously. Instead of Silicon Valley, Manhattan or London, today's centres of progress are in Asia. Economic power, however, has never been handed over without a fight.

A Sleeping Giant

Throughout history, China has experienced extended periods of world domination. During the Han dynasty (BC 200–200 AD), China conquered parts of the Korean peninsula, Vietnam and areas along the original Silk Road, which was used for trade with, among others, the Roman Empire. Paper, porcelain and other Chinese inventions also travelled west along the Silk Road. Between the seventh and ninth centuries—during the rule of the Tang dynasty—China flourished again with economic, political, scientific and cultural supremacy. The invention of printing turned China into the first information society on Earth. During the Ming dynasty, which lasted from the 14th to the 17th centuries, China excelled once more and became one of the world's most powerful trading nations, building settlements along the Indian Ocean and in Africa.

In the early 1400s, a Chinese fleet comprising hundreds of ships with the best cartographers, sailors and navigators aboard, set sail to map the world, reaching the coasts of Australia, Antarctica, the Americas and West Africa, where they established settlements to collect plants and animals for the emperor. However, when all the ships that had survived the perilous voyages returned home two years later, loaded with a treasure trove of international knowledge, China had changed. The population had rebelled against the high taxes imposed to finance the fleet and build a new capital city, Beijing. Amid the rebellion, a fire destroyed the imperial palace, and many believed the gods were punishing the emperor for his arrogant desire to conquer the world. China had become a 'sleeping giant', as Napoleon Bonaparte is thought to have later said about the once-imperial superpower.

Most of the fleet's maps and logs were destroyed, but a few reached the West and were used for Columbus's trip to the Americas. With the help of Chinese maps, he knew exactly where to go and what to explore. European powers would thereafter rule the seas for centuries, and European culture would dominate the world until the beginning of the 21st century.

Beyond China

Parag Khanna provides an extraordinary list of superlatives about Asia. With 60 per cent of the world's population (ten times as many people as in Europe, and 12 times as many as in North America), Asia now represents 50 per cent of global GDP and two-thirds of global economic growth. It produces more, exports more, imports more and consumes more than any other region. Asian countries also trade with and invest in one another far more than Western countries. Today, Asia is home to several of the world's largest economies, most of its foreign exchange reserves, many of its largest banks and businesses, and most of its biggest military forces.

Khanna argues that since Asia's fortunes follow significantly different paths from those in the West, global financial crises are not actually 'global'. Asia continues to see a surge in growth rates while others slump. In 2018, the world's highest growth rates were reported in India, China, Indonesia, Malaysia and Uzbekistan. Similarly, Western populist politics—from Brexit to Trump—don't infect Asia, where pragmatic governments focus on inclusive growth and social cohesion. While US and European citizens see walls going up along borders, Asian citizens see them coming down. Instead of being 'backward-looking, navel-gazing and pessimistic', billions of Asians are 'forward-looking, outward-oriented and optimistic'. Despite that, many prefer living in the West because they love the freedoms it offers. A high-ranking Chinese businesswoman once remarked that while they send their kids to study in the US, Asians would rather live in beautiful, clean Europe where they feel happy. Within the future Eurasian economy, Europe should be rebranded as the region of happiness.

Emocracy

Emotion plays an increasingly powerful role within and between countries. Historian Niall Ferguson noted that we 'no longer live in a democracy. We live in an 'emocracy', where emotions rather than majorities rule, and feelings matter more than reason.' This sentiment applies not only to personal space but also to politics. Nowadays, we rarely see election campaigns fought purely on notions of party-political ideologies and policy differences; rather, candidates rely on the delusions of the day. Political parties are rapidly losing members, and there have never been so many floating voters who, driven by emotions, make impulsive decisions at the time of casting their ballots. Consumers act similarly, making purchases based on emotions. Suppose consumer X has a wonderful experience with producer Y's electric razor. Consequently, consumer X will most likely presume that producer Y's espresso machine will provide the same satisfaction, even though these products are not at all related. We choose products (or rather their producers) based on emotions, which are usually linked to a belief that certain brands fit our lifestyle or ambitions. Feelings can also influence our job preferences or choice of employer. Pragmatic considerations like salary, prospects or security are less important today than more nebulous requirements, such as job satisfaction, workplace environment or shared values with an employer.

The Emotional Revolution

Despite the amazing technological developments of today—or perhaps because of them—emotion remains a critical factor in every aspect of the economic world, as it does in the social world. As mentioned earlier, consumers want a 'buying experience' and employees increasingly view 'fulfilment and self-development' as more important than salary. The earlier approach of managers to 'go by the book' has also evolved over recent decades, with emotionally intelligent leaders now engaging with EQ (Emotional Quotient) rather than IQ (Intelligence Quotient) in the workplace. A key factor for success, according to today's management narrative, is skilfully overseeing the emotional elements of employer–employee relations.

Two complementary developments are at the heart of this evolution-cum-revolution. First, effective competition has put pressure on producers, with products now becoming 'commodities' in objective terms. There are no longer bad cars, just as there is no longer bad fuel to power them. The difference in production costs, and therefore in prices, has narrowed across all sectors, leaving less room for a rational selection process. Second, people have reached the top of Maslow's pyramid (the hierarchy of needs, which will be discussed later) and are now able to let emotions dictate their decision-making process—in developed economies, at least. The feel-good factor of a purchasing decision is thus far more important than an objective, factual comparison.

The real impact of the emotional revolution is far more extensive than most commentators are willing to accept. There is no dimension in business life anymore where emotions do not play a significant role—whether it is inspiring employees, trusting advisors, relying on suppliers, stirring customers to buy or showing admiration for the boss! One could describe the evolution of business—or of any organization for that matter—in three phases, the focal points of which are respectively found at the turn of the 19th century, in the late 1900s and in the early 2000s.

1. **The Industrial Revolution.** The primary focus of management during this phase was on using standardization and mass production to increase productivity through artificial power and economies of scale. Emotions were disregarded and even actively discouraged. Charlie Chaplin's 1936 comedy film *Modern Times* offers a wonderful glimpse into the impassive mindset behind the Industrial Revolution.

2. **The Information Revolution.** A world of information without boundaries triggered a new business perspective during this phase. Focus shifted to the role of, and interaction between, key stakeholders in a company, particularly employees, customers and suppliers. With the rise of the internet, PCs, iPads and iPhones, companies began to use modern technology to rediscover the freedoms that the Industrial Revolution had restricted.

3. **The Emotional Revolution.** While the impact of the Industrial Revolution and the Information Revolution is still felt in certain industries and regions around the world, the Emotional Revolution increasingly dominates the management landscape. It permeates every aspect of business, from R&D to after-sales service, and everything in between.

The Emotional Revolution is most visible to stakeholders through an enormous increase in the importance of brands and reputations. For many consumer-oriented companies, the value of the brand, as estimated by retail experts, represents a sizeable portion of the business's total worth. Even at a business-to-business level, the importance of emotions should not be underestimated. With products and services achieving commodity status, the emotional profile of buyer–supplier relationships often becomes the deciding factor. Trust and empathy are increasingly valuable in any business nowadays.

For employees, the Emotional Revolution may determine the difference between a successful business and a mediocre one. Companies are competing in a war for talent, and the victors are those whose fight inspires employees the most. The consecutive levels of aspiration seen in Maslow's theory can be easily applied to the average employee. The far-reaching implications of moving from the phase of the Industrial Revolution to a world filled with emotion demand senior management's careful attention.

A Post-Truth Society

A fear of loss—loss of security, loss of living standards, loss of identity—is a key emotion in an emocracy. Deference to fear is not good for decision-making, but respect for feelings holds legitimacy in an emocracy. As the survival instinct reacts more strongly to fear than to positive emotions, people give credence to doomsday prophets and tend to ignore more reasoned perspectives that confirm things are not as bad as they seem. The emocracy conforms to every element of what is often called the 'Post-Truth Society', in which fact-based truths, logic and reasoned arguments are absent. The shift to a Post-Truth Society did not happen overnight; the term *post-truth first appeared in an essay by the Serbian-American playwright Steve Tesich* in 1992 and has since gained momentum because of (1) social media's growing influence and omnipresence, (2) the alternative media giving a platform to conspiracy theories, (3) an information war with Russia, and (4) a generation of politicians who claim to distrust fact.

Experts can no longer expect to win arguments with fact or truth when public judgement is based on 'who' is making the argument. This has become the new norm; fact-checking has turned into a big business in the quest to stem the flow of disinformation and shield citizens from (supposed) fake news and 'alternative facts'. However, this battle will certainly be lost because people are not inherently reasonable beings. Israeli psychologist and Nobel Prize winner Daniel Kahneman claims our ability to reason is hampered by inbuilt prejudices, and hence, instead of listening to well-argued statements that challenge our beliefs, we hear, believe and repeat only unfounded statements that confirm our own prejudices. This primal dysfunction of human beings is an engine powering the prevalence of online (and offline) nonsense. We are, however, all too often fully aware of these thought processes and behavioural weaknesses, subconsciously choosing ways to disguise them instead. Even if exposed for telling blatant lies, few people take accountability; someone caught in a compromising act is more likely to seek damages in court than acknowledge their wrongdoing. Such is our brazen society.

Somewheres and Anywheres

In his book *The Road to Somewhere: The Populist Revolt and the Future of Politics*, David Goodhart divides the UK population into 'Somewheres' and 'Anywheres'. The former are rooted in one place, such as a small town, and are quite socially conservative and often less educated. The latter are rootless, urban, socially liberal and university-educated. Polls suggest around 50 per cent of the population are Somewheres, 20–25 per cent are Anywheres and the remainder are 'Inbetweeners'. These groups have fundamentally different views on issues like immigration. Somewheres, who value social cohesion rooted in established, slowly changing populations of similar ethnicities and backgrounds, want to limit migration, whereas Anywheres welcome multicultural communities and have no concerns about an ever-changing population. We saw these divisions play out in the Brexit referendum on the UK's membership in the EU: metropolitan and multicultural Londoners overwhelmingly voted 'Remain', while their fellow citizens in more monocultural regions voted 'Leave'.

Goodhart leans towards the Somewheres' viewpoint, suggesting that we should all have a hierarchy of concerns at family, community and nation-state levels, which prioritize the needs of those within our own circle. He argues that migration is a problem for not only the receiving countries but also the countries of origin that often lose their best and brightest to emigration.

The Age of Anger

Another aspect of the emocracy is, as Moïsi notes, a blind rage flaring up internationally, acting as a driving force behind radical Muslims. Indian writer Pankaj Mishra identifies a worldwide trend towards anarchism, with its sole objective being the destruction of liberal systems in the hope that something better will rise from the ashes. He claims that the forces driving Brexit and the popularity of anti-establishment political parties stem from the same feelings of anger and revenge that drive teenagers into the arms of terrorist groups. We are living in the Age of Anger, characterized by an intense mix of envy, humiliation and powerlessness that creates 'an existential resentment of other people's being'. Lingering resentment runs deep and poisons society, undermining political liberty and 'presently making for a global turn to authoritarianism and toxic forms of chauvinism'. The source of this anger is universal: the failings of a market-driven capitalism barely regulated by authorities. Apart from a happy few who successfully chase profits and amass wealth—aided and abetted by an army of henchmen—there is an enormous number of socially excluded individuals who are economically and politically marginalized. They are the losers of globalization who do not see international interaction and integration as progress, but rather as a catalyst for mobilization in a global civil war—a protest against elites who snatch 'modernity's choicest fruits' without any thought for traditional norms and values. Meanwhile, the people who see these 'choice fruits' slip away seek 'cultural supremacy, populism and rancorous brutality'. Mishra's Age of Anger is Kali Yuga (the Iron Era) at its darkest and most violent.

Divorced from One Another

French geographer Christophe Guilluy suggests over 50 per cent of Westerners are the real losers of globalization. Comprising primarily the impoverished middle class, this growing cohort struggles to maintain its standard of living and is gradually sinking, a decline reflected in where they reside. The lower middle class—artisans, the self-employed, retirees—are less likely to live in urban centres where big money is made in today's globalized world. Two-thirds currently live in the suburbs, where property costs less and social mobility is limited—especially for those hoping to climb the social ladder.

A globalized economy doesn't need those living on the periphery, so project development tends to stop short of reaching the outskirts. Eventually, it is in these areas that political challengers gain electoral victories. The 'deplorables', to borrow Hilary Clinton's terminology, are confronted daily by a shimmering vision on the horizon: goodies the elite denies them. Those at the top no longer show interest in those at the bottom, while those at the bottom want nothing to do with those at the top who look down on them, preaching the value of a globalized world and a multicultural society. This rupture is catastrophic, and fittingly enough, Guilluy's 2018 book is titled *No Society: La fin de la classe moyenne occidentale* (The End of the Western Middle Class).

Guilluy sees populism as the political manifestation of a social and geographical divide that could overturn economic and cultural order, as demonstrated by the recent *Mouvement des Gilets Jaunes* (Yellow Vests Protests) in France. This popular uprising began in rural areas and protested against rising fuel prices and the general high cost of living.

An Age of Inequality

There is much to be angry about in certain ongoing trends. A recent edition of the Wealth-X *Billionaire Census* shows that the number of billionaires went up by 15 per cent to a record 2,754 in 2017. Not only are there more billionaires today, but also they are much richer. Their overall combined income reached a frightening US$8.9 trillion (in 2017), with the wealth of the 12 richest billionaires increasing by US$175 billion in the previous 10 years. Some of them even doubled their income in that time. For instance, the US businessman Stephen Schwarzman increased his wealth six-fold to $13 billion. In *The Corruption of Capitalism: Why Rentiers Thrive and Work Does Not Pay*, Guy Standing argues that although this huge increase in wealth is at the heart of capitalism, it is not generated through the production of goods or the provision of services but rather results from the ownership of both physical and intellectual assets, aided by subsidies and tax breaks.

The eight richest billionaires are now wealthier than the poorest half of the world's population. Data from Oxfam shows that while the world's billionaires increased their wealth by 12 per cent in 2018, the bottom half of the population got 11 per cent poorer that year through wage stagnation, outsourcing, automation and the on-demand economy. The number of people in marginal or precarious employment thus increased as the rich got richer.

The super-rich, those of whom are now present more in Asia than in North America for the first time, enjoy an increasing influence on the global economy. In contrast to the members of this restricted group who are thriving, things are going downhill for those with less wealth, particularly the middle class, left footing the bill for the financial crisis. In the last decade, societal inequality has increased globally. Oxfam reports that inequality is now as great as it was in the 19th century. In the McKinsey Global Institute report, *Poorer Than Their Parents? Flat or Falling Incomes in Advanced Economies,* findings show that between 2005 and 2014, more than two-thirds of people in 25 Western countries saw a decrease in real income. As mentioned earlier, it cannot be guaranteed that today's Western youngsters will be more prosperous than previous generations—a situation McKinsey & Company suggests is partly due to financial crises, but also due to demographics and changes in the job market. Both these factors, along with ageing populations, smaller households, proportionally less GDP spent on salaries, and loss of jobs to technology and automation, are having a knock-on effect on future economic growth. The middle class is still flourishing in Asia, though the march of progress and rising inequality in the region have put them under considerable pressure.

The struggles of younger generations also have a series of impacts on parents. Across the world, more and more young adults are choosing to stay with their parents longer because they cannot find work or, if employed, do not earn enough to set up a home independently. In areas with high employment, residential prices are rising faster than wages. The Pew Research Centre claims 52 per cent of those aged over 60 in the US—some 17.4 million people—are financially responsible for an elderly parent or an adult child, and atleast 1.2 million baby boomers are looking after both. The figures for this so-called 'sandwich generation' have doubled in 10 years. There are many reasons why adult children turn to their parents for support. Sometimes there are health problems, but more usually it is a combination of low income and high cost of living, including the repayment of student loans—especially those sums incurred for qualifications that did not deliver the expected successful careers. Some US baby boomers are even delaying their retirement to support their adult children, but research by the Consumer Bankruptcy Project suggests it is putting such a strain on them that the number of US citizens aged 65 or above filing for bankruptcy has tripled since 1991.

Millions of people on both sides of the political spectrum now feel the game is rigged against them, that the 'system' is specifically designed to increase wealth for the rich. It is therefore ironic that when the world's billionaires meet at Davos each year, the risks that inequality poses to a stable society are always on the agenda. However, the initiatives that follow these discussions are far from democratic.

In his book *Winners Take All: The Elite Charade of Changing the World*, former consultant at McKinsey & Company Anand Giridharadas writes that these 'panels on injustice' promote thought leaders who confine their thinking to improving lives within the faulty system rather than tackling the fault itself. This genre of elites advocates social change that should be pursued through free market and voluntary action, but not through public life, laws or reform of shared systems. In short, they believe social change should be supervised by capitalist winners and their allies. The main beneficiaries of the status quo should play a leading role in its reform. Giridharadas advances ideas from a speech he gave at the Aspen Institute to 'changemakers' and 'thought leaders', arguing that the very people to whom he was speaking are not so much helping the world through their philanthropic efforts as supporting the broken system that made their fortune. He challenges the idea that those best equipped to protect the interests of the poor are the rich, concluding that even when the initiatives promoted by the elites have brought about positive change, the fact remains that they simultaneously increased income disparity. Giridharadas points out that there is a choice between reform achieved through democratically elected, accountable governments or reform attempted by wealthy, unaccountable elites who claim to act in our best interest.

We have seen this type of shift before, of course. In *Mortal Republic: How Rome Fell into Tyranny*, Edward Watts explains how the Roman Republic transformed into the despotic, corrupt and anti-republican Roman Empire. Watts reminds us that citizens will revolt if they feel the game is rigged against them, with many gravitating towards strongmen for security. He tells how Rome's governing institutions, parliamentary rules and political customs succeeded in fostering compromise and negotiation for centuries, until politicians started misusing Rome's consensus-building tools for personal gain. Selfish political decisions irreparably weakened the Empire by obstructing crucial efforts needed to address the growing social and economic inequality. Moreover, the politicians' opponents responded by engaging in constitutional trickery to bypass the obstruction. Watts's point is clear: the well-being of a system should not be taken for granted. If we are to prevent a similar end for our own society, we must reinvent capitalism so that everyone benefits.

From Henry Ford to Elon Musk

Karl Marx did not expect the middle class to grow beyond a small section of society—an understandable conclusion in the 19th century. The situation changed when the growth of capitalism provided better education and higher wages, enabling more people to escape the working class and join the burgeoning middle class. As early as 1914—six years after the legendary Ford Model T was released—Henry Ford increased his workers' salaries because he realized that he could only sell his cars to the masses when they had enough money to afford them. Other industrialists followed his lead, creating a virtuous circle of well-paid employees that stimulated consumption, enabling factories to employ more people (consumers) and increase production. This created strong economic growth, and the poor proletariat, who Marx imagined would power a communist revolution, became a flourishing middle class instead. However, modern capitalists have abandoned the ideas of Ford and his fellow industrialists and now concentrate on strategies that enrich themselves and their shareholders, to the detriment of wider society. We tend to associate this level of greed and irresponsibility with hedge funds and the financial sector in general, but it is also seen in tech entrepreneurs who have a solid presence in the Wealth-X *Billionaire Census*. Mark Zuckerberg of Facebook, for instance, has always refused to apologize for the social network's secret marketing of tens of millions of users' personal details.

A culture of sexism prevails in many of the IT companies where the nerds who never had a lover turned into sexual predators as soon as they became wealthy. The sheer decadence of Silicon Valley, where restaurants serve dishes worth US$1,200 on 24-carat gold plates and where millionaires can be overheard calling the working class 'a bug in the system', is symptomatic of a capitalist elite community divorced from society. While old-school elites cared about their employees, the new ones are not in the least interested. Jeff Bezos, the owner of Amazon, earns every second what one of his warehouse employees earns every month. It is regrettable that his employees are paid so poorly that they cannot even afford to buy anything from his company.

But the billionaire business owners do not lie awake at night worrying about injustice in the world. Speaking at a summit for the *Financial Times*, the owner of Cartier, Johann Rupert, who is worth an estimated $7.5 billion, revealed that a nightmarish fear of the poor rising up to overthrow the rich keeps him awake. 'How is society going to cope with structural unemployment and the envy, hatred and social welfare?' he asked. 'We are destroying the middle class at this stage, and it will affect us. It's unfair. So that's what keeps me awake at night.'

Skin in the Game

Former derivatives trader-turned-author Nassim Nicholas Taleb believes the lack of responsibility prevalent among people making big decisions in government or business is due to a lack of 'skin in the game'—meaning, as others deal with the negative effects of their decision-making, they never personally experience the fallout. In his book titled the same, Taleb describes politicians, intellectuals, advisers, journalists and decision-makers who don't give a second thought to their terrible decisions or poor advice because they still get paid while never having to suffer the consequences of their actions. As Taleb puts it, a bad decision-maker or adviser can 'continue his practice from the comfort of his thermally regulated suburban house with a two-car garage, a dog and a small play area with pesticide-free grass for his overprotected 2.2 children'. This lack of symmetry between risk and reward leads to moral decay and has devastating financial consequences. Taleb is perhaps too dismissive of the dangers resulting from having *too much* skin in the game—tunnel vision or prioritizing one's personal interests, for instance—but he makes a good point in identifying a sensitive aspect of modern society.

The Fourth Sector and NGOs

If we reverse Henry Ford's logic, consumption will decrease if most people have less purchasing power, creating a negative spiral that is hard to break. In 2013, the International Federation of Red Cross and Red Crescent Societies released a hefty report, appropriately titled *Think differently: Humanitarian impacts of the economic crisis in Europe*, which concluded that the continent is sinking into a dark period of poverty, mass unemployment, inequality and social exclusion. Around the same time, in *A Cautionary Tale: The true cost of austerity and inequality in Europe*, fellow NGO Oxfam warned that 146 million Europeans risk living below the poverty line in the following 20 years. Both reports were written in the wake of a major financial crisis and commented on overly cautious austerity policies being pursued by European governments, primarily hurting the middle class. These reports are still relevant today. In response, Oxfam has been strengthening the 'Fourth Sector', an idea also adopted by the World Economic Forum (WEF) in its Fourth Sector Development Initiative. The fourth sector comprises enterprises that see advancing societal benefits as their primary purpose, in much the same way as non-profit organizations do, albeit the former operate for-profit. In doing so, they are breaking down barriers between the three traditional sectors of public, private and non-profit. Marilia Bezerra, a founder of the Fourth Sector Group, explains that it need not matter if the for-benefit entity is a massive global corporation as long as it 'decides that everything it does is something that is done with a purpose of creating a positive impact in the world'. The philosophical starting point is acknowledging that the world faces massive economic, social and environmental challenges, for which the only route is to channel the spirit of Henry Ford.

One of the biggest problems facing for-profit organizations is access to investment capital. In general, investors must be patient because for-profit organizations tend to grow slowly. Over the past two decades, these investors have been hard to find, but that may be changing. Today, many wealthy people donate part of their income or capital to enterprises that can deliver the biggest impact from their funds; they approach philanthropy in a business-like manner, not swayed by sad tales. One of the more positive pieces of news from the Wealth-X *Billionaire Census* is that the super-rich are increasingly embracing altruism, not only in traditional areas such as art, culture or health, but also in social and educational projects.

The New Machine Age

Humanity is embarking on a new technological revolution that will impact incomes and the job market. Dubbed the

'Second Machine Age', the period we are now entering will be characterized by a new wave of automation, digitalization and robotization. Renowned economists and researchers working in prestigious think tanks are casting doubt on whether the adage 'innovation creates wealth' still holds true in this new industrial era. The rise of Artificial Intelligence (AI) and, more significantly, Machine Learning (ML) has, for the first time, led to automation in areas that were formerly the province of humans—observing and drawing conclusions, reasoning and deciding. Previously, automation concentrated on taking over clearly defined tasks and routines that were easy to capture in computer code. Early automation tended to replace employees in the lower working classes who undertook repetitive administrative and assembly line work, but machines are now increasingly capable of replacing non-routine cognitive tasks, putting pressure on various jobs across all sectors of society. Graduates are likely to see the most impact, but postgraduates and low-skilled workers are also at risk. Machines are already capable of driving cars, constructing legal documents, making judicial decisions and writing sports or trading reports. The US computer scientist Ross Goodwin recently directed an autonomous Cadillac loaded with computers to drive from New York to San Francisco, during which it authored a fascinating novel called *1 the Road,* inspired by Jack Kerouac's classic *On the Road.*

A couple of years ago, the University of Oxford economists Carl Benedikt Frey and Michael Osborne predicted that in the next 20 years, 47 per cent of professions would disappear. At the top of their hit list are telemarketers, followed closely by accountants and financial controllers. Pilots and train drivers are also at risk. There is even a 43 per cent chance of their own academic profession disappearing. Professor Erik Brynjolfsson of the prestigious Massachusetts Institute of Technology (MIT) has long been a champion of the positive influence of Information Communications Technology (ICT) on the economy, but having predicted the loss of more jobs across different sectors, he is now concerned. He says the number of jobs in the West has been falling steadily since the 1960s, despite increased productivity and population growth. He calls this 'the great economic paradox of our time', in which production has reached record heights and innovation has never happened faster, yet middle-level incomes are stagnating, along with a structural loss of employment opportunities. He concludes that machines are indeed stealing our jobs.

The Acceleration

IT has two unique characteristics, both of which have a significant impact on the modern technology revolution. Firstly, ICT, which is synonymous with IT on which it piggybacks, is a so-called generic technology with wide-ranging applications. This is in stark contrast to the steam engine, for example, which transformed factories, mines and transport but had little application outside these areas. The growth of ICT can streamline production processes, increase output and reshape the earning model in many sectors, with an impact equivalent to that of the introduction of electricity at the beginning of the 20th century. The digital character of ICT further heightens the capacity for disruption; once a computer has been successfully programmed to undertake complex tasks, the technology can be duplicated and deployed on a massive scale, even to other industries. By definition, ICT innovations have an enormous reach.

The second characteristic is digital technology's exponential progress. In other words, every new step forward is equivalent to the aggregated sum of all previous steps. Although a few major steps were taken in the recent past, progress was limited and barely noticeable. However, we have now reached the acceleration phase. Suddenly, things deemed impossible a few years ago are either being realized or already in effect. Think of drones, 3D printers, self-driving cars and ships, hyperloops and environments where the physical and digital worlds blend—VR and Augmented Reality (AR). As the changes brought about by automation and digitalization follow one another rapidly, this snowball effect will lead to many far-reaching consequences.

Inspiration from Tech Giant Israel

When we talk about modern technologies, we tend to focus on Silicon Valley. However, in the past 30 years, Israel has emerged as a leading technology centre between the East and the West and can play a significant role in the new economic order. The country is sometimes referred to as the 'Start-up Nation' because it has the world's highest density of start-ups per capita—one for every 1,844 citizens, which is 2.5 times as many as that of the US. According to *The Wall Street Journal*, Israel is Europe's 'main technology hub', with more Israeli businesses listed on NASDAQ than from all European nations combined. In relation to the availability of venture capital, Israel ranks third in the world, and it holds second place for the availability of qualified scientists and engineers. Israel also has a long history of innovative technology. For instance, the chip that powered the original IBM

PC was designed at Intel's lab in Haifa, Israel's third-largest city, and it was Israeli engineers who later created the Pentium and Centrino chips. Every major technology giant has a research centre in Israel, and Steve Ballmer is reputed to have said that Microsoft is as much an Israeli business as it is a US one.

There are several reasons why technology is booming in Israel. Many of the country's founding fathers were scientists and intellectuals who successfully managed to merge a pioneering, enterprising spirit with a culture that valued knowledge and science. Most importantly, perhaps, Israel is a small country with limited natural resources in the middle of a hostile region. Israelis, in order to survive, need to be more inventive and better equipped than their neighbours, who easily outnumber them. With a huge defence budget that enables many technological breakthroughs, the Israel Defense Forces is one of the main drivers behind innovation. Some of its military advancements are also used for peaceful civilian purposes, which stimulates further innovation.

To be a knowledge-based economy, however, Israel will have to deal with some issues. Only some 8 per cent of Israeli employees work in the hi-tech industry around Tel Aviv, and it's a sector that so far hasn't created many jobs. Although many international businesses have research centres in Israel, they do not have headquarters there. According to economic journalist David Rosenberg, the tech sector has reached its ceiling, resulting in only a few people using their specific skills to earn high salaries, thereby widening the income inequality gap. Rosenberg warns that while Israelis may be successful at setting up innovative companies, they are less efficient at growing them and distributing the benefits.

There is also a demographic threat to Israel's success as a global technological powerhouse. The fastest growing population groups are the ultra-Orthodox and the Israeli Arabs, whose population percentages are expected, by 2059, to increase from 10 per cent to 26 per cent and 20 per cent to 23 per cent respectively. The ultra-Orthodox focus all their learning on religious scriptures and traditions instead of Science, Technology, Engineering and Mathematics (STEM) subjects. The Arabs, on the other hand, face discrimination and receive an inferior education in Arabic schools, which don't offer lessons in Hebrew, resulting in less funding. Both groups participate in the labour market at much lower levels than that of other Israelis and consequently suffer higher rates of poverty. This creates a risk of limiting Israel's potential; it is a lesson India should learn—treat minorities better. The payoff is stability and happiness.

Technological Unemployment

We must ask ourselves if we are in charge of these developments. Prescient UK economist John Maynard Keynes warned of what he called 'technological unemployment' in his essay *Economic Possibilities for our Grandchildren*, first published in 1930. He described what happens when the speed of technological progress has the potential to replace human labour with machines faster than new ways to employ people can be created. In other words, technological production processes change so fast that the economy is unable to adapt. Seeing technological unemployment as a temporary phase, Keynes anticipated that people would reorient themselves, adapt to changing circumstances, return to education, upskill and then find new work. He also expected the economy to adapt as well, keeping affluence and employment stable. Keynes's long-term prediction was that only the introduction of a 15-hour working week would ensure enough work for everyone. Back in the day, Keynes's colleagues reacted to his ideas with scepticism since received wisdom equated technological innovation with economic growth. Now, standing in the Second Machine Age, we are more likely to see Keynes's technological unemployment become a (semi) permanent feature in many societies.

Positive Noises

Many people agreed with Frey and Osborne when their ideas were published at the height of mass unemployment during a financial crisis; however, economists and politicians are adopting a more positive stance, now that the economy is recovering. Recent research papers are even downplaying the threat of technological unemployment. In 2016, researchers at the Organization for Economic Co-operation and Development (OECD) stated that Frey and Osborne had overestimated the risks of automation because their starting point was the loss of all professions. Every job role comprises multiple duties, not all of which can be automated, so machines will only replace people in specific tasks. Residual tasks will continue to be undertaken by people and new tasks will be developed to complement the machines' operations. It would therefore be more accurate to suggest that job roles will remain but the nature of the work will change. Researchers predict that a mere 9 per cent of jobs in developed countries can be completely automated, with nothing to indicate the number will even be that high.

Although innovation is developing faster than ever, progress in implementing modern technology on a mass scale is slow due to societal, legal, ethical and economic barriers. This gives working populations time to adapt to new circumstances. Researchers also suggest that increasing demand for modern technologies, by definition, creates more jobs. On one hand, more and more people are needed to build and maintain technology, while on the other, technology makes businesses competitive, leading them to produce more, increase their profit and involve a larger workforce. According to the WEF's *The Future of Jobs Report 2018*, worldwide jobs in 'the emerging professions' likely increased from 16 to 27 per cent between 2018 and 2022, while 'declining roles' likely fell from 31 to 21 per cent in the same period. The WEF estimated that during those four years, 75 million jobs would disappear worldwide through automation but 133 million new ones would be created. New roles and functions are also better adapted to the changing division of labour between people, machines and algorithms, which means innovation in the Second Machine Age creates growth and increased prosperity.

Does the Past Offer Hope for the Present?

Although the WEF report has given a more positive indication than the ones published by Frey and Osborne, a note of caution is needed. The authors don't mean to be prophets of doom; rather, these figures merely illustrate a scenario, a calculation of what *could* happen in an ideal world. As the researchers emphasize, arduous work is needed to give substance to the hypothetical if it is to be made reality. There must be significant investments and societal changes to ensure the workforce reskills and upskills. In 2018, the WEF suggested 54 per cent of those in employment needed significant training, with at least 10 per cent of those workers needing to train for at least 12 months. At the same time, 33 per cent of employers said they were unwilling to invest in workers whose jobs were at the greatest risk of being replaced by machines. The most vulnerable group in the working population is therefore the people most at risk, and if the extra training does not materialize, they could be unemployed permanently, swelling the disenfranchised, angry ranks of those who feel they lost out to progress.

Most importantly, the OECD assumes the new technological revolution will follow the trajectory of previous large-scale technological changes because more jobs were created in the long term than were lost. It feels like creative accounting—or, as Nassim Nicholas Taleb would say, it is like assuming all swans are white because you have never encountered a black one. There are similarities between the current and previous technological revolutions, of course, but today's rapid pace of change and the reach of modern technology mean the consequences are greater—unrest could last much longer than before. Furthermore, the new wave of automation is much different from that of the 1980s or what happened during previous technological revolutions. As mentioned earlier, the new technological revolution is not limited to one sector, but rather stretches across the whole economy. A 19th-century weaver who lost his job could find work in a mine or on the railways but those made redundant in one sector today may find other sectors equally constricted. It could be that the adaptation phase will last much longer than anticipated, meaning Keynes's spectre of technological unemployment may come to haunt us yet.

The research by the WEF and the OECD looks primarily at loss of jobs due to automation, but automation per se is not the main reason jobs are lost to technology. They are also lost because companies are unable to make the leap to a digital economy, ultimately failing. By factoring in these losses, we find the speed at which jobs are created by the technology sector itself (at start-ups, for instance) is many times lower than the speed at which they are lost. Take Instagram, for example, which was barely two years old when it was sold to Facebook for US$1 billion. At that time, it employed 13 people, but now it has 450 employees to facilitate 800 million people sharing their photographs each month. Then consider photography giant Kodak, which filed for bankruptcy in 2012, resulting in 8,500 job losses. Kodak was a pioneer, bringing the first domestic cameras to market, but it fatally missed an opportunity in the digital era. In the 10 years before Kodak closed its doors, the business had already laid off 47,000 employees—roughly as many people as worked for Google at the time (Google was 15 years old then) and nearly 20,000 more than Facebook expected to employ by its 15th anniversary (in 2019).

Job Polarization

Automation is best suited to routine work that is easily subdivided and translated into computer code. This type of work is found in the middle management sector of the service economy. Starting in the 1980s, automation has led to job polarization, resulting in lower demand for graduate personnel but a rising need for both postgraduates and low-skilled workers. Postgraduates work in jobs that are more difficult to automate, and although machines could take over a number of their menial tasks, there are no substantial savings to be made. Low-skilled employees are needed where wages are low and the cost of investing in machines is high. Automation is also impractical where low-skilled work either requires social skills or is site-specific, such as park-keeping or cleaning. The big win for automation is in the middle-income bracket. In the West, the number of jobs in this middle-income bracket has been falling steadily since the 1990s, and the trend is likely to continue. Tens of thousands of jobs are expected to be lost in the financial sector alone; cashiers, managers, accountants, tax investigators, traders, financial analysts and data-entry clerks should all be worried about their job prospects in the long term.

Working in the Dark

In recent years, some Chinese factories have replaced up to 90 per cent of their workforce with robots—a consequence of the pressure from rising salary costs. With no presence of people, there is no need for lighting, so they are known as dark factories. Often thought to exemplify automation's worst-case scenario, their reputation is not entirely fair. If this happened in the West, where laying off 90 per cent of workers is much more difficult, business owners would either soon find themselves embroiled in legal battles or face generous redundancy packages, both of which would barely leave enough money for a screwdriver, let alone a robot. It does not mean there will be no dark factories in the West, but rather that new factories will be built instead of repurposing existing ones, creating new jobs. This also means a chance for extra production capacity, which is where the real profit lies, and the possibility to recover businesses lost to low-cost outsourcing economies.

While factory owners in China were first switching off the lights, Adidas was switching on its first

'Speedfactory' in Germany covering 4,600 square metres, where robots produced sports shoes and T-shirts with barely a human on the premises. It was a type of work that had not taken place in Germany since the 1980s. The sportswear manufacturer also opened a Speedfactory in the US, with further ones planned for France and the UK. The Germans claimed there would be enough work for everyone because demand for Adidas products had been greater than supply for years, with Speedfactories being a way to address the shortfall. Contrary to the claims, these hyper-modern factories threatened the employment of half a million people in Asia who worked for Adidas. The question arose: how would the hardworking Asian people survive when their jobs were replaced by robots, whether foreign or domestic? In China alone, the jobs of more than 100 million people could be at risk from automation. Ultimately, the Speedfactory experiment failed because it was unable to meet the growing demand for a large number of models.

Digital Taylorism

Even work that would prove difficult for machines is not safe from automation. At opposite ends of the work spectrum, jobs that rely on intellectual or emotional ability, as well as creativity, are difficult to automate, although there is scope for major change. Work processes in these jobs will be increasingly split into smaller, specific tasks that are more repetitive and require less human input, opening the way for automation in the long term. This phenomenon is known as 'Digital Taylorism', named after the 'father of scientific management' Frederick Winslow Taylor, and it is already being applied in many professions. Technology is forcing doctors, teachers, call centre workers and shop assistants to follow stricter policies of inspection and control, leaving much less room for professional judgement and independent decision-making. Subjected to monotonous work, workers are experiencing job dissatisfaction, unhappiness and even psychiatric problems. It is well documented that the best ways to prevent burnout are taking pride and pleasure in work and being allowed to make independent decisions.

Pessimists predict that today's 'brain' workers will end up like the 19th-century artisans who saw industrialization reduce their craft to servicing a machine or standing at an assembly line. As computers develop better 'thinking' abilities, this will, in turn, lead to improvements in 'hand' work, meaning more scope for automation.

Leadership in the Age of Anger and the Second Machine Age

To make the Second Machine Age a success, we need good leadership. Manfred Kets de Vries, who draws on economics, management and psychoanalysis in his work on leadership, suggests that leaders need to know themselves, understand the effect they have on others and reflect to be more humane. In his article *Reflective Leaders Needed for the Age of Rage*, Graham Ward adds that 'the case for reflective rather than reactive leadership, in society and organizations' has never been stronger. He notes we are no longer human beings but rather 'human doings', and leaders are battered with information, making reflection both undervalued and impossible. As a result, rage, anxiety and sadness are building up—invisible, untapped and prone to explode. Ward concludes that leaders need to connect emotionally with those they lead—they must actively listen, while also acknowledging their own defensiveness.

Similarly, they also need to understand those outside their business. For example, political leaders failing to understand the people 'allow demagoguery in through the backdoor', while crafty opportunists are permitted to 'tap into popular anger, polarizing opinion'. Business and political leaders, therefore, must keep close 'to society, their teams and themselves through "reflective" action'.

A Time Similar to the Dark Ages

Modern times resemble the Dark Ages in many ways—through incompetent elites, lack of leadership, erosion of (moral) authority and the implosion of empires. The difference is that these events are happening on a worldwide scale today, rather than just in Western Europe or Italy during the Early Middle Ages. A new renaissance, which will put an end to the present dark age, will be global too. To usher in this new era, we must first address the perfect storm that is gaining momentum. A 'perfect storm' occurs when events smash together and strengthen one another, much like the way wars begin. Currently, there are six megatrends gathering pace, preparing to collide. A perfect storm is coming, and it could pit humanity against humanity, which pessimists believe could even lead to another world war. In the sixth century BC, Chinese general Sun Tzu advises in *The Art of War* that if you know your enemy and know yourself, you will avoid being 'imperilled in a hundred battles'; if you know yourself but don't know your enemy, you will win one battle and lose another; if you know neither your enemy nor yourself, you will be 'imperilled in every single battle'. The authors will leave it to our readers to decide whether they know themselves, but to guard against defeat, we shall introduce the enemy—the megatrends gathering force—which could create a perfect storm soon.

COLUMN THE FUTURE OF AGRICULTURE AND FOOD

At the end of the 19th century, Europe was flooded with cheap grain from the United States, plunging it into a deep agricultural crisis. While most countries, led by France, responded by closing their borders to protect domestic farmers, the Netherlands chose a different path. The Dutch government established a State Commission for Agriculture and sought expert advice, recognizing that the only viable solution was to compete with the US by becoming equally—if not more—efficient.

Embracing the commission's recommendations, the government prioritized agricultural education and research. This led to the founding of the National Agricultural School and the establishment of agricultural experimental stations—both of which would later evolve into Wageningen University & Research. This early focus on knowledge and innovation laid the foundation for the Dutch agricultural sector's remarkable success.

Through the collaborative efforts of government, industry, and research institutions—later referred to as the Golden Triangle—Dutch agriculture rapidly transformed. Today, the Netherlands is the second-largest agricultural exporter in the world, with an export value of approximately €125 billion. The agri-food sector accounts for nearly 10 per cent of the nation's GDP and employment, making it the largest manufacturing industry in the country. Wageningen University has become a global leader in agricultural research, attracting students from over 100 countries.

The sector's strength lies not only in mechanization and automation but also in the extraordinary increase in productivity. Over the past century, grain yields have grown from 2,000 kg to 10,000 kg per hectare, while average milk production per cow has risen from 2,500 kg to 10,000 kg—a four- to five-fold increase. This progress is driven by advancements in breeding, improved nutrition, disease control and preventive healthcare, among many other innovations.

Beyond boosting productivity, these advancements have also reduced the sector's environmental footprint. More efficient production means lower greenhouse gas emissions per kilogram of food produced. As a result, Dutch agriculture has become a model of sustainable and efficient food production, offering a blueprint for feeding the world's rapidly growing population with high-quality food while minimizing environmental impact.

By adopting Dutch agricultural innovations, India has the potential to become a food superpower. Increasing the number of Indian students studying Dutch agricultural technology through scholarships and exchange programmes would transfer valuable knowledge and expertise to India's farming sector.

The future of agriculture holds even greater possibilities. Breakthroughs in genomics and CRISPR-Cas technology will enable the development of stronger, more resilient crop varieties and improve animal health. The integration of artificial intelligence will further enhance efficiency, optimize resource management and unlock new potential in food production.

As the world faces the challenge of feeding billions more people in the coming decades, the need for continuous innovation in the agri-food sector has never been greater. By embracing cutting-edge technologies and fostering global collaboration, the Netherlands will continue to lead the way—benefiting not only itself but also the world.

—**Dr Aalt A. Dijkhuizen**
Former President & CEO

WAGENINGEN
UNIVERSITY & RESEARCH

2

Jihad and the Islamic Reformation

Saudi Arabia will host the FIFA World Cup in 2034. Crown Prince Mohammed bin Salman (MbS) hopes this event will present his country to the world as a beacon of modernity, stability and peace. The authors believe this promising young leader will succeed. However, to achieve this goal, MbS must crush the jihadists. An Islamic jihad—or holy war—fought by radical Muslims intent on subjugating both liberal Muslims and non-Muslims is endangering the world. While almost all Muslims are peace-loving, a radical minority is cleverly exploiting widespread anger in many Islamic countries to set its own agenda—anger about the Western cultural, economic and military dominance; anger about corrupt leaders; anger about the lack of future prospects; anger about the situation in the Middle East, and so on.

India enjoys cordial relationships with many states and stakeholders in the Middle East, such as the UAE, Saudi Arabia, Israel, and others. However, Islamism in neighbouring Afghanistan, Pakistan and Bangladesh might become a danger for India in the future, as previously demonstrated by the 2008 Mumbai terrorist attacks.

After independence, India was led along socialist lines by the Nehru-Gandhi dynasty, like many other newly independent nations in the Global South. So it remained as poor and inward-looking as its neighbours, with no major aspiration to stand alongside the other world powers. However, visionary prime ministers Manmohan Singh (2004–2014) and Narendra Modi (2014–present) changed tack, making India one of the world's top five economies and much wealthier than its neighbours. Today, if we fly over Pakistan and other northern neighbours of India, we see countries that resemble India in the 1970s. In contrast, flying over India reveals a modern nation with hundreds of new buildings and a far superior infrastructure compared to the 1970s. This progress, however, makes it easier for terrorists in poorer neighbouring countries to recruit and train young boys, making India a potential target. The Chinese often say that Mao Zedong enabled China to stand, Deng Xiaoping helped it walk and Xi Jinping enabled it to run. Perhaps a similar trajectory can be seen in India—where Nehru enabled it to stand, Dr Manmohan Singh helped it walk and Narendra Modi set it running.

Tensions between India and Pakistan over Kashmir could be resolved peacefully. India can now afford to buy Pakistan-occupied Kashmir, and Pakistan needs the money. This approach is not unheard of: the US bought Alaska from the Russians and Louisiana from the French. The problem lies in Kashmir being a religious issue for jihadists. Whether called IS, Al-Qaeda, Boko Haram (Africa) or Islamic State Khorasan (ISK) [Afghanistan], jihadists are mostly led, armed and financed by Iran. The Iranian regime was strong until the Israelis defeated its allies Hamas (Gaza) and Hezbollah (Lebanon) in 2024, indirectly causing the fall of Iran's Syrian ally Assad—who supported India on Kashmir. We don't yet know if the new Syrian regime will allow IS and other jihadists to regroup there and plan global terrorist attacks. What we do know, however, is that IS has already regrouped in Somalia, which overlooks India's important shipping routes. Syria will also become an exporter of jihadists. Some jihadists from the Chinese province of Xinjiang, who fight for the current Syrian leader, have already threatened to attack China with missiles launched from Syria. So jihadism and terrorism are here to stay, dear readers, much like the global drug trade. In fact, a growing nexus between terrorism and narcotics is already unfolding in Europe, which might spread to the rest of the world.

As mentioned, MbS is cautiously modernizing Saudi Arabia in line with the population's wishes, thus diminishing the power of the extremist Wahhabis. He is presenting Saudi Arabia as a modern nation and a peacekeeper in the Middle East, in contrast to a belligerent Iran. While the current Saudi Islamic Reformation is a beacon of hope for all Muslims, the UAE—India's close ally—has already turned its own reformation into reality. Even Indian Muslims show little interest in aligning with Iran.

According to Iranian-Australian scholar Imam Tawhidi, Islam must reform to survive. Tawhidi, who calls himself the Imam of Peace and can trace his ancestry back to the founders of the faith, describes jihadists as 'a cancer' and has urged for violence-inciting religious texts to be forbidden. He also speaks out openly against the oppression of women in Islamic culture. It is our hope that reformers like Tawhidi can unite Islam with the modern world, for that will be the only way to root out jihadism. At the same time, just as we know from our Christian history, religious reformation is likely to be accompanied by violence and a resurgence of conservative powers. It is quite possible that conflict within the Islamic faith will continue in the near future, with harmful consequences for the rest of the world.

Despite all, one positive outcome of this internal strife could be the Iranian regime's implosion.

The Surplus of Boys

German sociologist Gunnar Heinsohn argues that an excess of young adult males in a population leads to social unrest, war and terrorism. This happens because the third and fourth sons in a family fail to secure any prestigious social position—local economies generally offer opportunities for no more than two sons per family. In a traditional society, the firstborn son inherits his father's business or property; the second goes to school and becomes a priest or a teacher (or migrates). The options for subsequent sons are limited due to a lack of money, forcing them to rationalize an impetus to compete through radical religious or political ideologies. Heinsohn claims that most genocides and historical periods of social unrest can be explained through the youth bulge phenomenon. Recent history provides tragic examples, such as fascism and Nazism, conflict in Darfur and many other places, and the uprisings in Palestine and other Arab or Islamic countries. Men do not necessarily want to fight but do so when faced with a lack of economic opportunities.

Parents who favour male babies create gender imbalances that often mean their sons cannot find a girlfriend or marry. This is especially true in countries where same-sex intercourse is prohibited, where many young men, whether gay or straight, have no means to relieve their sexual energy. Heinsohn distinguishes two scenarios. In the first, superfluous boys fight one another to the death, reducing the surplus, after which peace is naturally restored (this happened in 1994 in Rwanda, where about 1 million excess boys were killed). In the second case, the boys turn to a violent ideology and a strong leader who offers them an opportunity to right some perceived wrongs.

A typical modus operandi of the latter ideology is to first speak out against a rich but militarily weak enemy, followed by targeting it to provide the boys with money and success. Next, it focuses on establishing power across an entire region. A clever ideological leader mobilizes young men to seize power, but then disposes of them before they can turn him in—the best way to achieve this is by starting a full-scale war. Hitler, Lenin, Stalin and Mao Zedong are prime examples of such leaders. In China, we see a surplus of young boys today, who could create trouble for the Chinese government in the coming years. There is a similar problem in the Islamic world, where millions of redundant boys are of fighting age. The surplus was the driving force behind the Arab Spring, and it is now the main reason for the success of violent Islamist ideologies and the continuing reign of terrorism. The millions of surplus boys are also behind the current waves of mass migration hitting the EU and the US hard.

Demographic Warfare

The coming decades will be characterized by mass migration. While some migrants are fleeing war, violence and persecution, others simply want a better life and seek their fortune. Furthermore, an increasing number of people displaced by climate change will join the waves of migration in the coming years, all because the weather is too extreme in their countries of origin. Europe is already facing an annual deluge of economic migrants from poorer parts of the world, with millions more awaiting their opportunity in Turkey and the Maghreb (Northwest Africa). As the authors write this, thousands of poor Latin Americans,

Indians and Chinese are making their way to the US through the dangerous Panama route. As economic power shifts further, Asia and countries in the East are also likely to be confronted with a large-scale influx of migrants.

In her book *Weapons of Mass Migration: Forced Displacement, Coercion, and Foreign Policy*, the US politico Kelly Greenhill explains how dictatorial regimes further their own political ends by using mass migration to manipulate the actions of other countries. It can be done in two ways: either by politically influencing target countries, emphasizing the risk that they may be unable to cope with such a large influx of refugees and migrants, thereby inciting rhetoric between opposing politicians, or alternatively, by blackmailing target countries, using international agreements or the law to force them to accept refugees and provide shelter. Dictators of any stature are, therefore, able to exert pressure on their democratic neighbours, giving themselves a tactical advantage in negotiations. According to Greenhill, the countries using 'strategically engineered migration' are weaker than their targets, which are usually liberal democracies proud of their record of upholding human rights. The threat of weapons of mass migration allows these dictatorships to play a bigger geopolitical role than they should rightfully be able to play.

Greenhill shows in her book that in the past 50 years, a developed country has been blackmailed or destabilized many times in this way—at least once a year on average. She notes that the most successful operator in this arena was the late Libyan dictator Muammar Gaddafi, who kept strict control over migration in the Mediterranean during his tenure. With his downfall at the hands of the West, this control disappeared, and Libya became one of the main jumping-off points for migrants into Europe. This development makes Gaddafi's downfall a classic example of the rule of unintended consequences, since it led to even greater chaos. The many weapons left by Gaddafi's army in the aftermath of the Libyan civil war have also found their way to other parts of Africa, especially into the eager hands of groups like Boko Haram in Nigeria and the defeated Tuareg rebels, who have decamped to Mali to continue their fight. The northwards migration towards North Africa and Europe has therefore received an extra push.

As discussed earlier, there is currently a surplus of boys in India, Brazil and countries within the Global South, some of whom are susceptible to jihadism—particularly those in Pakistan and Afghanistan. The BRICS countries are therefore investing in the Global South, creating positivity to override jihadism's negative purpose. However, with Iran also investing in the Global South, what will be the outcome? The authors believe that just as light prevails over darkness, positivity will prevail over negativity.

India can prevent homegrown social unrest and violent uprisings by offering alternative opportunities to its surplus boys. It sends many to serve in UN peacekeeping forces, as mentioned earlier, while also encouraging others to find work abroad. Although opportunities like this help, communist ideology still appeals to poor people and commoners, as demonstrated by the success of Maoist rebels in Nepal.

Greenhill describes how North Korea threatens China with weapons of mass migration. For more than 50 years, it has threatened to unleash millions of border-crossing migrants, unless it gets what it wants from China. India can learn from these threats and build border walls (à la Trump) to discourage its poor northern neighbours from blackmailing it in the same way. Preventing new tensions with Pakistan or Afghanistan, as well as stopping the social unrest in Bangladesh from spilling across the borders, is therefore one of India's top geopolitical priorities.

Capitalism of Greed

The unchecked Anglo-Saxon capitalism that has so far dominated the world is accurately described as 'greed capitalism'. As mentioned earlier, a small elite is reaping the rewards of our economic systems, while the majority is descending into poverty, uncertainty and dependency. Anger at this self-serving elite class is further fuelled by the knowledge that they hardly pay any tax in fair proportions. According to the Tax Justice Network, worldwide tax evasion by the rich has reached astronomical heights.

The Greek philosopher Aristotle taught his pupils that a large and thriving middle class safeguards social stability, while disparities in affluence within a population inevitably lead to political instability. As we've already seen, Johann Rupert, owner of the luxury brand Cartier, has similar worries. He believes the elites are busy 'decimating' the middle class, which carries grave consequences. Rupert's nightmare about the deprived revolting and attacking the rich is not surprising—greed capitalism not only serves the elites but also dominates politics. This is clearly reflected in this age, where politicians are busy serving these elite groups instead of the common people.

The feared revolt would cause a political, economic and cultural earthquake, and today's all-powerful elites would be shoved aside. The liberal democracy that has served Western countries so well for decades, making them rich, is no longer an example to the rest of the world. It is no longer a source of hope and solace for its own people, so it is destined to disappear. The clearest indicators of this are the political challengers emerging all around the world, mobilizing the masses with messages promising change—something that established politicians can no longer deliver. The authors will explore how this process works later, but for now, we urge our most egalitarian readers to wake up, connect with fellow citizens, reach out to the losers of tomorrow, defuse their anger and transform greed capitalism into karma capitalism, which is beneficial for entrepreneurs, their employees, suppliers and customers, and for society as a whole. The chasm between the elites and the rest of society will otherwise become so vast that we all will inevitably fall into it. Don't forget that many brilliant individuals are born into poor families or lower castes, yet rise and succeed because of their talent. India's current prime minister and his predecessor were born into poor families, as were many Indian entrepreneurs. So, in some ways, India is already more of a meritocracy than it was in the past, though too many people still live in poverty-stricken slums without any opportunity to nurture their talents. This needs to change. India can benefit much more from its demographic dividend.

The Netflix film *Yeh Ballet* provides an inspiring example: two gifted teenage boys (one Hindu, one Muslim) from a Mumbai slum are discovered by an eccentric ballet master and go on to pursue their dancing dreams despite facing bigotry and disapproval. The inspirational Hindi-language series *Class*, also on Netflix, raises questions about class differences and wealth. An adaptation of the Spanish series *Elite*, *Class* is a young-adult drama that pits three working-class children against the powerful elite at a prestigious international school, exposing the dark underbelly of wealth. Although fictional, the class differences it portrays need urgent attention. While more scholarships and funding should be reserved for poor or working-class youngsters, true stories of talented people born into poverty who reached the top must be told and retold in various formats across today's multimedia platforms. India's 21st-century dream can be the new 'American Dream': a dream of the poor becoming rich. India could be the birthplace of tomorrow's leading entrepreneurs who reshape the country and global standards.

Wealth is, however, not the only key to success—it is mostly happiness. Many people feel lonely, depressed and disengaged lately, as love, friendships and intimacy become more complicated. Therefore, the authors advocate for *Happynomy,* or the Economy of Happiness. If all people in society—irrespective of whether they are educated theoretically (higher) or practically (lower)—feel valued for their skills and talents, and if individuals from one class or caste don't look down on those from a lower class or caste, society becomes more stable and less tense. If people in wealthy regions stop ignoring those in slums, and urbanites stop disregarding rural communities, society becomes a lot happier. Each and every person has some value and worth in the eyes of gods, so why play god ourselves and (mis) judge others?

India must invest more in mental health, otherwise it will fall into the same trap as other countries. In the US, 50 per cent of citizens say they have no friends whatsoever— zero friends in a modern superpower—because they are too busy working, sometimes in several jobs simply to make ends meet. Adding to that, they may get only two weeks of paid holiday per year, if they're lucky. That is not the definition of happiness.

In the Netherlands—the authors' country—one in every three marriages now ends in divorce. Even if people are still married, many admit they are not happy. Up to the 19th century, people, on average, lived until they were about 40. If a couple got married at 20, they were together for 20 years. That was doable, even for arranged marriages. Now people live to 80, 90 or even 100. This means one could be married for 60–80 years, which is hard work, especially if your mother-in-law lives to a ripe old age too. In Mexico, the parliament has discussed a proposal that marriages should last only seven years, as people now live longer. If a person marries today, their marriage ends automatically after seven years, when they can renegotiate another seven-year term with the same spouse, or choose someone else. Maybe India could consider this idea too. Besides, it should legalize gay and lesbian marriage, just like Taiwan and Thailand have done. India, the land of the *Kama Sutra*, could become the superpower of love!

A Reset of the Financial System

The current West-dominated monetary and financial system is due for a massive overhaul. Some economic experts argue that the current system is bankrupt. The amount of cash flowing through financial markets has increased enormously in recent decades, though technological advances have made it difficult to pin down this flow. Enormous amounts can be traded in an instant from any global location, while national and international monitors, who barely have control over this lightning-fast capital, are unable to react to or modify the situation.

Suppose the Fed uses its favourite tool (increasing interest rates) to prop up the dollar, which would attract capital from India, Turkey and Brazil, quickly denuding these countries of essential finances. While money is just a means of enabling economies to simplify the exchange of goods and satisfy needs, it has become an end in itself in the current financial system. To rectify the faulty pattern that has crept in and now runs throughout capitalism and our monetary system, we need a complete reset. Ever since the Ukraine war began, the US has weaponized both the US dollar and the global financial system, including SWIFT (the global standard for payment and securities trade), against Russia—an unwise move that will have consequences. In response, the BRICS countries are expected to introduce new gold-backed currencies and a rival to SWIFT, which will enable them (along with others in the Global South) to increasingly trade without the US dollar, leading to the end of the dollar as the only world currency.

Bitcoin and other cryptocurrencies are also important financial elements of the future. In Israel, the Diamond Stock Exchange launched the CARAT, a cryptocurrency whose value is based on the diamonds in its vaults. This interesting idea (although terminated now) dates back to the time of the Egyptian pharaohs, who issued the first banknotes as coupons linked to a certain amount of grain in their warehouses. Similarly, we might see cryptocurrencies linked to oil, gas, uranium or other commodities in the future.

Such a reset typically involves a shock to the system, resulting from the revaluation or abolition of existing currency, or the creation of new money—a process usually accompanied by devaluation and expropriation.

New Technology

Wars and technology have always been closely related—the former is an engine ensuring the latter is developed and implemented quickly. While the established order is more likely to put the brakes on innovation during peacetime, modern inventions like the internet, GPS and night vision have their origins in the military industry. Ironically enough, the introduction of modern technology, which leads to people losing their livelihoods, can also create unrest that may ultimately trigger war. Although both winners and losers emerge from technological revolutions, it is the losers who try to sabotage change. The rise of Donald Trump can be correlated to social unrest created by today's technological revolution.

As mentioned earlier, humanity is now at the beginning of a new technological revolution—a Second Machine Age. Algorithms and robots are threatening employment opportunities and creating widespread poverty, causing people to lose hope for the future. In response, anger directed at the establishment could, in a worst-case scenario, lead to civil war. In the early 19th century, English weavers in the textile industry attacked and destroyed the mechanical looms that had replaced their labour. Known as Luddites, these protesting workers travelled from town to town, county to county, leaving a trail of destruction in their wake, until the army restored order.

Modern technology also enables people to cut themselves off from the diverse world and only associate with like-minded individuals. Modern ICT makes it possible for people to connect only with those who share similar views and avoid others whose opinions could challenge them. Everyone is looking for their own 'tribe' instead of feeling any affinity with their family, social class, neighbourhood or country. This phenomenon is known as 'tribalization', and we don't expect tolerance or mutual understanding between these diverse groups and tribes to be restored anytime soon. People feel safe within their own tribes, but out on the street, especially in big cities, they are increasingly lonely and inclined to see others as a threat.

At a time when more people are likely to lose their jobs to computers and robots, our intimate relationship with modern technology could go sour. Voices within unions and left-wing parties are calling for action to protect jobs by taxing robot usage, by making it expensive to replace human labour or even by imposing fines. Meanwhile, the wider public is losing sympathy for technology-based businesses. Those who are rejecting technology are not the losers of progress, but rather men and women who proved their mettle as software developers in Silicon Valley before they realized how businesses were using technology to create tech addicts. A large number of people are, therefore, turning their back on the IT industry, comparing the sector to the cigarette industry, which does everything in its power to create addicts for its products and promote the habit. These former techies have eloquently made their point, which is another factor contributing to the growing aversion to technology in wider society.

Enlightenment Now

As we have seen earlier, there is ample cause for concern in the modern world. However, as psychologist Steven Pinker points out in *Enlightenment Now: The Case for Reason, Science, Humanism, and Progress*, humanity has only improved since the Enlightenment in the early 17th century. Today, people are healthier, live longer and are more intelligent with rising levels of literacy. Contrary to what we often think, the world is now a safer place: warfare claim fewer victims than ever before and there is less violent crime. Failed harvests and famine are no longer prevalent; poverty is declining, and more people are now able to enjoy simple pleasures, such as a glass of wine or a visit to the cinema. Pinker credits the Enlightenment for our current situation because it encouraged people to use their intelligence and ability, follow a humanistic ideal and make the world better for everyone. If we keep a tight grip on this principle, we will undoubtedly succeed in the future, albeit with a bumpy ride.

Pinker also uses impressive data and numerous statistics to claim that many people are led by emotions and prejudice instead of information or facts, leading them to believe incorrectly that much is still wrong with the world. We have been around for 3,00,000 years but have experienced abundance only during the last 200—that's 0.07 per cent of human existence. Is it any wonder we are predisposed to pessimism and believe the distorted picture presented by politicians and the media? We long for the 'pure knowledge' attained by Hindus in their *Satya Yuga* rather than being dominated by an academic viewpoint of the world. The authors believe it is unhealthy to completely cut off emotions and that much of today's global unrest is due to humanity's neglect of sentiment—a point we shall explore in detail later. Humanity should not allow itself to be held back by fear and predictions of doom, but rather embrace change, even if it sometimes goes against our instincts. Jobs will certainly be lost in the coming years, but new ones—some better than we ever imagined—will emerge to fill the gap. The inevitable shift of world power towards the East will be mourned in the West, where populations should remember that not everything emanating from the West in recent centuries has been positive, healthy or beneficial for the world. For instance, the West created the spark for two world wars! They can learn much from the East—traits like optimism and enthusiasm, which have continued to shine from the East for centuries.

After the dark age of Kali Yuga, humanity can expect a new golden age of Satya Yuga. The transition between eras will be seamless, but our choices and behaviours will dictate whether populations remain stuck in one era or progress to the next. Today's positive signs suggest humanity is cautiously climbing upward. The authors believe humanity is finally ready to leave the dark age behind and embark on a new Renaissance—a rebirth that can benefit the entire world this time, rather than just an elite few in Western Europe.

Part 2

The World Megatrends

3

The New Renaissance:
The World Revived

As mentioned earlier, we no longer live in times of change, but in a change of times. We are at the beginning of an era that will reshape people and society, with an impact as significant to humanity as that of the Industrial Revolution in the 19th century. It will go down in history as the Second Machine Age, signifying a period when machines take over many rational tasks and activities. Integral to this new era is the Emotional Revolution, in which human emotions will become more important than ever before.

The digital workplace will put an end to inefficiency and time-consuming administration; software like the AI+FR will eliminate much of the bureaucracy for insurance companies, banks, tax departments and others; the complete digitalization of money will also gather pace. Central banks around the world are currently undermining money's value by constantly creating new currencies that are not backed by physical assets. Former president of the Dutch Central Bank (De Nederlandsche Bank, DNB) Nout Wellink expects that this devaluation will result in the implosion of the current financial and monetary system, allowing new cryptocurrencies to emerge and take its place. For example, CARAT was a cryptocurrency based on the value of diamonds, while the Kinesis Monetary System is based on the value of gold and silver.

The digitalization of healthcare will accelerate over the next 30 years, and we can look forward to tiny minicomputers swimming along our veins, checking our cells and immediately repairing any sick or injured parts of the body. We are close to seeing the end of illness, which is incredible. Moreover, nanotechnology and biotechnology may enable a Reproduction Revolution. As Elie Dolgin writes in 'Making Babies: How to create human embryos with no egg or sperm' for *New Scientist*, artificial wombs and embryos made from skin cells—remarkable new techniques discovered in only the last couple of years—could revolutionize reproductive biology and help bring an end to infertility. Bioethicist Henry Greely, foreseeing a day when IVF clients will be presented with a list of characteristics for their embryos, says that such technology sets the stage for 'very, very widespread use of embryo selection'. Greely suspects that given such choice, IVF might eventually become the default method of human reproduction, as he concludes his book *The End of Sex and the Future of Human Reproduction* by claiming that sometime in the next 20–40 years, 'sex (for reproduction) will largely disappear'. This technology could even transform the entire concept of family. By growing babies in artificial wombs and paying the elderly to care for them, an ageing country like Italy could quickly rejuvenate itself. Mass migration is no solution to ageing either—immigrants are often already too old, and the future cannot be built upon the children of others.

This quick sketch assumes the future will be quite like our human past. However, in his book *The Age of Em: Work, Love, and Life when Robots Rule the Earth*, Robin Hanson proposes a future in which robots may one day rule the world. Along with others, he believes the first truly smart robots will feature brain emulation (EM). By scanning a human brain and then running a model with the same connections on a fast computer, a recognizably human-like robot brain could emerge. After training an EM to perform a job and copying it a million times, an army of robot workers will be readily available.

Since technology will help us reset and renew humanity, the Second Machine Age will, in fact, usher in a new Renaissance.

SEEDS OF CHANGE

'India—you either love it or you hate it!' With this message I was sent to India to investigate the market for hybrid vegetable seeds in 1985. At the time, I worked for a seed company expanding into Asia. My research revealed that importing seeds into India was prohibited—a major challenge. Yet, young and ambitious, I pressed on.

For those unfamiliar with the industry, there are two seed markets: farm-saved seeds and professionally produced seeds. When properly handled, farm-saved seeds offer great potential. Farmers select the best plants, refrain from harvesting them, and instead wait for them to bloom, collecting seeds for the next season. However, cross-pollination with neighbouring plants often degrades the original quality. Worse, if the field has diseases, they transfer to the seeds, spreading the problem the following year.

Poor seeds are a farmer's worst enemy, as their livelihood depends on quality seeds and healthy young plants. No matter how much effort is put in, if the seeds are poor, the harvest is worthless. Professional seed companies, therefore, prioritize disease-free, uniform seeds with guaranteed germination.

My first task was to identify the diseases and challenges in India's vegetable industry. What I found was disheartening. The British had introduced ancient European varieties, while local crops like brinjal (aubergine) had seen little selection. The heavy use of chemical pesticides further complicated matters. Yet, India's predominantly vegetarian population made it a seedsman's paradise.

One difficult-to-produce crop for farmers was white cabbage, which requires cold temperatures to flower. Though India has cold regions, they differ from the production areas. As a result, seeds were often smuggled in from Japan via Hong Kong or Singapore. Japanese cabbage thrived in tropical conditions but was poorly suited to Western climates. I discovered that India straddles the meeting point of East and West—humid in the east and dry in the west, thanks to the Deccan Plateau. This western region, with its South European climate, was perfect for European seed varieties. Demonstrations proved that Dutch cabbage thrived there Ironically, its success caused traffic accidents—Dutch cabbage, being denser, was much heavier than its Japanese counterpart, breaking truck axles or brakes under the unexpected weight. With typical Indian humour, this became our best advertisement! Though still prohibited from exporting seeds to India, the vast Indian diaspora ensured they found their way into the market. Soon, Parliament heard of the "miracle seeds" and debated opening the market to international companies. Local seed monopolies, of course, opposed the idea.

The game-changer came with a tomato variety resistant to a mysterious disease. Having worked globally, I recognized it as a virus previously seen in the Jordan Valley but unknown in Asia. Trials using virus-tolerant tomato genes from the Middle East succeeded. It wasn't fully resistant but yielded enough to be profitable.

At farmers' gatherings, we showed a film about a Big Mama scolding her tiny husband for buying only one pouch of the expensive tomato seeds—after they saved half their crop during the outbreak. The humour made it relatable and impactful.

Eventually, India granted import permits, and modern seeds are now widely available. The Indian seed industry has since modernized, and agriculture is on the right track.

Though I left India at the turn of the century, I still maintain strong ties. India is complex but brimming with agricultural potential. With education, better logistics and countryside empowerment, it can become Asia's vegetable basket. I love India!

—Rob Baan
Dutch Food Guru and Non-executive Board Member

K

KOPPERT CRESS
Architecture Aromatique

4

The Digital Workplace

Jack and Ashwin, happily married to each other, are in Rome on holiday. It's a hot summer morning in 2035. They are at the Vatican. Pope Madonna, who was elected head of the Roman Catholic Church a year ago, addresses all the Catholics in the world this morning through several media simultaneously. She will fly this afternoon to attend the Berlin Council of Spiritual World Leaders, which aims to establish a long-lasting peace. The event in Berlin—the spiritual and political capital of the renewed European Union—will see the Pope meeting many eminent personalities representing all religions in the world: Hinduism, Buddhism, Islam, all Christian denominations, Judaism, atheists, agnostics, humanists and the believers in the Hodgepodge God.

In front of St Peter's Basilica, thousands of worshippers applaud the Pope's fierce speech. Jack and Ashwin admire her. As always, she is dressed impeccably, although she is almost 100 years old now and a walking Egyptian mummy, according to her critics. She looks stunning. Fine silks cover her, while her papal crown glitters. Jack remembers when the pope was still a singer and lived in the UK before her 10th divorce. 'I adored her even then. Now, she is able to reach my inner self, my longing for spirituality in this fast-moving, high-tech world. Who am I? Who are we? Where are we going? What is the goal and meaning of life? How can we dea with all the moral aspects of the new world order? What can we learn from the spiritual past of humanity and from ancient civilizations? How can we end stress, burnouts and anxiety? She helps me rethink my values, and in this way, she has lured me back into the Catholic Church after Pope Benedict XVI expelled all the gays in 2008. A remarkable achievement indeed.'

When it comes to machines replacing workers, there are two sides of the same coin, of which one is automation. The other side, which tends to be overlooked, is machines that complement people, even as they take over certain human tasks. As mentioned earlier, jobs consist of many elements that depend on people possessing a number of qualities. One task may require more physical exertion, while another may rely on cognitive skills; one requires repetition, while another demands creativity. To a greater or lesser degree, the ideal employee possesses all these qualities.

The US economist David Autor says every unique input to the work process is equally important to completing any job successfully. This means improving one aspect does not necessarily lead to deterioration elsewhere. In fact, the opposite is often true: if improvement in one task, such as introducing a computer to manage number crunching, leads to higher productivity, then one knock-on effect is an increase in economic value for other tasks. Take the increased mechanization in construction, for example, which has led to fewer construction workers on building sites nowadays. This is not only a result of using machines, but also because builders are now more skilled. Builders with machines—cranes, drills or nail guns—are obviously able to complete more work per day than workers without these tools. That said, these machines are also likely to cause more damage on-site, so other qualities, such as the ability to assess risk and a sense of responsibility, have become more valuable. Mechanization in the building trade has thus reduced the number of construction workers but increased the economic value of individual builders. In general, the rule is that where technology complements the worker, productivity goes up. This means when salaries increase, consumer consumption rises and employment opportunities grow in the long term.

A new wave of automation can therefore be the harbinger of good news. According to Autor, the potential of innovative technology to complement people is recognized less than its potential to replace them, and the effect of the latter is overestimated. Despite job polarization and Digital Taylorism, he believes semi-skilled work does have a chance to survive and even increase. Jobs requiring technical skills in combination with other skills, such as literacy, numeracy, common sense and problem solving, are especially likely to survive well into the future. This is because they are not the kind of jobs that can be easily broken down into individual tasks for a machine to manage without a significant loss of overall quality. While breaking down jobs into their constituent parts can lead to deterioration in certain fields, it can mean creating work for more people in other fields, especially for people who may possess some, but not all, of the requisite specialist skills. In the health services, for instance, medical assistants are now able to take over some tasks that used to be performed only by doctors. This means doctors can now concentrate on more complex matters, while medical assistants are enriched with more interesting and varied tasks. Accordingly, patients also benefit from having access to medical professionals who can devote more time to them.

Permanent Adaptation

Research in the 1980s revealed that instead of working fewer hours because of automation, people used their time differently. They switched from spending time on repetitive, routine tasks that could be automated to activities that complemented the machines. In other words, they adapted. Considering that, just as it was then, it won't be possible to automate all jobs even now, a similar shift will occur. McKinsey & Company predicts that by 2030, approximately 50 per cent of all work tasks will require technological, creative, cognitive and human skills, compared to just around 37 per cent today. The enormous speed at which technology can achieve this shift will be a semi-permanent feature, with the nature of work continuously evolving.

Learning Will Be Easy

In a world where machines are constantly learning, people must continue to improve as well. Learning keeps us one step ahead, and with technology making knowledge and training easily accessible, we are all becoming lifelong learners without even realizing it. The distinct boundaries of our daily lives are becoming less defined, and education is no exception. It is no longer necessary to attend a course held during set hours; with digital technologies like Skype, YouTube and Facebook Live, we can learn where and when it suits us. It is also increasingly easier to share knowledge with others. For almost every activity, instructional videos made by professionals or skilled amateurs are available on YouTube. In the future, we will undoubtedly receive instruction and guidance from the machines we work with, which, thanks to AI, will be able to share tips on how to work more efficiently in less time. Before we know it, learning will become an integral part of our lives, something we will do naturally.

Online Learning

The front runners in organized online education are those providing a Massive Open Online Course (MOOC). Lessons are viewed (or reviewed) via the internet, tutorials are held at set times via Skype, exams are completed digitally and marked by computers. There are also online discussion platforms where lecturers and students discuss the subject matter—an essential part of most online courses. Khan Academy, set up in 2006 by mathematician and computer expert Salman Khan, is one of the most popular MOOC platforms, currently offering thousands of lectures that have been viewed over 1.5 billion times on YouTube. Lecturers from renowned universities like Stanford and MIT give the lectures, and students can get advice and take exams via Khan Academy. The organization is also making inroads into offline education by offering training to teachers on how to use technology (and the lesson materials provided by Khan Academy) in the classroom. Other big players, such as Coursera, Udacity, FutureLearn and EdX, also work with renowned universities—but unlike Khan Academy, they try to profit from education.

Free AI for Everyone

The University of Helsinki now offers a free 30-hour online course for beginners, entitled 'Elements of AI'. While primarily aimed at Finnish people, the course is given in English to appeal to a larger base of students. It starts with the basics, explaining what AI is and how it can be applied to problem-solving, presenting real-life examples. The second part of the course covers ML and neural networks. While Finns completing the course earn study points towards an Open University degree, non-Finns only receive a certificate for posting on LinkedIn. The University of Helsinki hopes this course will alleviate people's fear of AI. It is a fantastic endeavour, and we agree that people are scared of what they don't know. Eventually, we will all need to embrace AI, so this course aligns perfectly with Finland's ambition to be a knowledge-based country, where people are its greatest asset and investing in them is worthwhile.

Don't Neglect Soft Skills

Education around the world is increasingly focused on STEM subjects as the demand for well-trained technical employees continues. However, potential employees need more than just technical skills to remain relevant. Such knowledge and skills age quickly, with technology itself being open to automation. Hence, the importance of mastering hard skills is set to decline. Soft skills, on the other hand, are difficult to automate, so people who excel in this area will always have an advantage over machines. Furthermore, as technology continues to pervade every corner of society, about 70 per cent of IT professionals already work outside the technical sector, and this trend is expected to continue. As IT expands into other sectors fields, qualities like empathy, language ability, cognitive skills and the ability to communicate and interact with others become increasingly important.

The need for multi-talented people will increase, and those who not only speak fluent technical jargon but also can seamlessly translate it for business directors, crisis managers, politicians and shop floor workers will be in high demand.

These are people who can also see the non-technical side of technology; people who understand what IT systems can do for a business; people who grasp concerns and fears and understand how things are organized, both legally and in an international context. There will undoubtedly be a plethora of ethical and legal dilemmas associated with the increasing use of AI, such as questioning who can be held accountable for autonomous decisions made by the system. It is only fair that the training materials used by AI systems are free of human prejudices. Businesses will therefore require people with both a good grasp of technology—how to develop and operate algorithms, for example—and a thorough knowledge of other areas such as law, economics, organizational skills, psychology, philosophy and ethics. In short, we should not neglect what makes us human by allowing education to focus only on providing as many people as possible with a technical grounding.

From Workplace to Meeting Place

Mobile technology, cloud computing and the Internet of Things (IoT) are creating huge changes in the workplace. We can now work *where* we want, *when* we want and using *what* we want—desktop, laptop, smartphone, tablet or even the dashboard of a self-driving car. Many skilled workers are already mobile, working from wherever they prefer: home, a service station, a café, a train or a shared office space. If there is internet access, coffee and electricity, they can work with peak efficiency. Many organizations already consider it normal for employees to work from home at least one day a week, and permanent office bases have either shrunk or, in some cases, disappeared entirely. While work is now increasingly divorced from a specific location, some companies and employees still prefer an office space—a high-quality setting that makes the time spent there worthwhile. We want our time to count, both professionally and personally, so the office must be an environment tailored to our specific needs, which won't necessarily be 'work' in the traditional sense. Workplaces therefore must be transformed into meeting spaces where employees can discuss projects, make new contacts and network.

The Office Experience

In recent years, we have already seen many changes. Offices have become lighter and more colourful, with cosy lounges and intimate corners to sit and talk; some organizations have installed table tennis, pool tables or yoga and fitness studios. Nothing gets the creative juices and cooperation flowing more than a jam session, so the Dropbox office in Dublin has even installed a music studio. Whatever the function of workplaces, they all have several common features: excellent internet connection, spaces to screen presentations and hold videoconferences and even whiteboard walls to write and share ideas on (as seen in the Cisco Toronto Innovation Centre, the smartest building in the world according to some). When inspiration strikes, no time should be lost looking for a flipchart pad or a piece of paper.

Innovation and new ways of working are not restricted to the workplace; developments in the wider environment are also relevant. It is perfectly possible to hold a brainstorming session at a park or a café. In between meetings, one may step out to do some shopping or have a massage, and after work, they may stop off somewhere—maybe for a chat, to take a bite, to exercise or to relax. The physical experience of going to work can be emotionally taxing to some extent. So, instead of draining employees' energy, the workplace must offer an inspiring and energizing ambience. Businesses will increasingly consider the wider picture when choosing a location, even going as far as building the perfect environment if nothing else is suitable.

Younger Generations Enter the Job Market

Younger people, in particular, care about their workplace. They want to work somewhere that reflects their lifestyle and provides easy access to the facilities they need. By 2025, 75 per cent of working people will be from the millennial generation. Compared with its predecessors, this generation has very different behaviours and expectations. Young people today need to believe in their work, enjoy it and feel they are contributing to a wider society. For many, this is more important than having a well-paid job. Millennials also ignore the strict separation of professional and private life that previous generations maintained; they use social media throughout the day and chat with friends while working. Young people are highly tech-savvy and choose their preferred tools. The authors have heard stories about millennials who declined job offers because they didn't like the hardware used by the prospective employer. One may think they are stubborn, but employees with strict principles and strong ideas are often brighter and more creative than their less-demanding colleagues. Besides, employers don't want to risk alienating the best talent. Although it's a nightmare for IT security departments, a 'Bring Your Own Device Policy' is also likely to become the norm.

Out with Time Wasting

The term 'smart office' has been in use for the past decade or more, although it is now undergoing a revolution. We can expect to see offices and buildings that really *are* smart in the coming years. The IoT is once again the driving force, this time in conjunction with data analysis. While future workplaces are filled with sensors that accumulate information, automatically regulate lighting, control air conditioning and open doors, machines will also track how we work, where we are in the building at what time, when we log in and which applications we use. Buildings will also register how many people are present on a given floor, how they operate in the space and which rooms are least used. All this information gathered by the building control systems can be linked to the data collected by computers or the Wi-Fi network and analysed to support employees by streamlining work processes. A significant frustration with flexible workplaces is locating an empty desk or free meeting room when needed. So next-generation offices are capable of reserving desk space, as well as meeting rooms, when employees arrive, directing them to that space and even diverting them en route to pick up their favourite beverages. Nobody needs to wander around anymore trying to find a space while balancing a stack of files, a laptop and a mug of coffee. In the Cisco Toronto Innovation Centre, a lift is automatically dispatched as soon as someone parks their car in the garage—no need to wait in dingy hallways. When it's too sunny, the blinds are automatically drawn; when the light intensity changes, they are pulled back. In a truly smart environment, the system knows everything about everybody at all times. Privacy has become outdated, but who cares when the advantage is saving time?

Wearables at Work

Sensors also offer a new opportunity to improve our health and safety through particular wearables—sensors we carry on our bodies or within our clothes and smartphones.

Wearables can monitor an employee's heartbeat and blood pressure; they issue warnings if the employee lifts too much or repeats the same action for too long; they can tell us if we are obeying health and safety standards, much like cars remind us to fasten our seatbelt. The IoT network allows sensors in a particular environment to share data with one another, including wearables. Working together, they measure the temperature, check oxygen levels in the workplace, alert employees who need a rest, ask a colleague for help or open a window. By using wearables, employees have less privacy, of course, but it benefits their health and safety. Furthermore, data from wearables and environmental sensors are collated and analysed to determine if the patterns reveal that a positive change is needed in the workplace, which benefits everyone. Considering how successful and prevalent wearable heart monitors or step counters are today, we don't expect too many complaints about the introduction of these types of sensors at work.

THE INVISIBLE BECOMES VISIBLE

In the coming century, technologies will be developed to make the invisible visible. These five innovations have the potential to change the way we live, work and interrelate.

A. AI Will Forecast Our Health by Analysing Our Words

Within five years, what we write or say will be capable of analysing our physical or mental well-being. Cognitive assistants and sensors in our smartphones or other devices will 'eavesdrop', evaluate and warn us when there are signs of deterioration. Using ML, it is already possible to predict the likelihood of a psychotic episode by analysing about 300 words, and this research is being expanded to help patients who suffer from Alzheimer's, Parkinson's disease, Huntington's disease, PTSD and even those with conditions such as autism and ADHD. The current diagnostic protocols (of Parkinson's disease, for example) are prolonged and labour-intensive, but they can be accelerated by allowing computers to measure a patient's 'logo-genesis'—how people speak, what they say and what language they use while writing—and then look for certain patterns or a specific use of grammar. With 80 per cent accuracy, researchers have proven that this technology can determine the severity of motor dysfunction in patients by analysing a one-minute conversation. Using these results, in combination with data obtained from wearables and visual imaging systems such as MRI and CT scans, we can create an accurate picture of individuals, allowing us to identify, understand and treat any underlying illnesses.

B. Nanotechnology Will Warn of Illness before We Experience Symptoms

Early detection of a disease is crucial. The earlier we can detect and diagnose an illness, the more likely we are to cure or treat it. As 'nano-detectives' detect microscopic bioparticles in our blood, sweat, saliva, tears and urine, they can alert us to potential illnesses before we experience any symptoms. However, isolating and analysing these bioparticles, which are thousands of times smaller than the width of human hair, requires new specialist technology, such as the lab-on-a-chip (LoC) system currently being developed. The LoC is a mere 20 nanometres in diameter— small enough to access DNA, viruses and proteins. The LoC technique is known as a liquid biopsy; it is less intrusive and more comfortable than traditional screening techniques. This technology will eventually be available in a user-friendly handheld device. When used in combination with other IoT devices such as sleep monitors and smart watches, it will provide a complete picture of our health, enabling us to treat illnesses before symptoms appear.

C. Hyperspectral Imaging (HSI) and AI Will Give Us 'Integrated Super Vision'

Over the past 100 years or so, scientists have developed tools allowing us to see electromagnetic waves. These instruments translate different frequencies in the electromagnetic spectrum—radio waves, microwaves, infrared and X-rays—into familiar sounds, effects and images. The equipment for this will be smaller, more portable, cheaper and more widely available over the next five years, making it a part of everyday life. Using these tools with AI provides early warnings and better information about things we were previously unable to detect. For instance, hyperspectral imaging technology in cars can help us see other road users in fog, rain or snow, and warn us when an object is approaching or crossing the road ahead. Furthermore, it can determine whether the object is a fallen box from a lorry, a deer crossing the road, a pothole that could cause a blowout or an unsuspecting pedestrian.

D. Macroscopes and the IoT Will Help Us Understand the Complexity of Planet Earth

The physical world offers only a tiny insight into the infinite, intricately connected and complex world. After successfully digitizing business transactions and social interactions, the process of digitizing the physical world has begun. However, because information gathered from microscopes, telescopes and everything in between is already so vast and complex, it is hard for people to assimilate and understand. Therefore, a 'macroscope' filters, magnifies and accentuates connections to make information understandable to the human brain. For example, there will be about 10 billion people by 2050, and consequently, food production will need to increase by 70 per cent to feed everyone. By combining and analysing data about climate, soil structure, the water table, irrigation, and social and political structures, we can give farmers new insights to help them determine what crops to grow, when to plant and how to achieve optimal harvests.

E. Sensors Will Assist in Managing Polluting Substances

Within five years, low-cost, readily available technology will measure methane around natural gas wells, storage tanks and along distribution pipes, enabling the industry to locate and repair leaks in real time. By linking networks of sensors in the IoT cloud, it will be possible to continuously monitor gas infrastructure. Over time, this technology will expand to detect all dangerous chemicals in the environment, such as oil residues in water or vehicle and factory emissions. Sensors placed on the ground or in autonomous drones will gather data, which could be combined with real-time wind speeds, satellite information and historical data to analyse complex ecological models.

The Virtual Colleague

In a digital workplace, we work alongside virtual as well as real colleagues. Many businesses already use chatbots to manage some of their client contact; banks have virtual counter staff and even virtual financial advisors; IBM created Watson to help doctors examine medical information and advise on possible diagnoses and treatment—this computer system is capable of analysing 200 million pages in a second, something that would take many years for a human.

Such virtual colleagues will become increasingly important. The Digital Workplace Report found that 62 per cent of managers in multinationals expect virtual assistants to play an advisory role in their organizations within two years, and about 58 per cent expect to be actively investing in this development over the same period. Virtual assistants can help us make decisions and can also take over practical tasks, such as updating diaries and placing orders.

Amazon introduced 'Alexa for Business' at the end of 2017 to meet this need. Werner Vogels, CTO and vice president of Amazon, asked why the human voice is not the natural interface for interacting with equipment at work, when people already use such technology at home. This is a logical question because, with an increasingly blurred line between private and work life, it makes sense for us to use the same hi-tech equipment wherever we are. Many millions of people use Amazon Echo while millions of others use Apple's Siri or Google's Assistant. All this doesn't even factor in the hundreds of millions more who use their smartphone assistants. Research by Ovum suggested that by 2021, there would be 7.5 billion virtual assistants active around the world—a frightening number that has only increased since then. Today, there are more assistants in the digital world than people, so it's no wonder that businesses like Amazon are cashing in on this growing market. Alexa for Business can print documents, place orders, make appointments, book meeting rooms, initiate conference calls, report faults and do a number of other tasks that would otherwise consume a lot of our time. Soon, virtual assistants might be able to take on the frustrating tasks that often go wrong if we attempt them ourselves, such as physically connecting peripherals to our desktops or laptops.

Speech Technology Is Developing Rapidly

Before we reach this stage, there are some practical obstacles to overcome, such as security. Businesses don't want to run the risk of Alexa for Business autonomously recording an important meeting and sharing it with clients or competitors—something the home version did with a private conversation a few years back. Speech recognition could also be problematic in open-plan offices or outdoor spaces. Imagine the booming voice of a colleague, who's relaxing in the office garden, activating not one but 10 virtual assistants. Employees would also be knocked off their stride by machines around the office suddenly starting to speak. Despite these difficulties, speech technology is developing rapidly, and the human voice is likely to become the most important interface in the workplace. For some of us, it will take time to get used to, but the virtual colleague is on its way.

A Deep-Sea AI Colony

The Chinese Academy of Sciences in Beijing has announced plans to build an unmanned research station at the bottom of the South China Sea. Run entirely by AI, it would be the world's first AI colony. Reliant on ships or a surface platform for power, but otherwise operating autonomously, the station will send robot submarines on missions to survey the seabed, collect minerals and record life forms. All materials will be analysed in the station laboratory, before sending reports to the surface. Chinese scientists compare the plan—costing at least US$160 million—to building a space station on a distant planet, but with much more difficulty. The exact location has not yet been decided;

it might be built at a depth of over five kilometres, meaning all materials must be newly designed to withstand the enormous pressure. It is a gargantuan task, though the benefits of knowing what is going on deep beneath the ocean's surface will be plentiful. It may help improve our understanding of climate change, build a more efficient and early warning system for tsunamis, and may lead to the discovery of new materials, new species and even new medicines. President Xi Jinping has encouraged Chinese scientists to undertake this groundbreaking project to help give China a technological lead. According to the *South China Morning Post*, at the deep-sea project launch, the president said that there 'is no road in the deep sea, we do not need to chase (after other countries), we are the road'—an ambitious statement, if not a little arrogant. The South China Sea is the most disputed waterway in the world, an area about which tensions regularly run high. Since an unmanned submarine base could also be used for military purposes, this project is bound to be met with suspicion by the US and China's Asian neighbours. China, however, has emphasized its peaceful intentions and says that it hopes the obvious research benefits will secure the support of other countries. The authors are all for it, since projects like this boost technological development and push humanity into a new era.

AI with a Human Face

To enhance our interaction with AI, virtual assistants will be given avatars. Some chatbots that manage client contact already have these features, such as AVA, the web assistant used by software company Autodesk. This digital human face was developed by the New Zealander Mark Sagar. He has also developed a number of other digital faces. More than just a facial representation for clients to look at during a conversation, these avatars, which Soul Machines calls a 'virtual nervous system', can recognize and smile or frown at human emotions, voice tones or facial expressions. At the end of 2018, Xinhua (the official state news agency of China) introduced an avatar as its news anchor, whose face was created using advanced AI software developed in collaboration with the search engine *Sogou*. This virtual presenter, based on one of Xinhua's human anchors, is capable of presenting television news 24/7 from any location in the world. These types of bots will become the model for the virtual assistants in our workplaces soon. In future, we will talk to virtual people, almost indistinguishable from real people, instead of to a plastic box. Humanoid robots will also enter society one day.

The Virtual Workspace

Not all virtual colleagues will be digital. Even though our flesh and blood ones may be located far from us, the advent of workplace VR and AR introduces a new era of virtual meetings or even holographic meeting rooms. It may sound like the realms of science fiction, but in the conferencing world, these new methods are already being tried and tested. Professionals who need refresher training, such as military personnel, pilots, surgeons or rescue workers, extensively use VR technology. Although practising and training in a virtual space rather than in real-life situations is much more practical, it may not always be cheaper—creating and realizing a VR space requires expensive equipment and computing power. However, there is no need to close roads or cause any public disruption; if something goes wrong, the exercise can be simply started again. Virtual meetings are already easier to arrange than physical ones, and once VR becomes fully integrated with other forms of tech, such as smartphones, the costs will fall. Mark Zuckerberg expects that VR will become the biggest communication platform in 10 years. Meanwhile, Microsoft has taken over companies like AltspaceVR, a start-up specializing in developing software for social VR environments. These are significant indicators that, in a world where employees and colleagues are more geographically distant, it makes sense to create virtual workspaces.

Flat Organizations

Many businesses still operate in ways reminiscent of those during the early days of industrialization—a time when workers were seen as dispensable, in need of constant supervision (to prevent mistakes or laziness) and judged by whether they met the daily production quotas. Nowadays, supervisory roles have evolved into management roles. Except for ensuring workers reach their targets (modern management speak for production quotas), what managers do in today's workplace is a puzzle to many observers. It seems like the days are numbered for the millions of managers around the world. Technology brings democracy to the workplace, making it possible, acceptable and even welcoming for employees to approach their colleagues and leaders with ease. Using modern technology, it takes seconds to chat online with colleagues who have more information, more budget, more contacts, more knowledge and more experience. They communicate in the same way as they do with family and friends—via social media rather than through their manager. Management intervention is thus unnecessary in this age when organizations are flatter and more flexible. This trend, driven by the younger generation, will continue as employees complete their tasks from a distance and become increasingly independent.

Flat Organizations Learn More Quickly and More Cheaply

Both MIT and 42 (the Parisian programming school established in 2013 that offers free learning for thousands of students who pass a strict selection process) no longer work in faculties, but rather rely on peer-to-peer and project-based learning. Colleagues and students with different specialities seek each other out to solve specific problems or work on joint projects. Such a model is not only extremely cost-effective but also encourages and optimizes knowledge sharing. By combining colleague feedback with an online platform that outlines every employee's expertise, the need to spend on expensive training courses is avoided. Instead, employees are able to directly consult colleagues with the relevant knowledge and learn exactly what they need to know. Looking further into the future, businesses can use employee DNA and neuro profiles to group colleagues into optimal working teams. Based on indicators such as patience, concentration ability, passion and an ideal mix of hormones and neurotransmitters, HR technology will be able to recommend which individuals would work well with each other, and who would make a suitable mentor.

In Conclusion

The most extensive changes in our workplace will happen out of sight. The machines we work with will remain the same, but the underlying infrastructure and technology will change. In the coming 10 years, smartphones, tablets and laptops will remain our main tools, but they will be smarter and more able to support our jobs through AI—often without explicit instruction. Employers and employees will need to be more flexible. The workplace must shrink or expand based on the number of employees while also accommodating an increasing number of robots. The electricity network must be sufficiently robust to allow extra machines and servers to be installed. Rigid hierarchy and top-down management are things of the past; democracy will enter the workplace, alongside increased freedom for working people to decide how, when and where they perform their duties. Employees must be prepared for lifelong learning, which organizations need to facilitate. Learning will become integral to everyday life because, more than any technological advancement, our education, knowledge and skills will determine whether we will still have jobs after the next wave of technology hits the workplace.

THE FUTURE OF FLYING

IndiGo has grown from 77 million to 112 million passengers over the past 2.5 years—a 45 per cent increase. Yet, this is just the beginning.

Boeing projects that South Asia will be the fastest-growing commercial aviation market over the next two decades, quadrupling its capacity with over 8 per cent annual growth. The International Air Transport Association recently reported an 8.3 per cent surge in air cargo demand—the biggest rise in nearly two years—driven by e-commerce and the growing goods delivery from China to Western markets. Seasonal events, like the Chinese Lunar New Year, will further boost both cargo and passenger traffic.

To capitalize on this growth, Asian aviation stakeholders are adopting best practices, including network optimization, digital transformation, fleet modernization and strategic partnerships. Airports such as Changi (Singapore), Daxing (Beijing) and Bengaluru (India) are leading the way through capacity expansion, smart technology, sustainability and passenger-centric services.

India, the third-largest and fastest-growing aviation market, has doubled its airport count from 74 to 141 over the past eight years. Although its fleet is only one-fifth the size of China's, the government is driving growth through relaxed regulations, reduced taxes and major airport investments. Airlines are boosting demand through fare discounts, regional connectivity, tourism partnerships and digital upgrades, while enhancing efficiency through cost control, network optimization and new revenue strategies.

At IndiGo, we are determined to evolve from a major low-cost carrier into a fully fledged global airline. We are actively exploring new opportunities, including acquiring aircraft to support this growth. The Netherlands is a key market due to its strong Indian community and business ties. We are in discussions to lease Boeing 787s for routes from India to Schiphol Amsterdam, and potentially Paris and London.

While we receive new aircraft weekly, they are limited to distances of around 6,500 km. To gain long-haul experience, we are leasing two Boeing 777s from Turkish Airlines, operating flights to Istanbul. Although we have ordered long-range Airbus aircraft, they will not arrive for a few years, prompting us to seek interim capacity for expansion into Europe and Asia.

Our move to Schiphol Amsterdam is purely strategic, as the aviation treaty between the Netherlands and India still allows for more flights. Currently, European airlines operate 70 per cent of flights between the two regions, but this will shift as Air India and IndiGo claim a larger share.

IndiGo's expansion is swift and ambitious. With over 100 new routes—including to the Middle East, Central and South Asia, and Kenya—we are also introducing business class on select routes. To support this growth, we are training 2,000 people daily, ensuring our planes are always ready for takeoff.

For IndiGo, aviation is more than a business—it is a vital driver of India's economic growth and job creation.

—Pieter Elbers
Chairman of International Air Transport Association and CEO

5

Energy in the 21st Century

Natural gas will be available for a long time to come. There is plenty of it, thanks to the shale gas revolution. The US and Australia are bringing huge volumes of natural gas to the market. Russia, a traditional industry giant, still has enormous natural gas reserves. Before 2022, about 80 per cent of the gas produced by Russia's state-controlled Gazprom was sent to Europe. To maintain its market position, Gazprom built two new pipelines to northern Europe—Nord Stream 1 and Nord Stream 2. It also built TurkStream for gas delivery to households and industries in southeastern Europe and Turkey. The European countries developed the Trans Adriatic Pipeline, which delivers gas from Azerbaijan through Greece to Italy, to reduce their dependency on Russian gas. There are numerous other pipeline projects under development and, for them to be economically viable, they need to be in operation for a long time to come. Gas pipelines also played a part in the Syrian civil war. By supporting the Assad regime, Russia was able to halt a plan by Qatar—which sits on top of the largest natural gas field in the world—to build a pipeline from the Arab Peninsula through Syria to Europe. It was a plan the Assad government strongly opposed, a plan that would have undermined Russia's energy position in the region. Qatar currently relies on tankers to export its gas, which is more expensive than pipe-delivered gas. Things may soon change in Qatar's favour though, as technologies for liquefying gas rapidly improve, making it much easier to transport without the need for huge investments in new pipelines and support infrastructure. However, terminals for LNG are not cheap. The LNG industry has matured rapidly in its 50–60 years of existence, disrupting the energy market now. According to consultancy company Deloitte, LNG trade has quadrupled in the last 20 years and is set to double again over the next two decades. The US is betting heavily on the LNG revolution to export its shale gas to Europe. It is also pressuring European countries to 'buy American', in return for NATO military support. Much to the annoyance of the Trump administration, the US pays most of Europe's defence bills. So now it wants gas deals in return. Since American LNG is 400 per cent more expensive for Europe than Russian gas, it leads to the highest energy prices in the world. This, in turn, leads to deindustrialization and high inflation, culminating in social and political unrest.

Meanwhile in India

Coal will remain in the global energy mix because many countries simply cannot afford to do without it. India, for example, is facing huge challenges in turning the country into a modern and prosperous industrial nation. To keep up with rising demand for electricity—approximately 300 million Indians currently live in the dark—it must connect an extra 15 gigawatts to the grid every year for the next 30 years. In 2017, about 78 per cent of the total energy generated in India came from coal-fired power stations, so it would be easiest to expand their capacity. Although the Indian government is certainly sensitive to arguments about not increasing carbon emissions—the country is already the third-largest emitter of greenhouse gases—it doesn't have an alternative yet. It must invest in coal, whether people like it or not. Luckily, the 50,000 coal-burning power stations around the world are being modernized to be more efficient and less polluting. According to Romanian architect Bogdan Chipara, existing energy infrastructure could easily be more environmentally friendly, so he launched the Coal Power Plant Mutation project. His imagined power stations are one kilometre tall, balloon-like chimneys filled with a series of filters that capture dirt and CO_2 emissions before they are released. Although so far only conceptual, radical ideas like his might work and transform existing power stations into more sustainable ones—a crucial step in the energy transition. We advise India to hire people like Chipara and build new coal-fuelled power plants based on his brilliant ideas. This will also lessen the massive air pollution that makes living in most big Asian cities quite unpleasant and unhealthy.

The Institute for Energy Economics and Financial Analysis has calculated that for newly built solar power installations, agreed energy prices have fallen almost 50 per cent in recent years to under 4 cents per kilowatt-hour. This makes solar power more competitive every day. India is therefore already investing a lot in solar energy. While India aims to produce 175 gigawatts of renewable energy—about as much as Germany's total generation capacity—solar power is expected to account for 100 gigawatts. Along with China's help, India has a current nuclear capacity of 8,180 megawatts. However, simple mathematics confirms these initiatives are not enough, and coal will therefore remain an important part of the Indian energy mix for at least another two decades.

Meanwhile in China

While India sticks with coal-fired power stations for the coming years, Asian superpower China is rapidly diversifying its energy mix. It currently still relies on coal for some two-thirds of its electricity production, though coal is rapidly losing ground in households and many industrial sectors, with gas and electricity becoming more popular. It is estimated that by 2040, coal's share will drop to less than 40 per cent. A main driving force behind this transition is air pollution, which in recent years has caused massive civil unrest and is now a grave concern for the Chinese government. Electricity will therefore replace coal first, then oil. By 2040, the share of gas in the total energy mix will more than double, from 6 per cent to over 12 per cent. This increase doesn't seem a lot, but with an annual demand of over 600 billion cubic metres, it is enough to turn China into the largest market for natural gas after the US. As for oil, China is expected to overtake the US as the largest consumer by 2030, although Chinese demand for oil will decrease over time, making India's demand for oil the highest in the world. At the same time, China is already a world leader in solar panel production. Solar installations are cheaper in China than both new and existing gas-fired power stations, and by 2030, they are expected to be cheaper than new coal-fired power stations and wind farms. By 2040, about 60 per cent of total Chinese energy generation will come from renewable sources—solar, wind and hydropower. Sometime in the next decade, China will also become the global leader in nuclear-based energy production, leaving the US and Europe far behind. All Chinese car and scooter manufacturers have developed electric cars and other vehicles, which are now being exported throughout Asia and Central Asia. These transitions, especially the electrification of scooters and auto rickshaws (or *tuk-tuks* as they are called in Thailand), will lead to less air pollution. Clean air and blue skies will become huge assets in the Economy of Happiness.

Breakthroughs in Nuclear Energy Research

Nuclear energy is back in fashion. Even though this horrifies many people, positive steps have been taken regarding safety and nuclear waste processing in recent decades, with further breakthroughs expected. The use of thorium as a fuel, for instance, looks promising. Thorium reactors are much safer than uranium ones. In a so-called Molten Salt Reactor (MSR), thorium is dissolved in an unpressurized salt mixture that also acts as a coolant. This means the fuel and coolant maintain the same temperature—if the temperature rises, the nuclear reaction automatically stops. The salt mixture is then redirected to another safe compartment in the reactor, making a meltdown (leaking or evaporating of cool water in the reactor) impossible. Furthermore, larger quantities of thorium are found in nature, meaning we would no longer be held to ransom by a few countries—including rogue dictatorships—that dominate the global uranium supply. An MSR also produces less nuclear waste than traditional nuclear power stations; what it does produce remains radioactive for *only* 300 years—an instant when compared with uranium waste that remains radioactive for thousands of years. An MSR can also reuse its spent fuel in the same way as uranium power stations. Moreover, it is impossible to make bombs using thorium directly—a win-win! Dutch nuclear solution developer group NRG is among the few organizations in the world currently experimenting with salt irradiation, and the global industry is following its progress with great interest. It will take a few decades to build working MSR power stations.

China Leads the Way

Japan, India, Germany, France and the US are optimistic about thorium, but it is China that has launched extensive research programmes. Seeing thorium as a way to produce cheap, clean energy on a large scale, Chinese ambitions could take a step forward with the help of Dutch practical knowledge. Under pressure from rapid urban growth, industrialization and significant levels of air pollution, China has become the front runner in developing alternative methods of energy production—from solar panels to nuclear reactors. It has embarked on a significant programme of construction, building new nuclear power stations capable of producing 58 gigawatts of electricity. Floating nuclear power stations to support its military and trade activities in the South China Sea are also under construction. A second university dedicated to nuclear power technology is planned for Tianjin (the first was established in Suzhou) to satisfy the growing demand for nuclear specialists. Nuclear energy is also powering the ambitious BRI project; trains serving the New Silk Road will be nuclear-powered, using energy from the three power stations that China is building in Pakistan. China's nuclear lead will give it a big geopolitical advantage. Its thorium-reactor technology, for instance, could be of immense importance to developing economies that need more electricity. These countries are already approaching China for knowledge, loans and investments, particularly in the nuclear energy sector.

Size *Does* Matter

Installing a nuclear reactor is expensive, but costs are decreasing because of SMRs, which make the process simpler. As SMRs are modular, they are easily transported in pieces by lorry, train or ship for assembly on site, much like Lego. Having long been used in inhospitable regions, such as the Arctic, SMRs are becoming smaller, simpler and cheaper, making them attractive to other remote communities that want all the pleasures of modern life powered by clean, responsibly sourced electricity. They are indeed cheap to produce, which is ideal for developing economies. These small modular reactors can also be installed underground, limiting potential for a terrorist attack. There are currently four main options: light water reactors, fast neutron reactors, graphite-moderated high-temperature reactors and various kinds of molten salt reactors, but further technological innovations are expected in the coming years. China is not the only key player in this market. The UK jet engine and luxury car manufacturer Rolls-Royce is active in the field, as are companies in Russia and the Republic of Korea. Of late, NASA is also developing Kilopower, a mini reactor with the capacity to create essential power for long space voyages or accommodation on the moon or Mars. The smallest version of Kilopower delivers one kilowatt—enough to make a toast sandwich—while, at 10 kilowatts, the largest can make toast sandwiches for the entire household. The brilliance is linking five or more of these together to produce enough electricity for a small community. With an increasing number of smaller investors and companies active in the SMR market, nuclear energy is no longer the sole purview of large government-sponsored businesses.

Further Down the Road: Nuclear Fusion

In Cadarache in southern France, the International Thermonuclear Experimental Reactor (ITER) is currently being assembled. In Latin, *iter* means 'the way'. Set up in 2007, ITER is a joint project between the EU, the US, China, Japan, India, the Republic of Korea, Switzerland and Russia. Albeit for experiments only, ITER has a very practical goal: to establish whether fusion—the nuclear reaction that powers the Sun, the stars and the hydrogen bomb—can be tamed to generate energy for domestic and commercial use. The idea is to form helium by fusing two hydrogen atoms using powerful magnets; a small quantity of mass is consequently lost during fusion, releasing vast amounts of energy. Fusion technology is often confused with fission—a misconception used by politicians reluctant to both abandon less expensive energy projects and spend billions for fusion reactors. During fission, one atom is split into two or more smaller nuclei, whereas two or more smaller atoms are joined together during fusion. Most importantly, the radioactive material left behind after fusion is no more dangerous than hospital waste. Fusion, therefore, offers a safe, abundant and environmentally responsible energy source. If the ITER process succeeds and the technology proves practical, the project partners will build a prototype commercial reactor named DEMO in 2040. After that, this technology could be installed around the world.

Crowdfunding New Energy Concepts

The Gaia Project acts as an interface between inventors and investments in the energy sector. This organization accepts viable prototypes, subjects them to rigorous testing and, if successful, uses money sourced from crowdfunding to develop the concepts further, to the point at which investors would be interested. The Gaia Project worked on the GBI-Powerunit—a generator that requires minimal electricity to get started and then runs independently with no emissions, producing energy using a magnetic field. Offering truly renewable energy regardless of weather, time or place, these units could be used in remote areas or isolated homes, generating up to five kilowatts of power completely free.

Deep Geothermal Energy

Deep inside our planet, the temperature at the core is in excess of 1,000°C (1,832°F). Stored in rock layers about 150 metres below the surface since the Earth was formed, geothermal heat can be transformed into energy. Only recovering a small percentage of the heat could supply the entire planet with clean, sustainable and safe energy for centuries. Low-temperature geothermal energy is already being exploited in many places, with the US, the Philippines, Mexico, Indonesia and Italy leading the way. The average temperature of the rock is 7°C (44.6°F), and the energy-generating heat is easily extracted using heat pumps. Eventually, the process causes the rock layer to cool, until, after approximately 30 years, it cannot produce energy. After another 10–20 years, it will be warm again and the process can start anew. Scientists also believe it is possible to extract heat from far greater depths—up to 10 kilometres or more—where 'supercritical water' (steam) with a temperature of at least 374°C (705.2°F) can be found. This deep geothermal heat, which can produce as much energy as a nuclear power station, is accessible from everywhere on Earth, making it a democratic source of energy that could help countries become more self-sufficient. Once the technology is fully mastered, the Earth's natural heat will be an important part of the future energy mix.

A Sunny Future

According to estimates from the International Energy Agency, the amount of solar power generated will increase 16-fold by 2040—a figure that could be an underestimate. Research facilities around the world are working to develop a new class of solar cell material, which may replace the commonly used silicon. Perovskite cells, as they are known, have huge advantages over traditional photovoltaic cells: they are not only much cheaper to produce, but also flexible. They can be printed on paper or added to paints and other solutions for spraying onto any surface, opening a wide range of possibilities. Perovskites could cover windows, walls or rooftops; they could even be used on moving objects such as cars, trains or aircraft. Solar transportation has already advanced significantly since Australia introduced the first solar-powered bus in 2013. Aircraft manufacturers and boat builders are developing new solar-powered prototypes, while several Arab countries are expected to experiment with the introduction of solar airlines. Solar fashion—clothes producing enough energy to power smartphones and other small devices—has been around for a decade or more, but the ease with which perovskites can be introduced into fabrics might suddenly make it more accessible to the public. Perovskites can also be added to existing solar panels to boost electricity generation. Traditional solar cells deliver no more than a 25 per cent energy return (in controlled laboratory conditions), whereas perovskites, being much more energy efficient, have a theoretical return of up to 40 per cent. Experts therefore believe that perovskites, once applied in the real world, will be a game changer, making solar energy highly competitive and widely available. In the meantime, work on photovoltaic cells continues as well. Researchers at the University of Cambridge have developed biological photovoltaics that use a photosynthetic material from algae to capture solar energy and directly convert it into electricity. These 'living solar panels' are environmentally friendly, low-cost and, being made from algae, are widespread and abundant.

Watch Out for the Blackout

In the past two centuries, solar flares have hit Earth several times, generating intense magnetic fields that cause electronic devices to burn out instantly, sometimes resulting in fire. In 1989, a small flare led to a blackout in Quebec, and in 1859, a huge solar flare disabled telegraph communication and caused fires around the world. The potential damage could be much worse today. The UK's Met Office, the national meteorological service, has warned the UK government that a solar flare could damage technology and power lines, resulting in data loss, which would cost the economy £16 billion. It recommended investing in a network of satellites that operate an early warning system to issue alerts when a major flare is building up, giving electricity utility companies enough time to prepare. Businesses and citizens could also be advised to switch their technology off. Researchers warn that without appropriate precautions, it could take up to five days to get the energy grid online again, following a strong flare and multiple substorms. The UK, like many other Western countries, still relies on outdated satellites that not only offer three days' advance warning but also are on the brink of falling apart. According to the Met Office, NASA and the European Space Agency are taking far too long to replace the faulty satellites, putting the entire Western world at risk of a blackout, the scale of which is unprecedented.

In Conclusion

The world is going through a major energy transition. This transition is necessary to end our addiction to fossil fuels and make everyday comforts like electricity available to everyone on the planet. Taking at least another two decades, this crucial change will be profound, creating uncertainty and fear, as all transition does. However, if we use an intelligent mix of the energy sources available to us, we will be better off. At the same time, we must not dictate to others what their choice of energy mix should be, because the situation differs from country to country, and it's unjustifiable to prohibit developing economies from using oil, coal or gas they so desperately need if they are to catch up with other wealthy nations. The future energy mix is diverse, with renewables and nuclear power playing a crucial role, though there is also a place for fossil fuels. Using all resources will create a surplus of energy, meaning that after 2050—when the transition is finally complete—we might begin an era in which energy is free to everyone. This prospect gives humanity an enormous boost. Welcome to the Age of Plenty!

COLUMN OVERTOURISM: BLESSING OR CURSE?

While the term 'overtourism' is relatively new, the phenomenon itself has existed for decades and has gained political attention over the past 10 years. Overtourism is often linked to crowded cities, but vulnerable areas like islands, coastlines and natural sites tend to suffer the most.

Tourism can be both a blessing and a curse, depending on one's perspective: business owners benefit, while local residents may face disturbances. Historically, tourism emerged as a leisure activity in the 19th century and grew rapidly after World War II due to improved safety, higher incomes, more leisure time and enhanced infrastructure.

Tourism has significant advantages such as driving economic growth, creating jobs and generating government revenue through taxes. However, it also has negative consequences, including disturbance, rising housing prices, loss of authenticity and environmental damage. Cities like Amsterdam and Venice, as well as natural areas and cultural heritage sites such as Machu Picchu and the Taj Mahal, serve as ideal examples of places affected by mass tourism.

Tourism has significant economic importance but brings with it complex challenges that demand balance and targeted solutions. Governments are continuously searching for measures to address the negative impacts of overtourism:

1. **Laws and Regulations:** Rules are enforced to reduce disturbances and environmental harm, such as banning

cruise ships from inner cities, limiting private rentals, capping hotel beds and implementing fines for violations.

2. **Pricing and Taxes:** Tools like entrance fees, dynamic pricing and tourist taxes are used to manage visitor numbers and attract specific demographics.

3. **Visitor Management:** Measures include booking systems, daily visitor caps, extended opening hours and closures of beaches or sites to balance crowd distribution.

4. **Marketing:** Focuses on attracting responsible tourists and promoting lesser-known areas through tactics like de-marketing (e.g. discouraging British youths from visiting Amsterdam).

5. **Awareness Campaigns:** Informing tourists about behaviour expectations and encouraging visits to less crowded destinations during off-peak seasons aims to influence long-term travel habits.

In conclusion, overtourism is a complex challenge that requires tailored solutions and collaboration among all stakeholders. Efforts are focused on balancing the benefits of tourism while minimizing disruptions through laws, pricing, visitor management, marketing and awareness.

—Henk Schüller
President, European Travel & Tourism Consultancy (ETTC)

6

Adapting to Extreme Weather and Climate Change

Arun is happy. He's just got a new job in Lisbon. However, he has to inform the virtual 31st EU state, which takes care of the portable social security for all citizens of the EU, of this career move. For the past three years, Arun has been working in France, and before that, he spent four years in Bulgaria. Since 2010, every European citizen has been entitled to portable social security. It does not matter where they live or work anymore; the contributions made by them and their employer are deposited in the bank account of this virtual social security state. Arun is happy about this. In the past, working in several countries was a disaster for one's social security, but as portable citizenship, part-time living and circular migrations almost bankrupted the old social security systems, a new system was necessary. In more ways than this one, it is truly the people's century.

This morning, Arun ordered his new coffee machine. Through the internet, he downloaded his personal code, which enables him to use the machine for his 25 favourite coffee flavours. Whenever he runs out of coffee, the machine notifies the supermarket, and he gets his coffee supplies on time—never without any of his 25 flavours. His colleague Jim bought the same coffee machine but with a different code, since he only has 5 favourite coffee brands. Nowadays, the consumer is in the lead—no manufacturer can make one uniform coffee machine anymore and dictate to the consumer how to use it. This is the age of tailor-made and portable 'everything'. Arun's portable lifestyle a ows him to live in Europe with his French husband Michel, while also frequently visiting his family in Tamil Nadu. Supersonic aeroplanes are the norm, so he can fly back home with Air India in just two hours.

Weather is one of the few topics that engage people in regular conversation. This is a leftover from the days when most people worked on land, when too much or too little rain or sunshine could make the difference between life and death. Plenty of angry gods or evil ghosts were worshipped to explain the weather's fickle, uncertain nature. Some people believed severe weather conditions occurred because humans had sinned or failed to thank the gods, while others thought someone had put a curse on them. For most, weather was the ultimate Act of God—one over which mere mortals could not hope to have any influence. Nowadays, the belief is exactly the same—climate change is happening because people have 'sinned' by polluting the air with greenhouse gases. Just as it was in the past, when every hamlet had its naysayer who sold his soul to the devil, there are freethinkers today who believe the climate has always been volatile and that climate change has little to do with the actions of people. This is hotly disputed by the believers of climate change whose entire identity is confined to the struggle against and taming of nature. We find it hard to imagine that anything in nature could happen without our leading the change or influencing the outcome. Our egos stop us from recognizing this. Furthermore, as mentioned earlier, we are inclined to listen to the prophets of doom rather than the harbingers of good news.

Nature Is Blossoming Like Never Before

The climate has been exercising its will on Earth for 4.5 billion years, whereas Homo sapiens have existed for little over a quarter of a million. Over those billions of years, the Earth has not only coped with cycles of violent weather and extreme heat or cold, but also learnt to evolve and adapt each time. Many lifeforms have come and gone; some of the oldest are still crawling about. The problem is that humanity doesn't like change and wants everything to be still and stagnant, including nature. To be more precise, we want nature to be what we imagine it was like when our parents, or even our grandparents, were young. However, nature is (and always has been) constantly changing and adapting to the present circumstances over billions of years, so Homo sapiens' influence, albeit real, is much smaller than we would like to imagine.

Chris Thomas, the UK professor of biology and ecology at the University of York, has spent many years researching the disappearance of plant and animal species because of climate change. He has found that more species have relocated to new habitats than have been lost. To his astonishment, this news was greeted with dismay rather than rejoicing—it was widely seen as a loss, not a gain. He then explained that people have an unshakeable belief in the thing called 'nature', which should be free of human influence. This is an *idée fixe (obsession);* ever since we left our indelible stamp on the environment, the planet has been drastically affected by human deeds. This was already true at the time of our grandparents; it was true in the days of Jesus;

it was true when Confucius formulated his philosophy; it was even true when Moses led his people across the Red Sea. The debate on climate change features only two facts: the climate does what it does and people influence their environment. While it does seem as if the climate is changing (becoming less predictable), we don't know why. Nor can we say with certainty what the direction of change is, or what the consequences will be. Adapting to extreme weather is necessary for all human beings. For example, wind catchers are used in Iran's Yazd province, where it does not rain for six months annually. The 'wind catcher'—a Persian innovation—is an architectural structure to create ventilation and cooling inside buildings, and such knowledge was transferred in earlier times through the Silk Road.

Having visited India more than 40 times, we have experienced extreme weather more than once. So, for Indians living in the country 24/7, adapting is a top priority. The north Indians have previously adapted to scorching heat by building houses with separate summer and winter parts. The summer section is partly underground and always remains cool. In Spain, where it becomes very hot in summer, architecture was developed in the Middle Ages to keep people cool, using water streams. The Mughals imported these technologies from Spain to India. In southern India, the wooden houses and specific architecture protect people against the heat. Of course, ventilators and air conditioning will help today and tomorrow, but most people work outside the air-conditioned offices. To ensure a happy future for the Indians, managing heavy rains, floods and their consequences is extremely important now, considering the fluctuating weather. The classic monsoons were manageable once, but the new ones create a lot of havoc. Moreover, the extreme heatwaves across northern India in 2024 and heavy rainfalls in many other regions will occur time and again. In China, rising sea levels and overuse of groundwater have led to the gradual collapse of skyscrapers in coastal cities. The same is happening in Florida. In the near future, India might also face a similar fate.

Das Große Waldsterben and Other Threatened Disasters

The climate debate may be more prominent now than a decade ago, but it's not a new conversation. Scary stories, distorted truths, scientific muddles and research results open to various interpretations have been around for years. For instance, remember the acid rain in the 1980s, which apparently threatened the world's forests? The acid-rain fear can be traced back to the research of German scientist Bernhard Ulrich, who concluded that *Das große Waldsterben,* or forest dieback, was caused by 'acid rain'—a result of industrial pollutants in the atmosphere. There were a number of methodological problems in Ulrich's research, but despite the shortcomings, German news magazine *Der Spiegel* massively spread his message of doom. Then the hype started. Governments in Western Europe and North America made substantial efforts to curb pollution, and to be fair, they have made a positive contribution to air quality. On the other hand, forests dying because of acid rain became the average citizen's major fear in the 1980s, second only to nuclear annihilation.

Matt Ridley, author of *The Rational Optimist: How Prosperity Evolves*, calls himself a 'climate Lukewarmer', a position he took by looking at past predictions of ecological apocalypse—'population explosion, oil exhaustion, elephant extinction, rainforest loss, acid rain, the ozone layer, desertification, nuclear winter, the running out of resources, pandemics, falling sperm counts, cancerous pesticide pollution and so forth.' He noted a consistent pattern of exaggeration that preceded a damp squib. It was never as bad as leading scientists predicted. This is not to say that all future predictions will be exaggerations, but Ridley encourages scepticism. We should all be a little more suspicious when faced with claims of impending disaster. Fortunately, in countries with an overwhelming young population, the natural optimism of the young wins against all doomsayers.

A Source of Life

Without CO_2, which is present everywhere in nature, life on Earth is not possible. Former Director of Greenpeace Patrick Moore, speaking on the subject for The Global Warming Policy Foundation, says that it is certainly beyond doubt that 'CO_2 is the building block for all life on Earth', without whose sufficient presence in the atmosphere, 'this would be a dead planet'. According to Moore, CO_2 levels were higher in the Earth's first four billion years than they are today, and because life on Earth was evolving at the time, CO_2 was unlikely to be a danger to life in itself. At the end of the Jurassic era, some 150 million years ago, CO_2 levels rose dramatically while temperatures fell, but 100 million years later, during the Eocene epoch, the reverse happened: temperatures spiked while CO_2 levels dipped. The amount of CO_2 in the atmosphere, therefore, appears unrelated to temperature, and to suggest otherwise is, according to Moore, 'dangerous propaganda'.

The French philosopher Bruno Latour believed we should rethink our relationship with the Earth and its nature. The authors agree. For years, humanity has believed it possible to keep consuming endlessly, but there are limits to what the planet can offer; there are consequences to our behaviour, although these are not always clear. If the Earth is overheating, or if a new Ice Age is coming, people must be creative enough to find solutions for either the problem or its consequences. Geoengineering offers a number of possibilities, though it is still in its infancy. There are also less drastic things we can do. For example, because trees absorb warmth, we can grow more forests if we want to cool the Earth. In any case, trees are beneficial for us, as explained later. We must plan spaces where excess rainwater can be held before being carried off and absorbed into the ground if we want to protect our cities from flooding. Large apartment blocks in Amsterdam, for instance, feature roof terraces with sand dunes (planted with traditional grasses), a beach and saltwater pool. This provides not only a beautiful place to relax in the city during pleasant weather, but also serves as a practical way to absorb rainfall. Furthermore, the plants clean the air and offer a habitat to butterflies, insects and birds.

While these are only a few examples of what we can do without excessive cost, the most important thing for us is to use our common sense and resist putting all hope in one expensive, unrealistic solution. Reducing CO_2 emissions is a useful ambition, especially as our rising energy demands are producing more emissions, but a world without emissions may not be the Promised Land. In fact, it is quite the opposite. We see people across Europe taking to the streets, voicing their rage at politicians who (obviously) must transfer the financial burden of reducing

CO_2 emissions to every citizen. If Dutch climate change expert Richard Tol proves to be correct in his assertion that climate change will primarily affect the poor, we would be better off spending time, money and creativity preventing an ecological disaster in the poorer parts of the world.

Towards a Food and Health Revolution

Around 350 years ago, Louis XIV, the Sun King, ruled France. He wanted the best of everything and enjoyed a daily choice of 500 dishes—a wish fulfilled by a full-time workforce of about 500, including growers, farmers, transporters, preservers (salting, drying, bottling, etc.), cooks and spit-turning boys. At the time, realizing such a wealth of culinary delights was the preserve of only the fabulously rich and, fortunately for him, Louis XIV was extremely well-off. Today, however, anyone in a developed country can live like the Sun King by merely visiting a supermarket where there is a ready choice of at least 500 meals. Furthermore, we no longer need our own workforce to eat well—a food revolution has occurred in the past 350 years. The democratization of food is a huge achievement for humanity, something that was inconceivable to average Europeans (regardless of class or status) three and a half centuries ago. Now, with the food revolution, the challenge is to feed 7–10 billion people in a nutritious, appetizing and sustainable way. While meeting this challenge may seem impossible, it could, in fact, become reality.

The Green Revolution

The food revolution has also faced numerous setbacks over the past 350 years. The 19th century saw terrible famines, most notably the Irish Potato Famine (1845–49)—a result of large-scale potato blight (*Phytophthora infestans*). Crises throughout the 19th century inspired food producers to improve their methods. Farmers joined forces to set up cooperatives and insurance schemes, while agricultural education helped pool knowledge and experience to improve the quality and output of crops. These initiatives led to a major advancement in food production and a virtuous cycle of improved understanding, resulting in greater investment and increased productivity. This worked well for decades, until further famines struck in the 1950s and 1960s, most notably in India, Ethiopia and Biafra. 'The poor children in Biafra would be grateful for this food,' said many Western mothers to children who left food at the side of their plates. 'They have nothing to eat. You are thoroughly spoilt. Eat up!' Such memories will resonate with many people of the authors' generation. Yet it was these famines that once again galvanized the food industry into launching renewed research and development, leading to further innovation.

What we now call the Green Revolution was an amalgamation of improvements in production, enabling much of the world's population to have access to decent, affordable food. The rise of intensive agriculture, for instance, increased the productivity and earning capacity of each acre of land, which was essential given the demographic changes that were taking place. While the world population was 2 billion in 1950, it has now surpassed 8 billion and is expected to reach 10 billion by 2050. This population explosion (a net global increase of 2,20,000 people per day) introduces an urgent need to protect our natural environment. We must stop cutting down rainforests and be more careful with energy resources. At the same time, we must acknowledge that without oil, we would never have been ab_e to feed 8 billion people. We must encourage healthier eating to prevent obesity, diabetes, cancer and other diseases of affluence. Environmental and health concerns will thus be the imperatives of the next food revolution.

Or Maybe Not...

The projected global of 10 billion by 2050 is almost an inevitability to which we should be accustomed. However, Darrell Bricker and John Ibbitson conclude in *Empty Planet: The Shock of Global Population Decline*—but what if we're wrong? In an interview with Megan Molteni at *Wired*, Bricker and Ibbitson explain how a never-ending decline in global population will begin in about 30 years, and how the UN has consistently omitted two factors from its calculations— urbanization and the education of women. They suggest the UN has a 'grim view of Africa' in its prediction that not much will change in terms of fertility. However, parts of Africa are urbanizing at twice the rate of the global average. In Kenya, for example, men *and* women reach the same elementary education level, and just as many girls graduate as boys.

Bricker and Ibbitson also discovered that women around the world want two children; the 'external forces' requiring bigger families are disappearing everywhere, especially in developing countries. In the Philippines, between 2003 and 2018, fertility rates dropped from 3.7 per cent to 2.7 per cent. 'That's a whole kid in 15 years,' they claim.

If Ibbitson and Bricker are correct, we need to reassess our future planning to consider ageing populations, depopulation and other factors. In their view, the problem is not an increase in mouths to feed, but rather a decrease in the number of people to produce food.

Rising Food Prices Push Innovation

Food prices have risen significantly in recent years and will continue to rise, so the poorest in society will have to tighten their belts or eat less. In a recent study, Goldman Sachs, one of the biggest and most influential banks in the business sector, predicted this rise will cause social unrest, political instability and even revolutions. In any case, many companies in the food sector must adapt to straitened circumstances by introducing smart, new business models that will encourage farmers, growers, transporters and other stakeholders to continue investing and innovating. We must also reassess what food is and how we should eat it: should we breed bacteria to make food tastier, or should we go back to the way our primal hunter-gatherer ancestors treated food? Human greed is an important driver of change because, after all, everyone responds better to a carrot than a stick.

A World Food Agreement

Influential Dutch agriculture and food expert Prof. Louise Fresco believes it is time for a world food agreement, just as there is a global climate agreement. In any case, climate and food are inextricably linked. If the northern hemisphere continues to get warmer, it will be possible to produce food at higher altitudes, meaning both Russia and China could be independent in food production. On the other hand, warmer temperatures in the Mediterranean and Africa will bring drought, threatening food production in those areas. A further temperature rise in the highlands would also threaten coffee production. A world food agreement is therefore needed to establish how we plan to feed the world by 2050 and who is responsible for what. According to Fresco, new food technology developments will be able to keep pace with population growth and increasing demand for food, but petty political arguments could disrupt the process. Today, farmers are consequently suffering. Meanwhile, as consumers become more discerning, food production and supply chains are being dominated by big businesses and increasingly controlled by bureaucratic governments. Regional conflict can adversely affect food production, while trade restrictions prevent food distribution. Fresco believes a food agreement could make the entire process more efficient by addressing these issues. It could also address the controversies and protests surrounding genetically modified (GM) food, particularly in Europe. This type of food is necessary to keep food production levels in line with humanity's needs. Along with adopting GM crops, time and money should be invested in making photosynthesis more efficient. Photosynthesis is an extremely complex process whereby plants convert CO_2 and light energy into food and oxygen. By improving its efficiency, food production could be increased.

Seafood, Vertical Farms, 'Vegetarization' and Lab Meat

Future food production will be diverse. Industrial farming will continue to play a significant role but will look different from traditional agriculture. Today, we obtain many nutrients from grains, potatoes, cassava and vegetables, which will be replaced in time by new sources of nutrition like algae and seaweed. Our planet is two-thirds water, though they currently contribute little to global daily calorie intake. Over the next three decades, however, the focus of food production will significantly shift from land to sea. We will also see industrial-scale farming in city centres, next to our homes. Standing many storeys tall, vertical farms in urban areas require far less space than traditional greenhouses and reduce transport costs. One vertical farm in the UK, for instance, compresses several fields into a regular-sized warehouse. Crops grow hydroponically (under artificial lighting in nutrient-rich water instead of soil) in racks stacked with 17 tiers, producing more than 500 tonnes per year.

Located in a former World War II air raid shelter in south London, Growing Underground cultivates herbs, microgreens and salad leaves 33 metres below the busy streets, using the latest hydroponic systems and LED technology. This prime location drastically reduces food miles for retailers and consumers. Also, it's not only plants that are grown in a laboratory-like setting. *In vitro* cultivation of animal cells produces cultured meat, also known as 'clean', 'synthetic' or 'lab-grown' meat—names the authors feel are far too artificial and clinical to sound appealing on a menu. Having been around since the beginning of this century, cultured meat was made popular by Oxford University researcher Jason Matheny, who in 2004 founded the NGO New Harvest, which supports the development of new agricultural biotechnologies, particularly for cultured animal products. Cultured meat is produced using many of the same techniques used in regenerative medicine, though it's one thing to develop pills and quite another to grow steaks. Research investment, however, has been limited, so we have seen only a few prototypes to date, such as 2013's lab-grown burger. It also remains to be seen whether consumers will welcome cultured meat on their dinner plates. One thing is certain: humanity cannot do without modern technologies like this if we really want to feed the planet. Connoisseurs need not worry, because there will always be farmers who raise cattle traditionally, such as those who raise Japanese Wagyu cows, although such delicacies will be costly.

Look After Your Bacteria

Not only will we produce future food in the same way we produce medicines, but also food will increasingly fulfil a medicinal function. Healthy lifestyles maintain healthy bodies, which involve much more than occasional exercise and cutting down on salt, fat and sugar. Scientists have proven there are multiple links between health and intestinal flora, which is damaged by excessive unhealthy food. Obese people can lose weight by undergoing a 'faecal transplant'—surgically receiving intestinal bacteria from slimmer people. A crucial connection between healthy intestinal flora and mental well-being is also well-documented. The Japanese keep their intestinal ecosystem healthy by consuming sufficient probiotics in fermented food and drinks. Yakult, for instance, is a Japanese fermented yoghurt drink.

Hipsters today maintain healthy intestinal flora (without even knowing it) by drinking the highly popular kombucha. For at least 1,000 years, people in Russia and Ukraine have been drinking kvass, a vitamin-rich fermented drink made from rye and malt. Kvass is even more popular than Coca-Cola in large parts of the former Soviet Union. Caring for our intestinal flora has become an important trend in the grey area between food and health, and probiotic innovation will be a significant future development.

Windy Pops—Better Out than In

Everyone farts. Some people may complain that fermented food or drinks make them windy. Some people find it embarrassing and only fart when they're alone. Of course, there is a world of difference between farting in public and letting one rip at home when your partner is there. The authors know of couples who are likely to have never passed wind in front of each other, or for whom farting would be such a crisis in their relationship that the culprit would be banished to the sofa for the night. All this fuss for nothing when it is so healthy to smell a fart! The hydrogen sulphide that makes our farts smell is naturally present in our bodies and has all sorts of beneficial side effects. Researchers at the University of Exeter have discovered that regular inhalation of hydrogen sulphide not only reduces the risk of heart attacks, strokes and even certain types of cancer, but also lowers the risk of developing arthritis and dementia later in life. So the next time you're sitting next to your partner on the sofa, instead of uncomfortably squeezing your bum cheeks together, suppressing a fart, just let it rip! Explain to your loved one that it is for their benefit, for their own good. 'Better out in the wide world than trapped in the darkness causing belly ache,' as one of the authors' late grandfather used to say. Amen to that.

Fasting Like an Athlete

When aiming to be fitter, many people look to athletes for training and dietary inspiration. This has created a trend for consuming more protein; all major dairy manufacturers have consequently introduced products with added protein. A steady intake of extra carbohydrates was once thought best for training and optimal performance, but a periodic intake—the so-called 'train low, compete high' concept of carb cycling—is now in vogue. Athletes follow a normal diet on training and rest days, taking on extra carbohydrates only when they need peak performance. This is not unlike Intermittent Fasting (IF), an eating pattern that has become increasingly popular. Such fasting helps people lose weight by restricting daily food intake to certain times of the day, such as eating only in the daytime. Many people find that fat melts away only through fasting without having to count calories or rely on slimming drinks and bland veggies. While a 'fasting' phase is beneficial for athletes because it trains the body at a cellular level, IF feeds into a growing need for togetherness, community and ritual among everyday people, who meet regularly (once a week, perhaps) to break their fast together.

The scientific health benefits of IF are unclear, but one crucial question is whether they are due to the fasting or the weight loss. Research has shown that health improves in subjects who intermittently fast but whose calorific intake enables them to maintain their weight. Scientists are discovering more about the benefits of eating less. Intermittent fasting can not only lower cholesterol and prevent diabetes, but it also stimulates the production of a protein that strengthens connections in the brain and works as an antidepressant. Researchers at MIT have recently discovered that intestinal stem cells reproduce faster in mice that are intermittently fed, which means fasting helps damaged tissue heal quicker. This might promise better recovery from infections and treatments like chemotherapy, so researchers now want to find out whether stem cells reproduce quicker in fasting humans too. If so, science can develop medicines to simulate the fasting process, even allowing people to maintain their regular eating habits. Expectations are high for the health benefits of fasting, and with good reason.

Diet for the Planet

Many books claim to describe the optimum diet, while many others suggest solutions for environmental issues. Aiming to collate all this information, the EAT-Lancet Commission on Food, Planet, Health, which includes 37 scientists from 16 countries, first determined what constitutes a good diet for healthy living, then assessed their findings against the global sustainability of food production in the future. They drew the conclusion that feeding 10 billion people is possible but requires the food system to be transformed through three substantial changes. Food waste must be halved by 2050; production must be more efficient and sustainable, with greater investment in healthier crops; everyone on Earth must adopt a 'planetary health diet' of 2,500 calories per day, which includes more fruits, vegetables, nuts and legumes, while significantly reducing dairy and red meat consumption. This planetary health diet of ample fresh fruits and vegetables is quite similar to the Mediterranean diet of a generation ago.

This research has started a discussion among all stakeholders (from farmers to consumers) about what we ought to eat, both now and in the future. The question is how future food systems can benefit, rather than harm our health and the planet.

Savour Your Food

Eating less doesn't have to be a challenge, and it certainly doesn't mean we must go hungry. Dutch researchers at

Wageningen University & Research have shown that feeling sated is not related to the number of calories ingested or any signal from the stomach, but rather a signal given by the workings of the mouth. Food that takes time and energy to eat is more satisfying than food that is either easier to eat or more calorific. Effort spent chewing low-calorie food tricks our brain, and we can lose weight without feeling hungry. Not only that, but it also lowers our temper and makes us less irritable and snappy with the people around us. We therefore avoid the guilt that leads us to indulge in crisps or chocolate.

People often mock vegetables for being 'rabbit food', but just think about it. Healthy and sprightly, rabbits take time to munch through a carrot. When all the chewing and swallowing get boring, our brains give us a signal: we are full. The same thing happens when we eat fruits. We feel sated if we eat the fruit whole, but pouring the same amount of fruit down our throats in liquid form leaves us hungry. It is therefore important that we are aware of what we eat. Instead of just shovelling food into our mouths, we must stop, pay attention, make some effort and enjoy it. Mindful eating sounds obvious, but it works.

Playing Games Is Good for Our Health

Using gamification is one of the new ways to help people get healthier. Everyone likes games, so this is an easy, painless way to reshape behaviours with positive lifestyle choices. Playing improves patterns of eating, sleeping and exercising. Just think about the tremendous success of *Pokémon Go* and how it made people active Games work as a positive motivator, as elements of gaming motivate sick people to take charge of their own health and recovery. Introduced into the care system, gaming encourages patients to be more emotionally and socially involved. They are motivated to try harder once they see themselves progress and improve. This model enables carers to function as coaches and motivators for self-improvement.

Games also make people more resilient. The US game *SuperBetter* teaches people how to react to life's challenges in a practical, engaging way. Shown to reduce stress, games can also help support hospital operations. For example, Dutch start-up Happitech developed *Skip a Beat*, in which a player's heartbeat affects gameplay.

The Elegant Death

In Switzerland assisted suicide is permitted. Swiss citizens who suffer in extreme pain can ask a doctor to help end their lives. This is also possible in the Netherlands. Switzerland now has introduced the Sarco pod, a self-assisted 'suicide pod' for those suffering from an incurable illness. Soon we will all be able to buy these euthanasia services online, irrespective of the laws in our own country. Euthanasia will also be available to elderly citizens who feel that their life is complete. They have done everything they wanted to do and just want to die peacefully. In our country one political party D66 has written a law that would make this legal. This law has not been passed by our parliament yet, but maybe it might be in the future.

Furthermore, within a few years, AI will make it possible for us to download our brains—knowledge, emotions and memories—into a computer, so that our loved ones may keep communicating with us after death. In Holland, we see that some Indians are afraid to ask their GP for euthanasia because they are afraid it might be against Hinduism. Is it? Or not? We do not know, but we think that the right to euthanasia should become one of the global human rights, regardless of what religious leaders think of it. It's every individual's own decision and we believe that everyone has a personal relationship with their gods.

A Data Revolution in Healthcare

Once in every 50 years, there is a healthcare revolution—a result of both scientific innovation and a general change in community behaviour. Once 19th-century scientists discovered that bacteria cause diseases, many governments launched campaigns to increase hygiene standards and improve public health. Hundreds of new medicines followed the discovery of penicillin in 1928. Another era of advancement in medicine occurred in the 1970s, thanks to better testing methods.

Now, after 50-odd years, the next big healthcare development is the use of data analytics ('big data'), captured not only by carers and health organizations but also increasingly by patients themselves using wearables and e-health applications. Collecting, collating and analysing vast amounts of data, along with the potential to create personalized healthcare plans, has a beneficial effect on diagnoses, prognoses and recovery. In addition, with constant healthcare monitoring using digital technology, treatments can be instantly amended to suit any change in circumstances. In general, digitalization and better use of information improve the efficiency, effectiveness and quality of healthcare, enabling many other benefits, such as e-care at home rather than in an institution. With big data at the forefront of the next healthcare revolution, the relationship between patients and medical professionals will improve, and superior-quality healthcare will be accessible to all.

The Healthcare Industry and Data Organizations Working Together

Data organizations are important future partners for hospital diagnostics. In another 10–20 years, they could even be responsible for our diagnoses, with hospitals and nursing homes providing only the follow-on 'care and cure'. So, while X-rays and scans could be undertaken in hospitals, results would be analysed by data companies using algorithms. How healthcare professionals react to this change is debatable, but it is certainly possible that with the advent of hospital supercomputers, fewer personnel will be needed. It is also possible that hospitals will consequently receive less funding or generate less income. The interdependency between healthcare professionals around the world and data organizations is thus vital. The former supply a continuous flow of information to the latter and then rely on data analyses using a large dataset far beyond national or regional reach. Patients, meanwhile, receive better diagnosis and treatment. A hospital in Newfoundland and Labrador already works closely with IBM and has been transformed into a hub for the IBM computer system Watson.

Whether it's hospitals or data companies that form the more powerful part of the equation, big data is undoubtedly a significant leap forward in health improvement and treatment.

The UK's Progressive Thinking: Free E-Health

In 2016, the UK's National Health Service (NHS) announced it would give away many thousands of free e-health tools and devices, including smartphone ECG apps that enable patients to monitor their heart. According to former Chief Executive of The NHS,

Simon Stevens, this initiative helped facilitate remote healthcare, saving thousands of lives in the process. Furthermore, the NHS made it more attractive for tech companies to offer their digital e-health solutions by adopting an easier procurement procedure, thus opening up UK healthcare systems to international business. This is a major step because healthcare technologization is a global development unhindered by national borders. Hospitals around the world will soon recognize the financial incentives of implementing modern e-health applications.

The Success of Robot Surgery

Today, robots play a significant role in hospitals. One in three operations could soon be conducted by a surgical robot, remotely guided by a human surgeon. These robots are mostly used for hernia operations, bariatric operations, hysterectomies and prostate surgeries, according to Intuitive Surgical Data. Surgical robots obviously don't come cheap. *Fortune* estimates the average model costs around US\$1.5 million, which explains why today's necessary technology is often quoted as the reason for soaring healthcare costs around the world. Surgical robots and other technologies, however, mean fewer medical errors, less need for doctors and nurses as well as faster patient recovery. People's ability to return to work sooner is an important economic consideration as well. Embracing medical technology makes financial sense and is a key solution for many of the current problems in healthcare.

Mini-Robots Will Undertake Medical Interventions Without Surgery

People swallow harmful objects that could cause untold damage to their insides, and it happens more often than we think. A watch battery resembling a sweet, for example, could easily be ingested by an infant. It has happened, it does happen and it will continue to happen in the future. Such objects require urgent removal, sometimes necessitating an intrusive surgical operation. However, that could soon be unnecessary. At the 2016 International Conference on Robotics and Automation in Stockholm, MIT scientists presented foldable mini-robots, small enough to be swallowed. Once in the stomach, they unfold, find the foreign object and guide it out through the intestines. A second robot can follow to repair any damage caused by the first. Having been extensively tested on living pigs, this technology could soon be integrated into our healthcare systems.

Care-Bots Can Help Older People and the Chronically Ill

Care-bots come in various shapes and sizes, performing a variety of tasks, from offering healthcare to the chronically sick to being a companion for lonely older individuals. They can assist nurses to lift patients out of beds or wheelchairs, and even wash a patient's hair. Developed by car manufacturer Honda, Asimo is one such robot nurse. Japan has a higher proportion of elderly citizens than most other countries, and since Japanese authorities have been unable to attract enough foreign workers, Asimo and others are filling the urgent healthcare gap. Every Japanese grandmother will soon be cared for by a healthcare robot possessing appropriate emotions to double as a companion. Robotics developers spend a lot of time modelling human emotions. The therapeutic robot PARO is modelled on human interactions with pets—cats, dogs and other domestic animals—to alleviate human loneliness and cheer people up. Resembling a baby harp seal, PARO is designed to fit comfortably on a human lap. This pet-type robot is used in more than 10 countries, providing comfort for patients with Alzheimer's and other diseases. Just like people, PARO is active in the daytime and sleeps at night; he is sensitive to noise, light, touch and temperature; he recognizes certain words; he bats his long eyelashes, wags his tail and makes seal noises when stroked.

Genomics Strengthen the Revolution

Research is making it easier to learn about our genetic heritage. Along with the positive traits that we are proud of, we are discovering hereditary weaknesses or defects: diseases cemented into our DNA or family characteristics like curly hair or long toes. Deciphering the first human genome—someone's individual DNA—cost a painful US$13 billion. Even a couple of decades ago, it still cost hundreds of millions of dollars. These days, thanks to continuous IT development, it can be done for a few thousand. Calculations performed on today's supercomputers are faster and less expensive—they can scan billions of lines of information, quickly isolating and analysing a faulty one. A genome contains about 3 billion lines of code, while the variance between one person and the next, which is key to finding inherited illnesses and health problems, is about a million. Furthermore, DNA sequencing machines break up the information and present it in many pieces, making analysis more difficult. After piecing together the information, today's computers can take days to complete the complicated task of comparing two genomes (otherwise known as 'read alignment'). To significantly reduce the time it takes, down to a couple of hours, the next-generation computers must work up to 100 times faster than those we have today, a feat that has been made possible by recent breakthroughs in hardware acceleration technology.

While the genomics industry focused on making sequencing technology faster and cheaper in the past, it now plays a pivotal role in healthcare and the development of medicines. Genomics has the potential to help treat specific illnesses in a precise, targeted way—at a genetic level. It can also recommend an optimal diet that is tailored to individual patients. Moreover, genomics is switching its emphasis from healthcare treatment to prevention, so we can expect significant advances in the area very soon.

COLUMN

THE INDIAN DIASPORA: YOUR GATEWAY TO BUSINESS SUCCESS IN THE CARIBBEAN AND EUROPE

The Indian diaspora is a powerful global network, bridging India with the Caribbean and continental Europe through culture, entrepreneurship and trade. For businesses and investors, this vibrant community offers more than opportunities—it offers trusted relationships that drive innovation and success.

Unlocking Caribbean Potential: The Caribbean is more than a tropical paradise—it's a land of emerging industries and untapped potential. With a strong Indian diaspora presence, countries like Suriname, Trinidad and Tobago and Guyana have become thriving hubs of commerce and culture.

At D World Advisory B.V. (DWA), we know the Caribbean intimately— it's home. We help you navigate this dynamic region, unlocking opportunities in:

- **Agribusiness & Food Processing:** Capitalize on organic farming, spice exports, and the region's growing demand for high-quality produce.
- **Cultural Tourism:** Festivals like Diwali and Holi offer lucrative tourism experiences that attract global audiences.
- **Trade & Export:** Leverage Suriname's strategic position as a gateway for Indian goods and as a platform for Caribbean exports like cocoa and rum.
- **Education & Skill Development:** Tap into the growing demand for vocational training and technology education, powered by Indian expertise.

Expanding in Europe: With a flourishing Indian diaspora, Europe is a hub of innovation and trade. Countries like the Netherlands, Germany and France offer vast business potential, from technology to healthcare and sustainability.

Our experience across Surinamese and European markets means we know how to open doors in this competitive landscape. We can help you seize opportunities in:

- **Technology & Innovation:** Collaborate with Indian-origin professionals leading advancements in AI, FinTech, and IT.
- **Healthcare & Pharmaceuticals:** Explore Europe's booming healthcare sector through strategic partnerships in telemedicine, research, and medical tech.
- **Cultural & Creative Ventures:** Enter thriving markets in Bollywood-inspired media, fashion, and culinary experiences.
- **Sustainability:** Partner on renewable energy and eco-friendly projects aligned with Europe's green innovation push.

Why DWA? What sets us apart isn't just expertise—it's our personal touch. As founders, **Sonny and Anand**, we take the time to understand your goals and challenges, building relationships that go beyond transactions. When you work with DWA, you gain:

- **Tailored Solutions:** Strategies aligned with your vision.
- **Deep Market Expertise:** Years of experience guiding businesses through complex regions.
- **Strong Networks:** Connections with policymakers and business leaders that open new doors.
- **Cultural Fluency:** Personal ties to the Indian diaspora ensure your business resonates locally.

Your Journey Starts Here: The Caribbean and Europe are calling. Whether expanding into Suriname or entering Europe's innovation hubs, **DWA** is here to guide you. Let us help turn your ambitions into reality. Contact us today—together, we'll build your next success story.

—Anand Ramkisoensing and Sonny Sheoratan

DWA

DWorld Advisory

7

The Convergence of Nanotechnology, Biotechnology and Neuroscience

Saddam Hussein, Joseph Stalin, Mao Zedong, Bashar al-Assad and Adolf Hitler are playing Scrabble together in Hell. During a break, they watch BBC World's live coverage of how the French police prevented a major terrorist attack in Paris. They watch in amazement as the BBC journalist unveils how the plotters were deceived by their VirtualMe avatars, using advanced technology from the French security agencies.

'What a world of wimps it has become without us,' Saddam laments. 'Why are there no real men anymore, like we used to be? How can they let some piece of technology with a damned Hindu name for an avatar prevent them from their manly work of terror? The whole world has become degraded. The real men out there must really miss us. Shall we ask the Devil if He could reincarnate us?'

Bioscience emerged during the first digital revolution in the 1990s, making it suddenly possible for computers with high processing power to analyse huge quantities of genetic data and discover patterns between genes and particular illnesses. Along with this, neuroscientists began using MRI scanners, which allowed them to observe the processes of a living brain for the first time. Then nanotechnology came along this century. These technologies slowly but surely integrated into a process known as the NBIC convergence—a significant scientific revolution that will totally transform our lives. In the future, it could be possible to combat depression or the effects of ADHD by inserting a nano-implant in the brain to regulate dopamine and serotonin production. Another technique to treat these disorders is Deep Brain Stimulation (DBS), which is already being used for patients with Parkinson's disease. The procedure uses a neurotransmitter—a 'pacemaker for the brain'— that stimulates certain parts of the brain and teaches it to suppress involuntary muscle spasms. While DBS can be effective in treating severe depression or obsessive-compulsive disorders, it could be extended in the future to treat people with addictive or aggressive behaviours and eating disorders.

There is an interconnected revolution in healthcare and food, which will become more pronounced as the 21st century progresses. While nowadays we visit a doctor when we're ill, we will look to our diet for treatment in the future. A big challenge is feeding a growing world population in a healthy and sustainable manner. We need to find ways to produce more sustainable food without putting further pressure on agricultural land, such as by shifting production to the sea or upwards in large-scale vertical farms. In Africa, however, there are vast tracts of uncultivated land that could be used for agriculture. With irrigation, large parts of the vast Sahel region (south of the Sahara) could be transformed into fertile land, which would not only boost food production but also help lift the local population out of poverty. For this to happen, technology is key. Food transportation, cooling and preparation techniques must be modernized.

In kitchens around the world, robots will replicate the movements and behaviours of celebrity chefs, simultaneously and repeatedly preparing high-quality, popular dishes from top restaurants in various locations. Hospitals (and patients) will be more reliant on robots, and we will gain better insight into our bodies and health with the help of AI and supercomputers. These necessary advancements will both help sick people recover and offer healthy individuals new ways of staying in their prime.

The Emotional and Spiritual Revolution

Even though we are now better off in some ways, many people are still unhappy, lonely, depressed, anxious, unheard, dissatisfied and rootless. Belgian psychiatrist Dirk de Wachter argues there is a vast chasm between our internal persona (lonely, insecure, unhappy at times) and external persona (Facebook-friendly, successful, always happy). While internal personas are not for public consumption, the success and happiness of our external personas—defined by wealth and possessions—have achieved the status of social norms. Everyone's supposed aim in life is happiness, which *seems* to be an easily attainable state. If we achieve happiness, we attribute it to our own efforts. De Wachter argues that if, however, we are unhappy or less successful, we can't cope with it and look to psychiatry for help.

Unhappiness is consequently medicalized, with psychiatrists making diagnoses and prescribing pills. Swiss emeritus professor of psychiatry Jules Angst said that unhappiness and adversity are as much a part of life as happiness and success. As we're not happy or euphoric all the time, unhappiness and adversity play their prominent roles.

De Wachter suggests we should once again learn to be unhappy. He believes that unhappiness is the route to a good life, whereas chasing happiness is 'the royal road to unhappiness', ending in the psychiatrist's consulting room. By simply trying to live a 'good' life, we will find spontaneous happiness on our journey. Mental illnesses arise from societal conditions, and vulnerable people are susceptible to what society denies them. As life becomes faster and society becomes increasingly competitive, de Wachter predicts that even more people will be neglected. Philosopher Roger Scruton believed we must take a broader, historical view of what is achievable, either in happiness or in society in general. A strange Western superstition suggests we can reset the clock—remodelling and remaking human nature, society and the possibility of happiness, as if our ancestors' knowledge and experiences 'were now entirely irrelevant'.

Social Media Is Making Us Ill

For her book *iGen: Why Today's Super-Connected Kids Are Growing Up Less Rebellious, More Tolerant, Less Happy—and Completely Unprepared for Adulthood and What That Means for the Rest of Us*, psychologist Jean Twenge analysed questionnaire data from thousands of young US citizens. She discovered that those who spend more time on social media tend to agree with the view that 'the future often seems hopeless' and they 'can't do anything right'. On the other hand, those who spend more time playing sports, doing chores or socializing are less prone to psychological problems. Twenge's research does not show cause and effect, so some young people may already be unhappy before turning to their smartphones for comfort. However, in 2016, a random selection of (adult) Facebook users were asked to avoid social media for one week. When asked about their mental well-being a week later, they reported feeling markedly less depressed. An earlier study had already found that Facebook usage correlates strongly with unhappiness. While it is possible that these people spent their time online only watching dismal clips of crime, death and destruction, it is most likely they were affected by an unrealistic, unattainable illusion of 'happiness'. Social media users often perceive other social media users to be happier.

Society Is Making Us Ill

Most people agree that the risk of developing a psychiatric problem is greater today than it was in the past. As countless studies show, people living in stressful environments are also more prone to mental disorders than those living in peaceful environments. Unfortunately, modern times can be defined by the increased amount of social stress. We live in large, busy urban centres; we are constantly in a rush; we are always busy playing different roles—as a parent, carer, employee, lover, partner, boss and so on. As we hurry through our cities, there are no longer pleasant stretches of green land to soothe our eyes; instead, we are faced with concrete buildings, roads, signage and shop windows. We breathe polluted air. Day and night, we're bombarded with all types of information, whether relevant to us or not. School classrooms are overcrowded. Work is disturbed by constant notifications, phone calls, messaging and emails; when we do find a quiet moment, colleagues start asking questions or the boss calls. Our sleep patterns suffer because our bedrooms are not dark enough or quiet enough. Life is not a bed of roses and we always find plenty to worry about.

Living in a Turbo Culture with a Reptilian Brain

Stress, which in itself is not serious, is our natural reaction to perceived threats, enabling us to act quickly and decisively, run away or avoid something unpleasant, and ignore pain and tiredness. Once we are alerted to danger, a signal is sent to our adrenal glands, which produce the stress hormone cortisol. Cortisol levels gradually die down when danger has passed, returning us to a state of calm. That was a fabulous mechanism for our ancestors who relied on it to escape from an angry mammoth or sabre-toothed tiger. Fight-or-flight mechanisms in the brain are primaeval and exist in most living creatures. Millions of years ago, fish and reptiles learnt how to react to fear and danger, and nature's alarm system is still operating today. Modern fish and reptiles are in little danger from the perils of city living, and for most people today—aside from soldiers, trauma surgeons and firefighters—stress is not a matter of life and death. Furthermore, we react to many imagined stressors as if they were real. We can't run away from a threat of war starting in North Korea, or from the US election results, or from a poison gas bombardment in Syria (unless we live there). But it's our reptilian brain that makes us worried and stressed about those events. The permanent presence of stressors deregulates our cortisol system, and that's where the problems begin.

Research proves that stress has existed throughout human history—only the causes of our stress have changed. Once upon a time, we got stressed about encountering vicious animals while out hunting the next meal, or about the plague, or about a failing harvest. Now, we get stressed about traffic queues, childcare, the conference in Tokyo, refugees and tight work deadlines. The authors are sure these are good reasons for us to be stressed.

Furthermore, modern life means stretching our nerves to the limit. Efficiency innovation in recent decades has saved time by speeding up business—a factor that ironically offers us less 'free time'. Taking less time to complete a task seems to save us more time, but it actually makes our lives more rushed. Despite theoretical time-saving practices, we are experiencing the ever greater pressure of time, with life's tempo accelerating constantly. Today's society could be described as a turbo culture in which many of us are running so fast that we're leaving ourselves behind.

Something Is Happening in Our Heads

One thing experts cannot agree upon is whether mental disorders are synonymous with brain illnesses. However, they do agree that mental disturbances influence the brain. Using neuroimaging, brain specialists can find the origins of and treatments for psychiatric problems by mapping which areas of the brain are active during certain mental disturbances. For instance, certain brain structures and functions in people who suffer from depression or phobias are remarkably different from those people of who don't. People with depression also have abnormal cortisol levels, suggesting communication between the brain and the adrenal glands is malfunctioning. While researchers are not yet able to isolate the malfunction, they can see from the neuroimaging that brains exposed to elevated levels of cortisol for extended periods risk permanent damage.

More Is Happening than We Thought

The new and improved imaging techniques allow us to see that more parts of the brain are active during mental disturbances than we originally thought. The rogue connections in some parts of the brain are causing people a social anxiety disorder (disproportionate fear of social situations) by which they misread other people's facial expressions. They also filter information differently, tending to focus on the negative aspects. Using the latest technology, it is possible for psychiatrists, neurobiologists, geneticists and endocrinologists to collaborate and explore these sorts of links in the brain. Even if they cannot isolate the actual causes, insight into the biology of mental disturbances enables more effective treatment and fewer side effects.

Depression Shrinks the Brain

By comparing brain scans from people with and without depression, researchers at the University of Southern California have discovered that the hippocampus shrinks when people are severely depressed. Responsible for memory, learning, spatial orientation, behaviour regulation and other essential functions, the hippocampus and its connections in the brain are important for survival. Changes to the hippocampus are barely noticeable during occasional bouts of depression, but the shrinkage is notably visible in people who experience depression more often or for longer periods. People who first suffer from depression before the age of 21 also have a greater chance of hippocampus damage.

Experiments show that animals with a damaged hippocampus are unable to adapt to changes in their environment. This is why people with illnesses of advancing age, such as dementia, which also damages the hippocampus, struggle with memory or coping with new surroundings. Researchers suspect the hippocampus shrinkage could be why people with depression are more prone to develop Alzheimer's disease and cardiovascular problems.

Stay Positive

A person's mood influences how they remember emotional information—a phenomenon known as 'mood congruence'. Happy people remember positive things that went well; unhappy people remember negative things that went badly. Psychologist and neuroscientist Jennifer Fee Arnold assessed this phenomenon in people with and without a history of depression. By looking at their brain activity using an MRI scanner, while asking them to remember positive or negative words, she found that brain activity in certain areas depends upon whether the words resonate with a person's mood or not. For those with a history of depression, trying to retain positive emotional information is much more difficult. What concerns Arnold most is that people who have experienced depression in the past also struggle to process positive emotions and are, therefore, at risk of entering a vicious, spiralling cycle of recurrent or long-lasting depression. One way to avoid this could be to stimulate the areas of the brain responsible for processing positive emotions through positivity training.

Increasing Loneliness

The number of single people in the world increases by 1.6 per cent each year, according to the UN. Approximately 200 million people live alone, most of whom are based in the US and Europe. This trend has reached Asia too; about 42 per cent of Tokyo inhabitants and 25 per cent of those in Seoul are single. Ageing populations are one factor driving this increase, but married women outliving their husbands is another. Around one-third of all people living in a single-person household today are thought to be over 65, and by 2050, this is expected to rise to nearly 50 per cent. Nowadays, people tend to marry later in life;

until then, they typically have more partners compared to previous generations. So, between partners and marriage, they temporarily live alone. Furthermore, after conducting a 10-year study into what he calls 'singletons', the US sociologist Eric Klinenberg suggests in his book *Going Solo: The Extraordinary Rise and Surprising Appeal of Living Alone* that single people are the inescapable outcome of a liberal society. Besides communication technology and urbanization, the principal factor for rising singlehood is female emancipation: women pursue careers instead of conforming to traditional gender expectations; they have children only if they want; they have no hesitation in seeking a divorce if they are unhappy in a marriage. However, it's now easier to switch between living in social isolation and having a social life, thanks to social media and the culture of big cities. Urban launderettes, gyms and cafés, in addition to on-demand meal deliveries, make single life more enjoyable.

The Single Person Society

If Klinenberg's analysis is correct, we can expect many more single households than might be expected from the demographics. More people than ever before are also choosing to live in the city: urban population growth increases daily by 1,80,000, according to UN figures. In 1950, about 730 million people lived in a city, but by 2030, the figure is expected to reach 5 billion, which is 60 per cent of the world's population. Living in cities offers hope, freedom, anonymity, economic security, social progress, better employment opportunities and entertainment. However, it also carries a higher risk of mental health problems. Chronic loneliness will be the inevitable outcome of tomorrow's 'single person society', unless we do something about it. Loneliness has a detrimental effect on society—it makes people ill and increases the risk factors for heart disease, type 2 diabetes, dementia and arthritis. There is also a significant link between loneliness and death. US researchers have found that older people who feel lonely are statistically more likely to die in the following six years. Lonely people tend to withdraw from their community, and consequently, they and the people they associate with become further isolated. Loneliness can thus be a contagious, self-fulfilling prophecy.

The Sexualization of Loneliness

Loneliness gets worse over time. Many lonely people believe they have failed to establish meaningful connections with others, which is often seen as an important purpose in life. They feel defective. By considering themselves as a burden to others, they are more likely to sit at home alone rather than go out and be sociable. Social isolation is increasingly problematic in other ways too. According to the UK psychologist Adam Philips, people are idealizing relationships and having unrealistic expectations of their partners. Many people with partners who fail to meet such expectations start dreaming of 'ecstatic intimacy', which they try to find in anonymous sex or pornography. Philips calls this 'the sexualization of loneliness', or a sign of despair at a lack of meaningful human interaction. International studies have shown that adolescents and young adults across the world are waiting longer to have their first sexual experience, while also engaging in less sexual activity. Some studies even suggest that all physical affection, including kissing and cuddling, is happening less. Finnish and

US studies have noted increases in masturbation among both men and women. In 2015, 43 per cent of Japanese people aged 18–34 were virgins. Japan, one of the world's most prolific porn producers with an annual turnover of US$20 billion (twice the size of the US market), is the undisputed leader in hi-tech sex toys that remove the need for a physical partner. The *onakura* shops, where men masturbate in the company of female staff, are also extremely popular in Japan.

Look for the Green Space

How do we improve our mental health? By walking in the woods? One may laugh, but research shows people are happier in rural environments. Schizophrenia, psychosis, depression or other psychiatric conditions are more likely to occur in people living in big cities. The same is true for eating disorders, such as anorexia or bulimia. Studies in the Republic of Korea and Japan suggest that spending time outdoors, surrounded by nature, is good for the body and mind. Being in a forest, for example, is believed to reduce stress, lower blood pressure, vary the heart rate, lower cortisol levels, activate the immune system and improve mood. Green environments are particularly healing for middle-aged men. In Japan, *shinrin-yoku* (forest bathing) is based on a practice that goes back to antiquity. Accompanied by a trained therapist, 'bathers' walk through the forest, sit or lie in the moss, relax and let the surroundings engage with all their senses. The 'bath' concludes with a traditional tea ceremony. Depending on the type of forest and time of year, it could be vitamin-rich, pine needle tea, green tea or berry tea.

While it is unclear why exposure to nature should be so healthy, scientists suggest it could be due to phytoncides—

chemicals emitted by certain bushes or trees. Others believe the rustling of leaves and birdsong have a calming effect. Either way, it doesn't matter. It's common sense that fresh air is restorative. It is also noteworthy that more doctors are promoting these methods. Shinrin-yoku has reached the US and Canada, where renowned cancer hospitals have adopted forest walks as part of the treatment. There must be a good reason why our ancestors found solace and spiritual enlightenment in nature.

Art and Kitsch

For those of us who would rather stay indoors, we should hang art on our walls. Looking at art is proven to be beneficial to us. According to one US study, regular museum visits stimulate children's ability to think critically, increase their empathy towards others and make them more tolerant. Semir Zeki, professor of neuroaesthetics at University College London, discovered that when people look at art, dopamine is released in the brain in areas associated with romantic feelings. Looking at art is therefore akin to falling in love, and it doesn't matter whether the art is a priceless treasure, a reproduction or a home-made piece. So one must hang that copy of Van Gogh's *Sunflowers*, the beach scene they bought in Crete or the Rembrandt artwork long stored in a vault. This effect is not limited to two-dimensional art—sculpture has the same impact. Most importantly, we should ignore what others think of our taste in art. Looking at what *we* find beautiful makes us happy, and happier people are better people who create a better world.

Art Inspired

Art has always inspired people to create new forms of art. The Egyptians, the Romans and later the Renaissance drew their inspirations from earlier societies. Nowadays, with the possibilities of modern communication, there is near unlimited access to art worldwide and throughout history. Art has had a big impact on society, both in free and forced ways. In the 20th century, art that forced people to subscribe to an ideology included communism and fascism. Both regimes used art to give their rule a human and justified touch. Opposed to this is the art that was used to protest against a rule that was not valued by the people. In general, one could say art has become freer with the progress of history, aligning with the democratization that has taken place across most of the world. Art is used to express what is happening in society. For example, the rise of abstract paintings from the mid-19th century was a response to the invention of photography. Since new forms of painting had to be invented, abstract artists received renewed praise from the public. Today, art is so diverse, and it is not likely to stop anytime soon. This diversity in art is a reflection of our complex and technologically advanced society. We are excited about the way new young artists will create works of art that fit this time and age.

Helping Each Other

Changes in society are necessary to combat loneliness. We must restore connections between people, which the US psychologist John Cacioppo—a loneliness guru—claims is simple to achieve. He suggests people perform 'random acts of kindness', such as telling strangers their hair looks nice, offering to carry someone's shopping or leaving your change behind in the vending machine. Whoever reaps the benefit is guaranteed to feel better, whether they're lonely or not. Other beautiful initiatives include local service exchange networks that match your skills and talents with people in your community who need those services. Whether young or old, everyone has something of value to offer. For instance, older people could request something on a community platform—guitar lessons, a bridge partner, a lift to a hospital appointment—and someone in the neighbourhood could offer their services in exchange for 'hours' that can be reclaimed later when they themselves need help. Programmes like this aim to connect generations, strengthen communities and build a social support network using existing resources. Reducing social isolation and loneliness improves everyone's quality of life, health and well-being.

Regular Exercise

The most important treatment a doctor can prescribe is regular physical exercise—nature's wonder drug. It keeps muscles and joints supple, reduces blood pressure and cholesterol, helps combat obesity and could lower blood-sugar levels in diabetics. In fact, avoiding a sedentary lifestyle is good for the mind and significantly reduces the risk of mental health problems. Staying physically active also lessens the symptoms of depression, although biological-mechanism scientists are still unsure how this works.

Doctors suggest 30 minutes of 'reasonably intensive' exercise per day is enough. There is no need to run a marathon, climb a mountain or spend hours in the gym. We don't even need to leave the comfort of our own home (although the authors recommend stepping outdoors). All we need to do is walk at 5 km/h, cycle at 10 km/h or climb the stairs. Vacuuming, shopping or mowing the lawn are eligible activities too. It is crucial that we burn calories and elevate our heart rate to 110–140 bpm.

Cuddling Helps

The first and most important thing we do in life is communicate through touch. A loving physical touch sets off a series of bioelectric and chemical reactions in the body, all of which have a relaxing effect on our nervous system. Touch consequently has a deeper and more immediate impact than words. Physical touch lowers cortisol levels (particularly in women), reduces blood pressure and lowers the heartbeat, thereby lessening stress and making us feel relaxed. Oxytocin is a calming hormone and neurotransmitter that helps us cope with stressful situations and is released in both men and women by a loving, non-sexual touch from a partner. As oxytocin levels are higher in females, women are better able to cope with stress, whereas men retreat into their shells, cutting themselves off emotionally or turning stoic. This male reaction is unhelpful and could lead to anxiety, depression or other psychological problems for which men are less likely to seek help. A meaningful hug could make men more resilient and keep them on a healthy path.

Unfortunately, touching has become increasingly regulated and physical contact is frowned upon, particularly between same-sex friends. Up until the late 19th century, it was considered perfectly normal for men to share a bed when staying in a hostel, which included the probability of occasional touching. Nowadays, even best friends panic about sharing a bed if the situation demands. According to the US psychologist Ofer Zur, physical contact for the modern-day heterosexual man is confined to sex or violence, with sports as an exception—men are permitted to touch each other on the playing field without provoking any suspicion of homosexuality.

Male behaviours are taught from an early age. As boys get older, physical contact between a father and son is reduced to a pat on the back, while rough-and-tumble games stop during adolescence because they have sexual connotations. These social limits are worrying because boys raised with little physical contact are less able to deal with emotional problems as adults. A lack of physical affection between parents and children also increases the likelihood of adult violence, according to a US study. Where children are regularly hugged, there is almost no evidence of violence in later life.

Professional Hugs

Men need platonic hugs but avoid them because of societal pressure. The US professor Kory Floyd argues that a lack of hugs leads to 'affection deprivation' and 'skin hunger', conditions which are more prevalent among men than women. In a 2011 Kinsey Institute study of a thousand heterosexual, middle-aged married couples across five countries, more men than women found kissing and cuddling important for happiness. An entire cuddle industry has sprung up in the US, with websites offering 'professional' huggers for therapeutic and relaxing (non-sexual) cuddling sessions. Remarkably, these services are most popular among well-educated, heterosexual, divorced men in their early 50s. In other words, men who are successful in the eyes of society still feel something is missing in their lives.

Marketing for Loneliness

In America, bars organize *hug-inns* or *hug-ons* where you can ask staff to hug you in return for payment. In China, there are agencies that arrange non-sexual company for lonely people—someone to accompany you to the cinema or a museum, a companion to talk with, etc. Loneliness has become a booming business in the single-people society with too many impulses, too much anxiety.

In Search for Meaning

Frequent stories in the media claim the number of people suffering from mental health issues is increasing, while the WHO has suggested for years that depression is the most prevalent illness in large parts of the world. However, there are also a number of studies disputing this, so it is difficult to say whether more people are mentally unwell than in the past. The good news is that many mental disorders are readily recognized today, largely because people are seeking help. If we walk into any bookshop (or browse through an online store), we will find shelves cracking under the weight of self-help books—books giving tips on how to be happier, how to overcome grief or how to cope with criticism. Even more self-help titles are published weekly. Psychology is discussed more often on television, while celebrities openly talk about their emotional struggles. This inner-life emphasis reflects the age in which we live.

Religion was traditionally *the* source of hope, inspiration and meaning to support people in times of trouble: rabbis were wise people giving advice about life's questions; Catholic confessionals were the forerunners of a psychiatrist's couch; the problems of depressed Protestants were, through the study of the Bible, put into perspective by the suffering of Christ. However, people in the West have moved away from the Church since the 1960s, and this has undermined religion's supporting role in society. This doesn't mean we no longer need meaning or spiritual solace—quite the opposite, in fact. Strongly connected to increased interest in emotions, the search for spirituality has seen a revival since the 1990s. Adolescents and young adults are at the forefront of this revival, though people of all ages are joining in. Religious academics now refer to modern society as post-secular. This trend is spreading all over the world. In countries such as Saudi Arabia and Iran, many people call themselves post-religious. Youngsters in these countries don't attend mosques any longer. In Thailand, they go to the temples less often than their elders.

Similarly, Hindus and Muslims in the Netherlands no longer visit temples and mosques. Hence, some Hindu temples are now marketing and reaching out to the youth in new ways.

The Hodgepodge God

In 1943, the US developmental psychologist Abraham Maslow arranged human needs in a pyramid-shaped hierarchy to indicate what motivates our behaviours. Starting at the pyramid's base, the first step is the physiological needs, or the basics upon which human survival depends—food, water, air, shelter and so forth. Once these needs are met, people start climbing. The needs assigned to each step of the pyramid become progressively abstract, from safety to self-actualization, via love and esteem. Western civilization reached the apex of the pyramid—the summit of Maslow's hierarchy of needs— at the end of the last century. Asian and Latin American countries are nearing the top too.

Primary needs are often the only things that matter to many people, so once basic needs are met, they have less interest in self-actualization or realizing their potential. This goes hand in hand with the search for meaning and spirituality. In this age of the individual, traditional churches and institutions no longer satisfy our needs. Instead, having a personal religious experience and inner psychological development is more important.

Globalization will give birth to a new universal religion, which the authors call the Hodgepodge God. In many ways, the Hodgepodge God will resemble the ancient Indo-European spirituality that is still visible in present-day Hinduism. It will be a multifaceted 'Hinduism-Plus', comprising yoga and meditation, finding solace in the woods like the Japanese, eating chocolate, using cannabis like the Incas, Mayas and Aztecs, reviving Jewish and Christian stories and embracing Sufi music, chants and dances.

In Conclusion

We are all likely to experience some form of mental illness at some point in our lives. Just like getting the flu, breaking a bone or suffering from some other ailment, some of us are more prone to it than others. No one finds it unusual for us to visit a doctor, consultant, physiotherapist or hospital with a physical problem, but many people are surprised when we mention mental health issues or ask for psychological help. All types of sickness, illness and injury—physical or mental—should have equal importance. Bombarded with constant stressors in a world filled with lofty expectations, we should perhaps have regular mental health checks. Physical health check-ups are a regular thing, so why not mental? Society expects us to fill a multitude of roles, which often conflict with one another, as we constantly process information to formulate the correct response. Life can be mentally exhausting, more so than ever before. The pressure to manage all these while achieving an idealized happiness makes the burden heavier. We forget that happiness is nothing but a series of fleeting moments, and real life happens in the troughs between those peaks. Life should not be a constant struggle, of course, but we need to make the best of it. Sometimes we won't succeed, yet that is no reason for succumbing to stress—or to worse. Adversity arrives more often than happiness, and by realizing this, we will immediately feel better. Unhappiness passes quickly too; it will pass quicker if we help each other.

We see this in Indonesia, one of the happiest countries in the world, where strong communal bonds foster a sense of belonging and mutual aid, easing loneliness. Bhutan, too, is often ranked among the world's happiest nations. Yet many of its youngsters choose to migrate, unwilling to settle for earning just $4 a day. At the end of the day, money makes the world go round.

NAVIGATING GROWTH: THE NETHERLANDS-INDIA TRADE CORRIDOR

Investor Warren Buffett once said: 'Beware the investment activity that produces applause. The great moves are usually greeted by yawns.' At Broekman Logistics, we do not know whether our plans to strengthen Dutch-Indian trade will be met with yawns or applause. What we do know is that they are rooted in megatrends shaping the Global South, and we are ready to invest heavily in India. For example, we are expanding logistics facilities at Mumbai's port, aiming to create significant value for India, the Netherlands and global trade.

For us, trade is not just about business—it is a form of peacekeeping. Buffett also said: 'Never invest in a business you cannot understand.' Logistics is in our blood. It flows through our veins, and we understand it deeply.

Broekman Logistics' connection to India runs decades deep. In 2006, we acquired an Indian company operating since 1988, with its first office in Mumbai. We quickly expanded, opening offices in New Delhi (1992), Chennai (1994), Ahmedabad (1996) and Bangalore (1998). Since 2021, we have operated with 18 offices across the country, with more to come as we continue our expansion.

The future of global trade lies in strategic partnerships, seamless logistics and market expertise—nowhere is this more evident than in the flourishing Netherlands-India trade corridor. We are dedicated to optimising the flow of goods between these two dynamic economies, offering reliable and innovative logistics solutions.

Our services include ocean and air freight, project forwarding and domestic logistics. With our own customs brokerage licence, micro warehousing solutions and strong local presence, we provide end-to-end supply chain services tailored to our customers' needs.

Currently, our primary focus is on growing ocean and air freight volumes between India and the Netherlands. Our efforts have already yielded strong results, solidifying our position as the preferred logistics partner for Indo-Dutch trade.

Looking ahead, we are expanding our warehousing capabilities in India. Drawing on our expertise in the Netherlands—where we serve major clients like Kubota, Liebherr and HG—we recognize India's rising demand for larger, high-quality warehouse facilities. The introduction of the Goods and Services Tax (GST) has made advanced warehousing solutions even more essential. By 2025, we expect to open our first state-of-the-art warehouse in India, supporting growing supply chain demands.

With a longstanding presence, innovative mindset, and a clear vision for the future, Broekman Logistics is THE expert on the India-Netherlands trade lane. We do not just ship cargo—we deliver the promises you make to your customers by looking beyond logistics.

—Martijn Tasma
Director of International Freight Forwarding

BROEKMAN LOGISTICS

8

Towards a Green and Great India

In this section, we will discuss some international trends—environmental, technological and cultural—that can inspire India to become greener and greater.

Towards the End of Waste

We generate around two billion tonnes of waste per year globally. By 2050, this figure is expected to reach 3.4 billion. A third of all global waste is currently dumped or burnt. Landfill sites and recycling programmes cannot cope with this growing problem, so garbage piles up on the streets. This century will therefore see an increase in the number of waste incinerators and recycling schemes.

Wealthier populations generally produce more waste than less affluent ones. With wealth increasing around the world, recycling has become more efficient and effective. We expect recycling to become a multi-billion-dollar global industry soon, involving every country—waste is, after all, an important resource.

With its robust infrastructure and stringent regulations, Singapore is extremely efficient in waste collection and hi-tech recycling. The city-state produces almost zero waste and is spotlessly clean. Singapore's waste management strategy minimizes waste generation and maximizes resource recovery through the three Rs—reducing, reusing and recycling.

From Waste to Energy

Singapore has invested in advanced waste-to-energy plants that convert non-recyclable waste into electricity, reducing the strain on landfills while also producing renewable energy. It has deployed smart waste management initiatives, driven by cutting-edge technologies and innovative solutions, to optimize efficiency and minimize environmental impact. The city-state has also invested heavily in research and development, exploring novel approaches to waste management. One notable innovation is the adoption of pneumatic waste conveyance systems that transport waste away from residential and commercial estates to centralized collection points through underground pipes. This reduces the need for traditional waste collection, minimizing carbon emissions and enhancing the urban environment's overall cleanliness.

Community Engagement

Community engagement and public education are important for fostering a culture of sustainability in Singapore. Through extensive outreach programmes and educational initiatives, the government encourages citizen participation in reducing waste. Public awareness and recycling campaigns incentivize behavioural changes, empowering individuals to make environmentally conscious choices on a daily basis. Singapore is thus setting the stage for continued progress towards a greener, more resilient future.

We expect India to follow a Singaporean model for waste management. This will happen through not only large-scale planning but also small-scale initiatives.

For instance, as people get wealthier, they tend to discard clothes more frequently. Although producing cotton is expensive, it can be recycled from manufacturers' waste (excess or unused yarns, fabrics and textiles) and consumers' discarded clothes.

Following systematic collection, sorting and assessment of cotton fibre quality, recyclable waste goes through mechanical or chemical processes to produce reusable fibres. Recycled cotton has shorter fibres and is less durable than virgin cotton, so it needs additional materials, such as polyester, to improve durability. Recycled cotton is therefore suited for casual clothing and home-building materials, which do not require high-quality fibres. Dyeing cotton with CO_2 also leads to less waste.

Inspiration from DyeCoo

Dutch company DyeCoo uses reclaimed CO2 instead of water as a dyeing medium in its patented and proven industrial technology. When pressurized CO2—recycled from existing industrial processes in a closed-loop system—becomes supercritical (SC-CO2), it has a very high solvent power that enables dye to dissolve easily without additional chemicals. The high permeability allows dyes to penetrate easily and deeply into the fibres, creating vibrant colours.

Implementing this kind of new technology should not be taken for granted because it could deliver great results on an industrial scale to cotton giants like India and countries across the subcontinent. DyeCoo is the only company that has been able to scale up CO2-based textile processing technology, winning industrial and commercial endorsements from both textile mills and consumers.

Old Cotton Clothes

We used to donate old clothes to poorer countries. However, the rise of BRICS and the Global South means there are fewer poor people who need our unwanted clothes, which are now often just dumped instead. Still, they could be used for cotton batting or wadding, quilts and home insulation against cold weather.

A Good Future for Wool and Felt

One of the most profitable livestock businesses in India is sheep farming. Sheep are reared for meat, wool, skin and manure. One can expect a 78 per cent return on sheep farming investments. On top of that, Indian sheep farmers have the capacity to produce even more wool if fashion designers and clothing manufacturers decide to use it more often.

In warm, tropical countries like India, people usually don't have many winter essentials. Increasing wool usage can change that. Old woollen sweaters can be turned into felt—a versatile fabric with wide-ranging applications, such as in insulation and other heat-retaining initiatives. Felt is also ideal for decorative goods, arts, crafts and soft furnishings; it is used in tents, yurts and clothing. Sheep are thus the future of warmth.

As discussed earlier, fresh fruits and vegetables for one million people can be produced daily in a single 10,000 m^2 vertical farm. Only 22 of these would be required to feed people in Mumbai (22 million citizens). Farmland is no longer needed and can be sold or repurposed by farmers—a vegetable farm could become a sheep farm or the site for new homes for the youth.

Alternatively, farmland could be returned to nature and remodelled as a new jungle or wildlife reserve for elephants, tigers, lions and other animals. They need their space too in the future India.

Plastic, Paper and Water Recycling

Recycling will proliferate in future. Over the next few years, several new ways to recycle waste will be developed by both big companies and start-ups. For instance, a Japanese professor has developed a small household machine that turns waste plastic into petrol for the family's scooters and cars.

Plastic, paper, steel and aluminium recycling will become more sophisticated in the coming years. Companies in China and the US are even turning human excrement into biogas for rural communities. India could also utilize this technology.

The price of paper in India is high, but, as seen in the Netherlands, it is significantly cheaper if all paper waste is recycled.

In a world where freshwater is becoming scarce, there are significant advances in reusing water recycled from sewage. Rainwater harvesting will also operate on an industrial scale, as it does in Bangkok. Even human urine can be turned into agricultural fertilizer!

Medical Waste

COVID-19 led to a significant ongoing increase in medical waste. Recycling, therefore, offers a new income stream for hospitals and professionals in the healthcare industry.

Inspiration from Hyderabad

Hyderabad's Pavani Lolla has developed an innovative, odour-free home composter that turns kitchen waste into compost in just seven days (regular composting takes 45–60 days)! A student at Vignana Bharathi Institute of Technology, Pavani embarked on a mission to tackle India's waste crisis after being inspired by her experience in the college's Eco Club. During an outreach programme, she witnessed how villagers neglected waste management and envisioned her solution.

Along with her peers Mahesh U and Siddhesh Sakore, Pavani founded Future Step—an enterprise working in the waste management sector. Their portable home composting product, small enough to fit anywhere, can handle up to 1 kg of organic waste daily, without the need for artificial heating.

Pavani's innovation not only addresses India's mounting waste problem but also empowers individuals to actively participate in environmental sustainability. This inspiring example will be followed by several new innovations in waste recycling. We can thus expect that by 2050, India will be as spotless as Singapore, without any waste whatsoever.

Clean Rivers

Over 90 per cent of plastic waste in our oceans comes from major rivers in Asia—a situation that will be rectified through efficient plastic recycling within the next 20 years. Since we cannot survive without oceans, keeping them clean is vital. The first step is reducing the amount of plastic in rivers that flow into the seas.

Industrial waste recycling has become a major business in Europe. European rivers are generally clean because fines and penalties are imposed on factories whose waste is identified in the water.

For many Indians, bathing in the Ganges and other holy rivers is a way to purify their souls. Hence, they can use this deep spiritual sense to keep their holy rivers clean and pollution-free.

The Future of Craftsmanship

After the 2019 Notre-Dame fire in Paris, France quickly mobilized. Thousands of carpenters, painters, artisans and other craftsmen fully restored this iconic cathedral within five years. This restoration feat was possible because France values craftsmanship. Artisans and skilled tradespeople are well-paid, respected and awarded prizes by the president.

India also has a long tradition of craftsmanship. Brilliant artisans built and decorated thousands of forts, palaces, havelis and historic city centres across the country—just think of the magnificent Taj Mahal! While some of these great buildings are now tourist attractions or renovated into hotels or resorts, many are dilapidated because maintenance costs were too high during a period when India was poor.

Preparing for a Tourism Boom

Tourism is on the rise in India, and national pride is growing. India can therefore afford to invest in its craftsmen and renovate these forgotten, derelict treasures. A revival of India's forgotten heritage will allow tourism to spread across the country, preventing the levels of overcrowding we see at a limited number of tourist hotspots in Europe.

Many significant buildings in India's historical past were never built, for one reason or another. There's a popular belief that Shah Jahan, who commissioned the Taj Mahal, also wanted to build a 'black Taj Mahal' on the opposite side of the Yamuna River as his own mausoleum. It was never built. So why can't it be built now? With two Taj Mahals, tourist pressure on the existing one would be reduced.

In 2001, the Taliban blew up the enormous Buddha statues of Bamiyan in Afghanistan, after rejecting India's offer to transfer the artefacts to India for safekeeping. Many ancient scriptures, including the Bible, mention giants who lived among humans, and these Buddhas were perhaps the last remaining physical representations of those giants. India, the birthplace of Buddhism, could reach out to the Taliban again, requesting permission to transport the ruined Buddhas to Buddha's birthplace in

Lumbini, Nepal, where they could be rebuilt by Indian artisans. This would certainly attract more pilgrims and tourists to the region.

Many Hindu monuments, palaces and havelis are also neglected in Pakistan and Bangladesh. Indian entrepreneurs could revive these architectural wonders by buying, transporting and rebuilding them in India. The tales, stories and history associated with these important antiquities make it a compelling option. Alternatively, replicas of these structures could be built in India—after all, many people don't see much difference between an original building and a faithful reproduction anyway.

In China there are lots of 'copycat communities' that attract tourists. For example, the Holland Village in Shanghai is a residential area that mirrors Dutch architectural styles, complete with canals, windmills and even exact replicas of buildings like the Netherlands Maritime Museum and the Bijenkorf department store.

We expect to see a rise of copycat communities and national 'restoration' events in India, like France's reopening ceremony of Notre-Dame de Paris in 2024.

The Future of Storytelling

The aforementioned tales, stories and history inspire people to visit the scenes, settings and locations they describe. If India wants to increase and diversify its tourism, many old legends from the *Mahabharata* and other ancient scriptures must be retold. At the same time, modern creative writers can craft new, inspirational narratives from which visual content could be generated through AI to attract tourists. So there is a great future for storytellers.

Most Christians are unaware that Jesus travelled extensively in India and was inspired by Hinduism. The Bible describes what he learnt in India. The Gospels of Thomas and Judas are also good examples. The Hindu concept of reincarnation was mirrored in the Bible, although the Christian church later erased it. Spiritual tourism already attracts Buddhists, who flock to India en masse, but tales of Jesus's travels could attract more tourists from other religions too. The Jewish heritage in India could also be used to market the country as a spiritual destination for Jews around the world.

Electric Aircraft

Today's small electric VTOL (vertical take-off and landing) aircraft do not need airports and can thus connect remote regions, further increasing India's appeal to both domestic and foreign tourists. Like flying buses, these VTOL aircraft can transport 20 or more people per flight, allowing craftsmen to access and renovate India's numerous remote, derelict sites.

Bullshit Jobs

Every country has its meaningless, bullshit jobs. According to anthropologist David Graeber, over half of all societal work is pointless, and it becomes psychologically destructive when paired with a work ethic that associates work with self-worth. He argues that the association of work with virtuous suffering is recent in human history.

Many of these bullshit jobs will thankfully end with the rise of AI, robotics and facial recognition, allowing the workers who spend their time doing crappy tasks to retrain themselves for more productive work.

Red tape in India exemplifies bullshit jobs. Now with advancements in AI, less bureaucratic needs will enable many civil servants to change careers and start afresh with meaningful work—as artisans or craftsmen, for example.

Supersonic and Hypersonic Aircraft

Fast aircraft—even faster than the famous Concorde—will enhance global tourism. These are being developed in the US and China, but India also has the technology and know-how to build its own.

Using China's new detonation engine, a supersonic jet could soon transport passengers at Mach 4 (over 3,000 mph) at altitudes above 65,000 feet, making it possible to travel anywhere on the planet within a few hours. Developed by aerospace firm Space Transportation (Lingkong Tianxing Technology), the JinDou400 detonation ramjet engine is an air travel revolution that will allow passengers to fly from Beijing to New York in just two hours.

Unlike traditional jet engines, this innovative design uses shock waves from detonation combustion, boosting the engine's thrust-to-weight ratio, reducing costs and simplifying its structure.

With plans to integrate this technology into its Yunxing supersonic civilian jet, Space Transportation aims to outperform past supersonic aircraft, like Concorde. The Yunxing jet will use boosters for vertical take-off, accelerate to Mach 4 at high altitudes and decelerate using a liquid rocket engine to ensure a controlled vertical landing.

The company expects its passenger aircraft to be ready by 2027, with the first commercial flights taking off in 2030. If successful, this innovation, with its potential for high-speed, point-to-point transport, could redefine global travel.

Populations are ageing fast in the West, China, Russia, the Republic of Korea and Japan. India can benefit from positive changes in tourism by attracting pensioners who can afford to travel. Like Thailand, India can create tourist opportunities specifically for elderly visitors—perhaps even exceeding what Thailand currently offers. For example, the popularity of combining high-speed travel with the comfort of cruise ships ('air cruises') is growing.

Airships

As technology advances, lightweight blimps and airships powered by helium are making a comeback. As mentioned earlier, this offers another convenient transportation possibility for reaching remote, inaccessible locations.

The blimp and the more rigid, cigar-shaped Zeppelin have been around since World War I, when they were used to transport supplies to colonies in German East Africa.

In 1917, the Zeppelin LZ 104, nicknamed Das Afrika-Schiff ('The Africa Ship'), set a world record by flying non-stop 6,800 kilometres in just 95 hours, spending almost four days in the air during its round trip from Europe to Africa.

However, the age of airship was short-lived. In 1937, the German passenger airship Hindenburg (filled with hydrogen) travelled to the US, where it exploded while landing in front of a large crowd in New Jersey. With public confidence in airships shattered, their main competitor (aircraft) then captured the freight and passenger market.

In the 1990s, after decades of research and technological improvement, a German company launched the Zeppelin NT (New Technology), making the airship much more than a colourful advertising novelty. From the military to the mining industry, today's airships are considered for any project requiring access to remote areas that lack paved roads or railways.

Airship manufacturers are now developing hybrid models with aircraft-type wings or helicopter-like rotors, which derive 80 per cent of their lift from helium and 20 per cent from motorized propulsion.

Given their high-load capacity, airborne resilience and versatile landing ability, the business potential for these new air freight vehicles is huge. Many commercial airship models are set to hit the aviation market in the coming years, as discussed by the writer Onyedimmakachukwu Obiukwu in African innovation and design magazine *Ogojiii*.

The US aerospace company Lockheed Martin has spent 10 years and over $100 million researching and developing its LMH1 airship. Over 85.35 metres long and nearly 25 metres high, LMH1 with its four 300 hp engines can carry more than 21 tonnes.

The Dynalifter from Ohio Airships can lift 200 tonnes, travel at 260 km/h and land in a mere 1,200 m (a short distance given its size). Like Lockheed Martin's LMH1, the Dynalifter is an ideal transport solution for Africa—it is already being marketed by Airships Africa, a South African company.

Funded by the US military, Aeros Corp launched a 250-metre airship in 2018 that carries 250 tonnes, travels at 220 kilometres per hour and has a 10,000 kilometre operating radius. This airship is ideal for the heavy construction industry, such as airlifting turbines to the Lake Turkana wind farm in Kenya—an area with little infrastructure.

The mining industry could also use airship technology for projects in distant, inaccessible sites, like the Mbalam-Nabeba Iron Ore Project in Central Africa that straddles the border between Cameroon and the Republic of the Congo.

India could either partner with these manufacturers or build its own airships to transport goods faster than by road, rail or sea. Airships reduce congestion, are better for the environment and have a significantly smaller impact on people's health than other forms of transport. Furthermore, they could deliver humanitarian supplies and essential medicines to remote communities, thus potentially saving thousands of lives.

The airship benefits don't end there. Google's Project Loon planned to use blimps and balloons to provide internet access to rural areas and telecommunications services across Africa and Asia. This demonstrates the airship's potential to reinvent mass service delivery at a lower cost by replacing expensive satellites.

Blimp versus Drone

The current craze for drones, which offer seemingly endless commercial applications, hasn't been capitalized well. Airships can be remote controlled too, and they don't suffer from the level of energy expenditure seen in drones. In fact, airships represent the only form of air transport that can immediately go carbon neutral.

However, airships don't come cheap. The cost of building large airships can be prohibitive; the considerable starting limit could be a show-stopper for many large-scale projects. For heavy-lift airships, Hybrid Enterprises estimates a starting cost of tens of millions of dollars, whereas manufacturers targeting social aid organizations would charge approximately US$1 million—the cost equivalent of a single aircraft supplying medicines to a few thousand people. Moreover, helium has more than doubled in price over recent years, reaching US$200 for a 500-balloon capacity tank.

If the financial challenges can be overcome, airships could be part of the solution to India and Africa's infrastructure woes. Rather than being a relic from a bygone age, airships could once again become industrial and social game changers.

Clean Air as an Asset

Europeans have clean air, but they take it for granted. India has clean air zones like Kashmir and areas in the Northeast; Delhi, Agra and Mumbai, on the other hand, have high levels of air pollution. Pollution is also a huge problem for cities like Bangkok and Jakarta. Air cleanliness within the next 10–20 years is essential for the health, happiness and development of tourism in India. Clean and pollution-free air reduces cleaning and maintenance costs for not only monuments like the Taj Mahal, but also major city centres.

New Coal Plants

Ultra-clean coal (UCC) from new processing technologies reduces ash to below 0.25 per cent and emits extremely low levels of sulphur. Instead of heavy fuel oil, pulverized coal could therefore be used to fuel huge marine engines. There are at least two UCC technologies under development, and underground coal gasification already happens in the UK. All these solutions contribute to clean air.

Blue Skies as Asset

China's air quality continued to improve during the COVID-19 era (2020–2022). According to the Ministry of Ecology and Environment, the average annual concentration of particulate pollution (PM 2.5) in 339 major Chinese cities fell to 29 µg/m³ (micrograms per cubic metre) in 2022. The average number of days classified as having good air quality reached 316. As China's residents and visitors will note, the clear blue skies are back.

Towards the End of Deserts

India has a desert area of 13.52 per cent. Covering about 2,00,000 sq km the Thar Desert alone forms approximately

5 per cent of India's total geographic area.

What we think of as a desert landscape is not a permanent feature. The African Humid Period, which occurred around 11,000–5,000 years ago, transformed the Sahara into a lush green landscape filled with vegetation, lakes, and abundant wildlife. This transformation was driven by changes in the Earth's orbit, specifically its axial precession—the planet's wobbly path—which dramatically increased summer solar radiation and strengthened monsoonal rains over North Africa.

Geological evidence—lake sediments, the Nile River runoff and reduced Saharan dust deposits—confirms the vast extent of this humid phase, stretching from the Sahara to East Africa. In this period, human populations thrived in the fertile environment, as reflected in extensive rock art depicting pastoral life and large animals.

However, the end of this period brought gradual death and desiccation, forcing populations to abandon the drying Sahara and migrate towards water sources like the Nile River valley, where complex societies such as Pharaonic Egypt emerged.

This Saharan region won't always be a dead desert. Over the past 8,00,000 years, the Sahara has periodically turned green. Every 21,000 years or so, thanks to the Earth's orbit and other factors, wet periods drench the usually dry desert, transforming it into lush greenery.

Inspiration from China

As part of a national initiative to end desertification and curb the sandstorms that plague parts of the country during spring, China has encircled its largest desert with trees. The *Three-North Shelterbelt* project, which began in 1978, created a 3,000-kilometre 'green belt' around the Taklamakan. The Great Green Wall, as it is known colloquially, contains more than 30 million hectares of trees.

Planting trees in the arid northwest has increased China's total forest coverage from around 10 per cent in 1949 to more than 25 per cent today. In Xinjiang alone (25 million inhabitants), forest coverage has risen from 1 per cent to 5 per cent in the past 40 years.

The *Three-North Shelterbelt* project involved decades of experimentation with different tree and plant species to determine which is the hardiest. Critics argue that tree survival rates are low and the project has been ineffective in reducing sandstorms, which routinely strike the capital Beijing. However, China will continue planting vegetation and trees along the edge of the Taklamakan to ensure desertification is kept in check.

A Xinjiang forestry official said poplar forests on the northern edge of the desert would be restored through the diversion of floodwaters, while new forest networks are planned to protect farmland and orchards on the western edge. According to official data, 26.8 per cent of China's total land is still classified as desert—a decrease from 27.2 per cent a decade earlier—despite the tree-planting efforts.

Inspiration from Israel

Water is crucial to life. Climate change is already depleting water resources for people around the world. Rising temperatures increase evaporation and cause extreme, lingering droughts. The water cycle is also affected by extreme weather conditions. Climate change thus influences where, when and how much rain falls.

The World Resources Institute says a quarter of the world's population live in 25 countries that face extremely high water stress each year. The situation will only get worse. By 2050, an additional one billion people will live with extremely high water stress, even if we manage to curb rising temperatures.

As the world continues to be assailed by challenges of climate change and increasing demands for water from growing populations, governments are searching for sustainable means to manage water.

Israel has become a global leader in water innovation and technology. As one of the driest countries in the world, it has the most advanced solutions for adapting to intense droughts and water scarcity.

Israel has turned its desert into productive land for efficient agriculture through desalination, drip irrigation technology and wastewater recycling. It has the world's highest levels of wastewater treatment and recycling—nearly 90 per cent. So continuous innovation and cutting-edge technology demonstrate that sustainable farming can flourish even in the harshest environments.

The article 'Adaptation lessons from Israel's Negev Desert: A source of climate hope' published in *Energy Monitor* highlights the need for effective adaptation strategies. It shows how a world grappling with the effects of climate change can look to Israel's innovative water management technologies and desert farming techniques for efficient climate adaptation. It notes that despite being more than 60 per cent desert, Israel has agricultural production surpassing that of its larger rival countries. For example, Israel's milk production is 13,000 litres per cow, much higher than that of North America (10,000 litres) and Europe (6,000 litres). Its tomato yield is 300 tonnes per hectare, compared with a global average of 50 tonnes.

According to data collected by the Tony Blair Institute for Global Change, it also produces 262 tonnes of citrus fruits per hectare, whereas North America and Europe produce 243 tonnes and 211 tonnes, respectively. Furthermore, more than 40 per cent of Israel's crops are grown in the desert.

Gideon Behar, ambassador at the Special Envoy for Climate Change and Sustainability at the Ministry of Foreign Affairs of Israel, believes much of what Israel has achieved can be replicated by other countries facing desertification. 'Israel has overcome climatic challenges with innovative solutions,' he explains. 'We are a small country with a limited impact; therefore, these adaptation solutions are our biggest contribution to the climate fight.'

Towards Smart Water Management

Israel began desalinating water 50 years ago and produces more than 700 million cubic metres now. In 2019, desalination provided 70 per cent of domestic and municipal water—a level the government is hoping to increase.

During an interview with Elon Musk, Bill Maher claimed that we are running out of water. Musk replied that the Earth is 70 per cent water. When Maher exclaimed that it is undrinkable water, Musk calmly stated that desalination is 'absurdly cheap'.

Cheap Desalination

How cheap is cheap? *Energy Monitor* notes that around 1 per cent of global drinking water is desalinated, but it's around 25 per cent in Israel. The Sorek B desalination plant, one of five in Israel, has an annual capacity of 52.8 billion gallons and a contract to produce water for $0.41 per cubic metre. With around 264 gallons per cubic metre, 6.4 gallons will therefore cost one cent.

But it's not only Israel leading the way. Dubai blossomed in the desert due to desalination technology, and today's municipal water in the United Arab Emirates is entirely desalinated. Around the world, there are hundreds of desalination plants either planned or under construction.

The cost of desalination was $0.75 per cubic metre in 2012, according to the website *Filtration and Separation*. The average hourly wage for unskilled workers in the US was then $10.87; it has increased to $15.72 by 2022. This indicates that the 2012 time price was about 4.14 minutes, whereas the 2022 time price was 1.56 minutes. In simple terms, we were getting 165 per cent cleaner water in 2022 than we did for the same time price in 2012.

The abundance of desalinated water is growing at a compound annual rate of 10.22 per cent, doubling every seven years. These gains happened while the global population increased by 860 million people. During this period, the population was growing at 1.14 per cent annually, while desalination grew almost nine times faster.

Humans are exceptionally clever at innovating. Knowledge is replacing salt and we're turning liabilities into assets. So long as we're free to discover valuable knowledge and share it with others in an open market, humanity will adapt and thrive. We should never underestimate our ability.

Thousands of desalination plants along India's coast could provide the country with enough domestic and agricultural freshwater. By capturing rain in underground caverns during the monsoon periods, the country can develop much smarter solutions for its water management (and prevent flooding). If India then utilizes the water abundance to plant forests, hot summers will become pleasant.

Every country will have to deal with extreme weather in the near future. Reverting desert to arable land is therefore crucial to ensure people's lives continue to flourish with fewer sandstorms and other climatic hazards. By making the desert land of 13.52 per cent arable, India can produce more than enough food for a growing population and an increasing number of tourists. India can become a food superpower in the future, easily securing third place among the world's top food exporters, after the US and the Netherlands.

Of course, these developments require a significant amount of energy. As discussed earlier, nuclear power will help India on this journey, as it helps Israel and China.

7 CHAKRAS OF MANAGEMENT: WISDOM FROM INDIC SCRIPTURES

In *7 Chakras of Management: Wisdom from Ancient Scriptures*, the author reflects on 42 years of professional experience, shaped by ancient stories shared by family members and a caretaker during childhood. These tales from Hindu scriptures—*Ramayana*, *Mahabharata*, the *Bhagavad Gita* and *Upanishads*—offered timeless guidance during moments of uncertainty.

Over time, the author developed the Seven Chakras framework to interpret these lessons, transcending religious boundaries by incorporating insights from Sikhism, Jainism and Buddhism. The Seven Chakras represent focal points in ancient meditation practices, each linked to physical, emotional, and spiritual well-being:

1. **Muladhara (Root Chakra):** Grounding and stability, fostering security and connection to the Earth.
2. **Svadhisthana (Sacral Chakra):** Creativity and emotional stability, promoting healthy relationships.
3. **Manipura (Solar Plexus Chakra):** Willpower and resilience, aiding stress management and goal achievement.
4. **Anahata (Heart Chakra):** Harmonious relationships, encouraging trust and empathy.
5. **Vishuddhi (Throat Chakra):** Authentic communication and empathetic listening.
6. **Ajna (Third-Eye Chakra):** Awareness and intuition, promoting deeper insights.
7. **Sahasrara (Crown Chakra):** Higher consciousness, fostering unity and purpose.

Interpreted through Indic scriptures, these chakras offer a holistic approach to self-improvement and navigating challenges.

The book highlights the adaptability of Hinduism, or *Sanatan Dharma*, encouraging questioning, self-reflection and continuous learning. It categorizes the scriptures into:

- **Shruti (That Which Is Heard):** Divinely revealed texts like the Vedas, which explore reality and knowledge.
  - *Rig Veda*: Mythological hymns.
  - *Sama Veda*: Hymns for rituals.
  - *Yajur Veda*: Ritual instructions.
  - *Atharva Veda*: Spells and incantations.
- **Smriti (That Which Is Remembered):** Texts like the *Bhagavad Gita*, *Ramayana* and *Mahabharata* that offer practical guidance for life.

The author draws on Adi Shankaracharya's *Advaita Vedanta*, which teaches that ultimate reality (Brahman) is eternal, while worldly experiences are transient. This perspective promotes mindful goal pursuit, grounded in a broader spiritual context. The *Bhagavad Gita*'s emphasis on duty and integrity further underscores the importance of responsible action.

Through storytelling, the author links spiritual wisdom to personal and professional life, advocating for introspection and the practical application of ancient insights. Stories not only convey lessons but also evolve with each retelling, enriching both the storyteller and listener.

Ultimately, the book offers a guide to integrating ancient Indic wisdom with modern challenges, inspiring readers to embrace timeless principles in their personal and professional journeys.

—Ashutosh Garg
Management Expert and Author

CHAKRAS OF
MANAGEMENT
WISDOM FROM INDIC SCRIPTURES

ASHUTOSH GARG

Part 3

Agenda Setting

9

Towards 12 Pillars of Power

Akaash and Anand take the tube together to their jobs in the city. They chat about life, hobbies, work, society and generally enjoy themselves. Both in their early 30s, they work in the creative financial industry and live in the brand new apartments in the Usk Complex. Built in the popular Art Deco style, yet featuring all the mod cons of the 21st century, the complex was designed by a real estate developer who blends retro taste with hi-tech. The apartment building is everything they both dreamt of. Everybody who lives in this complex shares the same lifestyle. Tim and James only mix with people like them, who think, feel and live like they do, whether they live in the same apartment building or elsewhere in the region or around the world. Their tribe connects through the internet, parties, VirtualMes, and of course, work. The mixed work-life balance of the new century makes work much less of a chore. In the post-material economy of their century, the GPS-ification of the passionate man is a thing of the past. Life is about living and experiencing passions now. Their multisexual lifestyle, typical for a metropolis, makes bisexuality normal; all other sexual deviations are looked upon with humorous indulgence. They have no kids, which is the norm in their tribe—kids are seen as too much of a hassle. They usually ignore people of other tribes.

'The only way to find your way in the postmodern world, where globalization and Europeanization have unified the un-unifiable, is to have a strong identity rooted in your own community. This community of our friends and family members, sharing the same culture, attitudes, tastes, values and lifestyles, gives us a strong sense of identity—like a village in a fast world, or an oasis of peace in a fast-moving environment. Great,' Tim says.

Staying forever young is the norm in their tribe; in some other tribes, the norms are different. In the apartment building next door, people are more attracted to nature and natural living. James calls them the 'Nature tribe'. He says, 'They only wear clothes made from natural fibres—not the ones we prefer, which protect us against bullets or knives due to the nanocells in our clothes that function as a harness. They only eat natural food, straight from the farms, and they are very proud of their lifestyle—totally vegetarian, no leather shoes, no furs, no alcohol and no fat in their food. They do breed a lot. An average family in this tribe has two to four kids.' People belonging to other tribes live in the neighbouring apartment buildings. Just in their part of town, Tim and James count about 50 different tribes. In the tube, the tribalization is clearly visible. People only talk to members of their own tribe or exchange text messages with tribe members outside the tube, ignoring the unknown people inside. Tribalization is here to stay!

Economic, political and military power relationships among countries have been established for a long time. The US and the Soviet Union were the only superpowers after World War II, and while the Cold War raged, most other countries sided with either of the protagonists. During the same period, Japan developed into the world's second richest country, although this was not translated into its political, diplomatic or military power. Then the picture radically changed with the fall of the Berlin Wall in 1989 and the disintegration of the Soviet Union in 1991. Now, a quarter of the way through the 21st century, the US still dominates the world order, but other countries are growing stronger, leading to the emergence of a new economic order. Twelve pillars of power will shape the future of humanity in this new, *slowbalized* world.

The First Pillar: Economic Blocs

In 1951, the creation of a six-nation European Coal and Steel Community laid the foundations for the EU, a bloc intended to bring lasting economic progress and peace to the continent. The scheme proved successful—today's EU accounts for an estimated 13.4 per cent of the world's GDP. As a unique hybrid of political theories, the EU relies on policy agreement between member states, although some agree to disagree. The bloc's intergovernmentalism allows members to cooperate in certain fields while retaining their sovereignty, whereas its supranationalism enables members to make certain autonomous decisions. The history of the EU is characterized by disputes, with some members seeking further political integration and others striving to keep their powers national (or reclaim powers from the EU). It is a precarious balance, which is always shifting. Nationalism currently sets the tone for the EU, due in part to economic crises and billion-euro bailouts that prevented Greece, Portugal, Italy, Ireland and Spain from going bankrupt, which would have otherwise dragged other member states and the Eurozone itself down with them. The process of European integration will thus slow and eventually halt. The euro as a single currency unit will also disappear. However, as an economic bloc, the EU will remain powerful. It will return to its origins as an economic union rather than a cultural and political one. As it lacks both political agreement and a powerful army to protect its economic interests, the EU will no longer play a significant political role in the new world order.

Copycats

Despite its flaws, the European model has been replicated across the world—a trend that will continue. An EU-like bloc not only provides economic advantage but also makes former rivals economically interdependent, minimizing their interests in war and conflict. For instance, France and the UK, which fought one another for centuries and still don't share friendly terms, are now enjoying mutual peace for the first time in their joint history. France and Germany, another pair of past enemies, are currently the EU's most influential countries, which jointly rule the bloc, particularly in foreign and economic policies.

Several blocs like the EU already exist in Asia: the Association of Southeast Asian Nations (ASEAN), the South Asian Association for Regional Cooperation (SAARC), the Asia–Pacific Economic Cooperation (APEC) and others. These blocs will merge in the future, forming an ASEAN-Plus model, representing a single Asian trade alliance. China's growing influence in recent years has reoriented Southeast Asia's power structure towards its own interests, with China becoming the number one trading partner for every country in the region while simultaneously expanding into Africa and Eastern Europe. There is strength in numbers, and Southeast Asia's governments are not only striving to tap into China's new wealth, but also including Beijing in a plethora of organizations or dialogues in the name of 'community building' and closer integration. While Japan, India and the Republic of Korea are participating in this objective, Australia and New Zealand remain more reserved. In her book *Asia's New Regionalism*, Ellen Frost suggests we are witnessing the resurgence of the 'precolonial Maritime Asia'—the sweep of coastal communities, port cities, towns and waterways connecting Northeast and Southeast Asia, India and Australia. Maritime Asia is the locus of Asian wealth and power. It is where 60–70 per cent of ASEAN people live, where the biggest cities are located and where globalization-driven investments are concentrated.

In 1992, the US, Canada and Mexico signed the North American Free Trade Agreement, which Donald Trump vowed to renegotiate during his first presidency but later replaced with the United States–Mexico–Canada Agreement. It is expected that three trade blocs in South America and the Caribbean—CARICOM, Mercosur and UNASUR—will eventually merge to form one economic counterbalance to the North American bloc. Russia, Belarus, Armenia, Kyrgyzstan and Kazakhstan formed the Eurasian Economic Union in 2015, while Africa is slowly working towards creating the world's largest free-trade area, uniting 55 countries with a total population of more than 1 billion people and a total GDP of more than $3.4 trillion. A stronger African Union might bring peace to the poorest continent. Economic prosperity and much-needed peace could also emerge in the Middle East if blocs were created there. There is room for two blocs in the region: one including Turkey, Saudi Arabia, the UAE and Israel—let's call it the *Ottoman Union*—and another more Islamist one, uniting fundamentalist forces in the region and in North Africa—*the Bloc of Doom*.

The Second Pillar: Superpowers

According to Goldman Sachs, the new world order will be dominated by six superpowers: the US, Japan and four BRICS countries—Brazil, Russia, India and China. Russia will be economically the smallest because its oil and gas exports are now one-sided. Many countries to which Russian resources are exported would also prefer to end dependency on the unreliable Russians, following Russia's war on Ukraine. A serious population decline is also diminishing Russia's status as a superpower. However, the global demand for gas is likely to rise, which is good news for Russia: its reserves are not only huge, but are also expected to receive a significant boost from the Arctic's natural riches.

To remain a key player, Russia has invested heavily in new pipelines to connect European and Asian countries, although attempts to exert the type of control it had during the Soviet period resulted in ongoing problems with its neighbours. In trying to prevent countries along its border from falling under the influence of the EU or NATO, Russia regularly interferes in domestic politics in the region. This is a dangerous game that creates the type of chaos we currently see in Ukraine, escalating the risk that Russia will lose control entirely. Nevertheless, its oil and gas reserves will ensure Russia remains wealthy for a considerable time to come. As the smallest superpower, Russia will be in the position of kingmaker, aligning itself with China in a 'Dragon-Bear' coalition. Other countries that align with Russia, such as North Korea, are also likely to be in the mix.

China: The Promise of the 'Red Dynasty'

China is one of the fastest-growing economies—the second largest in the world for the past decade. However, estimates suggest China will take first place from the US within the coming years. The Chinese know this, and their behaviour on the world stage has therefore become increasingly dominant. China is, for instance, an important source of raw materials for the hi-tech industry, but for political reasons, it has decided to reduce exports and increase prices. However, the Chinese government might seem less confident now after Japanese scientists discovered huge quantities of the same precious materials on the Pacific seabed. China is already the largest trading partner for many countries in Africa, providing both financial and technological support, and its dominance in the African market is steadily increasing. Chinese-African trade is currently worth more than US$170 billion annually, with China exporting more than it imports. The authors refer to communist China's rulers as the 'Red Dynasty' as a nod to the fact that, despite the ideological shift, China's governance remains as top-down and centralized as it was in imperial times.

According to *Jane's Defence Weekly*, China's military capacity, which could also surpass the US by 2090, is often thought to be the ancient Chinese clan system in a new guise. The People's Liberation Army is already characterized by an entrepreneurial spirit and, according to the US trendwatcher John Naisbitt, is heavily involved in business, owning many companies and becoming China's largest multinational.

India: A Rather Different Superpower

Until the 1990s, India never dared to dream of becoming a superpower. However, with the economic reforms of the Manmohan Singh administration, the nation gradually began to dream bigger. Yet, a cat that dreams about becoming a tiger first must lose its appetite for mice. If India truly aspires to become a superpower and stand on equal footing with China and the USA, there is still much work to be done.

The illiterates of the future will not be those who cannot read or write, but those who cannot learn, unlearn and relearn. So to transform from an Indian cat to an Indian tiger, India must embrace this cycle of continuous learning and adaptation.

Militarily speaking, the situation in India is different from that in China. India will, by 2032, surpass Japan and move into third place in the rankings of economic superpowers. For many decades, India has been at odds with its Islamic neighbours Pakistan, Bangladesh and Afghanistan. The conflict with Pakistan has led to India's army becoming the largest and most experienced in Asia, while India itself is best equipped to deal with terrorism. Although it is not a commonly known fact, India is the third-largest contributor of UN peacekeepers to countries like Sudan and Congo. The Indian navy also hunts for pirates off the coast of Somalia.

Already the third-largest oil consumer in the world, India is now believed to have overtaken China in this respect. Although it still lags behind China's economic presence on the African continent, India's annual trade with Africa is currently worth more than US$52 billion—an amount it plans to triple in the next few years.

Aiming to be less dependent on imports from the Middle East, India looks forward to strengthening its trading ties with Africa. However, while it is the Chinese government in Beijing driving the country's investments in Africa, India is led by private businesses, like the industrial giant Tata and the telecommunications company Bharti Airtel.

The role of private enterprise in India's international economic boom also reflects domestic reality. India's national economy is driven not so much by government as by private entrepreneurs who manage the transport infrastructure, the water supply and other public facilities. This model serves as an example of success for African countries—they must deal with their incompetent, corrupt or powerless governments. Indian businesses also have another major advantage over their Chinese competitors: after many years of serving the masses in India, they understand how to deliver what poorer people need.

Brazil: A Most Unexpected Rise

Ranked the 14th-largest economy in the world in 2003, Brazil has followed a different strategy from China or India. The country is rich in the raw materials that other countries are eager to obtain, while also being rich in human capital. Brazil is home to the largest populations of Japanese and Germans outside their respective countries. These communities and their international contacts stimulate the Brazilian economy, of which industry is an important pillar. Greater São Paulo is the world's second-largest German industrial base, for instance. As both countries attach immense importance to technological and scientific innovation, Germany and Brazil are partners on an equal footing—more equal than Germany would be with China.

Once the world's eighth-largest weapons exporter, Brazil has had ancillary involvement in many global conflicts. However, the country and its people are widely loved. Brazilians are considered harmless, carefree party-goers who make the best footballers—a reputation they cherish. Brazil's positive image on the world stage is likely to increase, not only because the country uses hydroelectric power and energy sources like biodiesel and oil extracted locally within South America, but also because it formally and politically distances itself from major conflicts. Brazil, therefore, has every chance of developing into a superpower.

The Third Pillar: World Governmental Institutions

A globalized world needs global institutions to govern people, planet and profits. Institutions currently attempting to lead this rapidly changing world are not performing well and are consequently facing criticism. Their legitimacy is eroding due to their inability to tackle global issues. The UN has been unable to limit population growth in an already overcrowded world; the UN Security Council has no permanent members from the BRICS countries, where power is growing; the UN peacekeepers and NATO forces often become embroiled in unwinnable wars (as demonstrated in Afghanistan); the World Bank, the IMF and other financial institutions are unable to govern the new players adequately in a complex world economy. At the same time, the need for an international financial and economic consultative body remains essential. The authors consider it probable that the new economic blocs will establish their own institution to negotiate trade, financial and economic matters.

This institution will deal with issues of morality and politics, including the division of earthly and interplanetary natural resources. Moreover, reaching a compromise would be easier because this institution would comprise a limited number of parties, unlike the UN, which was a lost cause from the outset—with 190-odd members, stalemate and disagreement are its main achievements. The authors also expect (and strongly advocate) the creation of a World Crisis Fund, to be used in times of need.

The Fourth Pillar: Multinationals and the Superclass

Many multinationals are already more powerful than some countries—over 50 businesses report annual sales of over US$100 billion, whereas only about 60 countries report an annual GDP of the same level. While sales and GDP cannot be taken as equivalents, these figures do give an insight into the economic power wielded by some businesses. Multinationals may have their origins in one country, but they are rarely nationalistic. International issues are more important for multinationals, many of which have become superpowers with considerable influence over life and work decisions, society and the national economy in countries where they operate. The executive board at a multinational can often be more powerful than a government.

While some multinationals, including banks and other financial institutions, are now downsizing because the globalized world has become too vast and complex, others, such as Google, Apple and Microsoft, are expanding. Chinese multinationals are also expanding and investing around the world, including in Europe and the US. Similarly, Indian multinationals like Tata and Mittal (although whether Mittal is truly Indian is debatable), and Brazilian ones like Embraer, are becoming global players. The authors expect multinationals to be a major pillar in tomorrow's world— their power and influence will increase, while their leaders become even more prominent members of the superclass that runs the world.

The Fifth Pillar: Tigers Are Moving Up…and Down

Tigers are regions in the Global South with a strong economic foundation and efficient talent management. They are ambitious, well governed, bursting with confidence and wealthy—but simply too small to play the role of a superpower. The key question is in which direction should they move.

Sometimes tigers are small, independent countries; other times, they are regions within a country. Tiger countries include Switzerland, Singapore, Chile, Taiwan, Vietnam,

Turkey, the Republic of Korea and Canada. Tiger regions include Bavaria in Germany, South China, Punjab and Maharashtra in India, and the southernmost region of Brazil. Australia is a tiger country with bigger potential, boasting a strong economy free from crises for decades. The foundation of Australia's prosperity is its abundant natural resources, which it successfully exports to Asia. Furthermore, Australia has low unemployment and a good education system, thus consistently attracting profitable immigrants. While Australia could be the biggest tiger in the world, some other tigers have lost their prospects.

Thailand, for example, was once a stable country, but has spent years in disarray because of strife between old and new elites. Likewise in Turkey, new elites seized power while old elites grudgingly accepted the reshuffle.

The Sixth Pillar: Mixed Power and Dormant Regions

In the future, regions, countries and cities will be divided into strong and weak zones. For instance, many big cities will have rich areas where highly skilled people live and work. These people are the *Anywheres* mentioned earlier who enjoy a liberal lifestyle, love the perks of globalization and technology, and consider a multicultural society enriching. Their skills also attract money and investments, making these areas even richer. On the other hand, the same cities house large groups of people who will lose out in the process of globalization. These 'angry tribes' (the aforementioned *Somewheres*) are becoming poorer, have no relevant skills for survival in the new world order and lack the spirit, ambition or intelligence to capitalize on opportunities. Technology has replaced their jobs and made them redundant. As a result, the tension is growing in the burgeoning ghetto neighbourhoods where they live.

While some regions and countries that reached sensational economic or cultural heights are now in decline, others are currently dormant. These latter regions and countries are stable and inhabited by a greying population that is no longer innovative, not excelling in any single field, performing averagely and living off investments made during better times. These areas have come to a standstill; their populations have little ambition to lead the world, and their institutions have withered. Thanks to peace and a stable political climate, life is pleasant for people in these areas. Their 15 minutes of fame are a thing of the past—a memory they are content to live on.

The Seventh Pillar: Lost Regions with No Future at All

History has never been fair, nor will the future be. Globalization produced both winners and losers—Slowbalization may do the same. Lost countries such as Chad, Pakistan, Afghanistan, Congo, Somalia or Sudan have no future despite their natural resources. Their populations live in poverty, afflicted by disease, war, corruption, overpopulation, human rights abuses, a permanent lack of water and many other challenges. Overall, these countries offer few prospects to anyone living there—the people are perpetually angry with themselves and with the rest of the world.

What these lost countries have in common is a prevailing mood of injury, often expressed as a combination of superiority and inferiority. Although not economically important, these lost regions filled with anger can make the rest of the world fearful. Wealthy countries fear they will be blackmailed by this anger. Lost populations desire to live elsewhere and are ready to be mobilized, leading to waves of mass migration, as discussed earlier.

The existence of lost regions and the anger of their populations is partly related to poverty, despite the large reserves of raw materials held by these countries. Here is the good news: poverty is declining like never before in human history, even in Africa. Half a billion people have been lifted out of poverty since 2005, and if the trend continues, there may be hope for the lost regions after all.

The Eighth Pillar: Peaceful Networks and Diasporas

Mass migration has changed the way we live. Anthropologists use the word 'diaspora' for a people—or even a single person—living permanently outside their homeland. The best-known diaspora is that of the Jews, which began after their first temple in Jerusalem was sacked by the Romans in the first century AD. The Jewish diaspora has grown and become influential all over the world. Another major diaspora is the Armenian one, which originated as a result of the genocide committed by the Turks. However, it isn't necessarily violence or persecution that drives people into diaspora. Due to voluntary emigration, there are currently more people of Italian descent living outside of Italy than within the country. Similarly, there are more than 60 million Chinese living outside of China, more than 35 million Indians living outside of India and more than 7 million US citizens living outside of the US.

Again, the term 'diaspora' is not solely reserved for people with the same ethnic or national background. A diaspora can be formed by people who share the same religion or the same sexual orientation. There has always been a gay diaspora, for example, representing homosexual men and women who are living outside of their own country. What most diasporas have in common is that they can build and maintain strong international networks. The gay diaspora is a good illustration of this. According to American sexologist Alfred Kinsey, around 5–10 per cent of the world's population identifies as gay or bisexual, and through globalization and new media, they have developed a global lifestyle and organized themselves into a powerful international community. Although not a diaspora in the traditional sense, the Freemasons constitute another global organization that seems to have existed for centuries, its power always hidden, much like secret associations of the Bilderberg Group or the Mormons. In the new world order, these communities and diasporas, with multiple parallel loyalties, will play an increasingly significant role.

The Ninth Pillar: Angry Tribes and Networks

Fear of the 'other' is nothing new. Whether it's fear in the guise of Jewish pogroms, fear of the 'Yellow Peril' or segregation, some societies have always been anxious to remain untouched by this culture of fear. Now, the fear has gone into overdrive; we are assailed on every side by anxiety about the purity of national populations, the threat of terrorism and 'white fears' of losing the struggle for existence. Donald Trump gave a voice to this last fear by suggesting that the fundamental question of our time is 'whether the West has the will to survive'. A fear of decline has intensified in Western countries that are losing power to globalization, which simultaneously empowers those previously considered the Yellow Peril. The anxieties of the powerless are being directed towards clearly identifiable social groups, whether immigrants or refugees.

Pankaj Mishra claims that in the past 200 years, Anglo-America has been the winner. As the UK's empire expanded, its home economy boomed, followed by the Industrial Revolution—all of which bestowed great power upon such a small country. Later, America found people in Africa to enslave and serve its growing economy. Anglo-American philosophies, defined by enlightened, rational humans or the commercial world, have mediated today's thinking. However, Mishra is right to claim that people committed to this Anglo-American way of thinking have 'often missed out on the fact that modernization and industrialization have been traumatic processes'.

The rest of the world had fewer resources and opportunities than the UK and America, but we forget that and assume modernization was inevitable, desirable and an Anglo-American model that other countries would 'benignly follow'. This modernization led people to move away from traditional structures and leave their homes and villages behind to embrace the big city industrialization.

This created a trauma, which gave rise to angry tribes or groups of people unhappy with the way the world was developing. Some are white Westerners who have lost their jobs to immigrants; others are immigrants who are disappointed in their new homelands; some are activists with a specific agenda that isn't in the mainstream, such as eco-terrorists; others have a separatist terrorist tradition (e.g. the IRA in Ireland); there are some with a political agenda, like the communists in India who oppose multinationals; others have a more nationalistic or even xenophobic agenda. All these tribes are opposed to globalization and respond with rage to a feeling of powerlessness.

Traditionally, one-third of any population supports change, one-third opposes it and the remaining one-third is indifferent so long as their own interests are unaffected. Those who oppose change are a multifaceted bunch who cross the political spectrum. What they have in common is a voice we will hear more in future.

The Tenth Pillar: the Tech Industry

Over the past 20 years, the financial services industry has expanded massively—a growth driven by technology, according to specialists. Technology has connected people, providing more mobility and flexibility than ever before. In the future, technology will continue to be crucial as one of the 12 pillars of power. Extensively reshaping the nature of our lives, governance and economies, technology will also merge with other industries—like finance—to become omnipresent in all aspects of our lives.

The Eleventh Pillar: Religious and Moral Groups

We live in an age of sharp religious boundaries—sharper than they have been for a long time. People today are more conscious of their identity and religious background. After a period of liberalization and secularization, there is a call in the West for clear, compelling moral values. Ethics are once again taking centre stage, mainly because they offer people something to grip on to in an uncertain world. In these hectic, vulnerable and uncertain times, people long for order and stability, characterized by respect and decency.

Kondratieff Wave patterns (hypothetical economic waves) indicate that following a period of emphasis on increased affluence, we are beginning to focus more on increased well-being, in which ethics play an important part. The modern world's moral views are often expressed by global organizations like Greenpeace or Amnesty International—voices with enough power and influence on public opinion to have a significant impact on how people feel about a wide range of issues. Large parts of the economy are consequently ruled by emotions.

Although many people feel religion is out of fashion in the new world, it is not so. Most parts of the world, including the most technologically advanced countries, are still religious, and the constant quest for moral and ethical boundaries will increasingly bring people back to religion.

The Twelfth Pillar: Financial Institutions

The world is expected to be richer, with traditional financial institutions like BlackRock, the Chinese Citic Group, the Norwegian State Investment Fund and many others, playing a leading role in financing the new economic world order. Banks, pension funds, credit card businesses, lease businesses, insurance companies and other financial bodies will all play a significant role in the future. However, they will have to share power with fresh players like hedge funds, private-equity businesses and even players from other lines of business, such as technology businesses. New coalitions and partnerships with businesses from outside the financial sector will strengthen the position of this pillar of power. The investment policies of these financial entities will be crucial in deciding the direction of global development. For example, a decision to invest in sustainability and alternative sources of clean energy is crucial for the development of a new energy economy. Within this pillar of power, we may expect a lack of clear focus and a continually shifting balance.

In Conclusion

The authors have presented you with 12 pillars of power. These will interact with one another, working together to model or remodel both people and the world they live in. In *The Return of History and the End of Dreams*, the US scholar Robert Kagan gives an impression of this interaction. Kagan argued—some 10 years *avant la lettre*—that the apparent triumph of liberal democracy in the 1990s was fleeting and that an era of renewed competition between great powers would be coming.

That competition would be marked by a tension between two political traditions—democracy and autocracy—primarily in the shape of a resurgent Russia and rising China. It's now safe to say that he was right.

However, the authors disagree with Kagan's idea that the new world will resemble the 19th century with its wars, revolutions and isolated nations. We are in for a bumpy ride, but we are not overly pessimistic about the future. If autocracies are to succeed, they will have to make their citizens as happy as democracies do. So we expect both systems to blend into *Happynomy*—the Economy of Happiness.

THE FUTURE OF HOSPITALITY: A VISION OF INCLUSION, SUSTAINABILITY AND EXCELLENCE

The future of hospitality lies in its ability to embrace inclusion, sustainability and excellence—ensuring that every guest, team member and stakeholder feels welcomed and valued. At The Lalit, we are committed to shaping this future by embedding Diversity, Equity and Inclusion (DEI) into our very DNA, transforming hospitality into a beacon of warmth, acceptance and responsible luxury.

Sustainability: Caring for Our Planet, People and Product: In a world moving towards more conscious living, sustainability is no longer optional—it is essential. The Lalit leads this transformation by integrating eco-friendly practices across our operations. From reducing our carbon footprint through energy-efficient infrastructure to eliminating single-use plastics and promoting ethical, local sourcing—we are committed to protecting the planet.

But sustainability extends beyond the environment. It also means caring for people and products. By investing in local communities, empowering our workforce, and adhering to ethical business practices, we ensure our impact is comprehensive and lasting. Our approach blends traditional Indian hospitality with modern luxury, offering experiences that are both grand and responsibly forward-thinking.

Building a Culture of Inclusion: DEI at The Lalit: True hospitality is about making every individual feel at home. At The Lalit, we are an equal opportunity organization, where everyone—regardless of gender, sexual orientation, neurodiversity or background—can thrive.

Our Aditya Nanda Scholarship for LGBTQIA+ individuals and Apna Heera Scholarship for neurodivergent individuals are key pillars of this mission. These initiatives go beyond financial support—they are about breaking barriers and redefining what inclusive education and employment can look like within the hospitality industry.

India as the Centre of Excellence in Hospitality: India has long been synonymous with warmth and generosity. At The Lalit, we envision India as the global epicentre of hospitality excellence. Through a seamless blend of traditional charm and modern luxury, we aim to create a standard that is traditionally modern, subtly luxurious and distinctly Lalit.

Our carefully curated experiences celebrate local art, culture, and heritage—while our collaborations across the tourism sector set new benchmarks that reaffirm India's leadership in global hospitality.

A Future That Welcomes All: As the hospitality industry evolves, the future belongs to those who champion the 3 Ps: People, Planet and Progress. Hospitality becomes a bridge—connecting cultures, preserving heritage and promoting peace.

At The Lalit, we are building an ecosystem that is not only luxurious, but also inclusive, immersive and sustainable. Through our commitment to DEI our educational scholarships, and our conscious practices, we are not just preparing for the future of hospitality—we are shaping it.

With care, creativity and conviction, The Lalit stands as a beacon of what hospitality can and should be: a space where everyone belongs, where the environment is honoured and where India shines as the epitome of world-class service.

This is the future we believe in—and one we're building, one experience at a time.

—Keshav Suri
Executive Director, The Lalit Suri Hospitality Group
Founder, Keshav Suri Foundation

THE
LaLiT

10

Actions

Evita Perón of Argentina muses to the Queen Mother of the UK on their joint pink cloud, while they both sip from their glasses of sherry.

'I'm a devout Catholic girl, yet I'm amazed at how Argentina is being reincarnated on your continent. You know, 80 years ago, Argentina was one of the eight richest countries in the world. But we became a bit lazy and spoilt because of all that wealth and a long period of peace. Decline started slowly. If you earn €5 less every month, why bother about decline? It was happening too slowly to alert people or inspire them to take action. You only try to reverse a trend when there is a deep feeling of crisis and a real sense of urgency. When Juan and I were elected to the Argentinean presidency, we knew in our hearts that the country needed reforms—harsh measures to stop the decline. We knew the liberal opposition party had the best plans for the country, but we also knew the people did not want to listen to them. We loved power so much that we chose the easy way. Government often offers more glory than opposition, hmm? Of course, that was true until President Javier Milei rose to power from nothing and reinvented the country. Now every country wants its own Milei, including India.'

The Queen Mother replies, 'My child, you can change a trend and still get re-elected, just as Maggie Thatcher did in the UK in the 1980s. Britain had been in decline for a long time by then. There was nothing left of the glory of the old empire, and a future as negligible as Africa on the North Sea seemed inevitable for us. But she came, decided to change all that, got elected and re-elected twice, really turning the tide. You could have done so too, my dear. You could have been the Thatcher of Argentina.'

The ladies sip their sherry and watch what's happening in their beloved Europe. The Queen Mother is happy with the way her great-grandson is performing as king. He connects well with Prime Minister Robbie Williams and even enjoys riding in the horse carriage. Since the introduction of the government's new environmental laws, the royal family hardly drives anymore. The horse-drawn carriage has returned, but the king can still use the internet aboard and the horse has been replaced by a robot horse. The UK has returned the Koh-i-Noor diamond to India. The 'coalition of the willing' of European leaders, who want to reverse the trend of a declining Europe, is working hard to prevent the Argentinean model from becoming a reality. Queen Máxima of the Netherlands, who is Argentine by origin is one of the strongest advocates against 'Argentinization' of the continent, at least in an economic sense. Yet she has introduced the tango in every European capital. The tango had only been popular for the past 80 years in the Turkish capital Ankara, ever since the great Turkish leader Atatürk introduced this Argentine dance there in the 1920s. Now it's popular in the clubs in Manchester, Paris, Mumbai and Shanghai. Viva Argentina!

We can look forward to turbulent times in the next few years, as economic and geopolitical power relationships shift and the West risks losing its dominant position. Asian countries are choosing their own path to progress, their optimism contrasting with the culture of fear that still dominates the old centres of power. Signs of wear and tear are appearing in the West's ideal of liberal democracy, sold to the rest of the world (even the West no longer sees it as ideal). Traditional political positions are being rewritten in the face of a Global Political Awakening among the masses. At the same time, the world is experiencing a new digital revolution and is poised at the threshold of a new energy transition. All these developments lead to uncertainty, sometimes anger and sometimes fear. However, they also provide fertile grounds for sowing seeds, whose germination can lead to the growth of a better, more beautiful world. If we nurture these seeds and allow them to germinate, we could be on the verge of an unimaginable period of growth, blossoming and progress: The New Renaissance. There are a number of steps we can take to ensure the transition to a new Renaissance happens as smoothly as possible. Only then can we all benefit from the fruits of a newly revitalized world in the future.

i) If You Are a Citizen:
   - If you decide to have children, have only two or three.
   - Raise your child(ren) to have passion for creativity and technology.
   - Free yourself from dogmatic religious values and organizations by creating your own personal God.
   - Embrace the knowledge economy; embrace *Happynomy*—the Economy of Happiness.

- Let go of anger and adopt a relaxed outlook on life; be positive; join the axis of hope.
- Be aware of nature and the Earth's vulnerabilities and behave accordingly.
- Be respectful and tolerant of other people and unfamiliar cultures, without neglecting your own. Adamantly oppose intolerance and teach your child(ren) to do the same.
- Organize or join groups that lobby against weapons of mass destruction, perverted subsidies and stupid political policies.
- Oppose political correctness at all costs.
- Be willing and flexible enough to learn and improve. There are no permanent jobs in the Second Machine Age, and the best way to keep at least one step ahead of the competition—be it machine or human—is through continuous learning.
- Embrace the innovative approach to working. Accept that the division between work and leisure is eroding. You can combine caring for loved ones with working from home part-time. Train yourself to multitask.
- Learn how to be happily bored. There will be less work in the Second Machine Age, so enjoy it.
- Empower your own mind and be an independent thinker. Don't believe everything you are told.
- Organize a network of informal home carers for the people you are close to. Build solidarity in your own circles.
- Learn about your health and discover your vulnerabilities. Set a healthcare budget based on your discoveries and start saving. Relying on insurance to cover all eventualities is no longer feasible. So start your own 'care piggybank'.

- Use AI to sharpen your talents.
- Work on your meta-cognitive skills: speed reading, mind mapping, meditation and concentration. Your brain is what matters the most throughout your whole life. A fully active brain prevents physical decay.
- Prevention is better than cure. Embrace exercise, healthier food and a healthier lifestyle. Cherish good fats and avoid bad ones. Better health and lower costs are the rewards for prevention of diseases.
- Use your CV as a talent passport. Besides listing what you've already done, highlight what you can do with your talents and ambitions. Use multimedia— personal introductions by video will be standard. Always mention any informal care duties you perform.
- Be financially independent. Check your financial arrangements and minimize your debt. Less debt allows you to pursue a job you love in the post-materialist economy.
- Allow yourself to dream.

ii) If You Are a Politician:
- Provide good leadership. Reflect on your role and connect with the emotions of those you lead.
- End perverted subsidies.
- Lead your region or country towards energy independence.
- Invest in new nuclear energy.
- Invest in fibre-optic networks, so citizens, institutions and businesses in your region or country can benefit from high-speed internet.
- Facilitate lifelong learning for the entire population.
- Embrace innovative technologies and set up

programmes for creating digital awareness. Make the entire population tech-savvy.

- Design a wise, sustainable population policy. End mass migration.
- Adamantly oppose religious fanatics and their dogmas.
- Invest in the middle class—the backbone of any healthy society.
- Make your government lean and mean. Use e-government, AI and technology to perform better.
- Set up mechanisms for citizens to govern themselves. This will strengthen social cohesion, narrow the gap between politics and society and help rid the feelings of dissent and anger among citizens. This can be organized easily and relatively cheaply by using mobile and internet technologies.
- Invest in strengthening the Fourth Sector or non-profit organizations (NGOs).
- Put your own 'skin in the game'.
- Forget the CO_2 hype. There are cheap ways to deal with a changing climate.
- Take climate change into consideration during spatial planning. Make room for parks. Remember that trees provide shade, absorb CO_2, emit oxygen, improve people's health, are nice to look at and help reduce erosion or flood risks.
- Join the axis of positive and hopeful countries.
- Recolonize lost regions in a coalition with others.
- Shift some food production methods away from the land to the sea.
- Strive to reach a world food agreement to feed a growing world population sustainably.
- Work together with other countries to create new

mechanisms and effective institutions for global governance.

- Collaborate with international communities to turn Africa's unused land into a profitable agricultural resource.
- Follow the German town of Liebenau and restructure town planning according to demographics. Let senior citizens live together in the centre, with younger families around them. The seniors can perform informal care duties where possible within their own elderly community and help with childcare.
- Invest in education.
- Invest in a new energy grid (a smart grid), which can power electric cars and the future IT and care infrastructures that will consume much more energy.
- Be brave: tell people they must continue working at a later age. You might find they prefer that!
- Create working incentives for older people, with a stay-at-work premium that insures employers against disability among their post-65 workforce.
- Encourage educational centres in your region to modernize and embrace technology. Think how to unite different generations, both socially and through informal caring associations.
- Embrace environments for elderly people of the same 'tribe', such as communal living for Chinese or Turkish senior citizens. It works.
- In the Second Machine Age, people will work less, so managing their boredom will be a major issue. Be good at it.
- Facilitate working from home and reconsider urban planning. The strict division between work and home activities is no longer relevant. It also

complicates informal care arrangements for the working population.
- Show guts and vision; be a leader! Serving the people comes before self-interest. Make sure you leave a legacy!
- Keep yourself up to date with new developments regarding science, technology and social networks.

iii) If You Are a Business Leader:
- Provide good leadership; be reflective rather than reactive.
- Rather than putting shareholders first, join the Fourth Sector.
- Embrace Karma Capitalism.
- Put your skin in the game.
- Invest in the permanent education of your workers.
- Embrace modern technologies.
- Oppose perverted subsidies in your own industry.
- Aim to be sustainable and independent by diversifying your energy use.
- Be aware of a declining world population.
- Invest in ethics and moral standards.
- Invest in futuristic leadership and creativity.
- Aim to be independent of banks.
- Create a coalition of willing businesses and consumers.
- Invest in your leadership diversity—include women, people of different sexualities and minority groups.

iv) If You Are a Banker:
- Go back to your roots. Finance economic growth, innovation, creativity and entrepreneurship. Stay away from voodoo economics and fancy products that are either unethical or beyond your understanding.

- Invest in people and put their interests above those of your shareholders.
- Embrace Karma Capitalism.
- Don't judge businesses solely on their financial performance but also on their social value.
- Invest in microloans for poor countries. You will create new markets, which become valuable for you at a later stage.
- Finance projects that work with renewable energy sources.
- Focus on one of these categories and be good at it: investment banking, retail banking, private banking or asset management. Don't try to be good at everything.
- Work together with technology businesses to create new financial products and solutions.

v) If You Are an Entrepreneur:
- An economic crisis is the best time to start your own business; many wannabe entrepreneurs don't have enough courage to do that.
- Locate your business where there is a surplus of boys—a cheap and willing workforce awaits you.
- Focus on those aged over 60—the fastest growing consumer group in the world.
- Differentiate your marketing between old-money consumers and new-money consumer groups.
- Look for alternative ways to get financing. Be independent of banks.
- Make your organization flexible and non-hierarchical.
- Surround yourself with a group of innovative businesses—big or small—and work together in networks.

- Embrace technology.
- Invest in your employees, even those who work on short-term contracts.

vi) If You Are a Philanthropist:
- Only invest in the First, Second and Third Worlds—not in lost regions, unless they are recolonized.
- Support Fourth Sector initiatives.
- Invest in causes that strengthen the position of the middle class.
- Do not finance projects or organizations that contribute to mass migration.
- Finance projects related to the decreasing population.
- Finance projects that support the expansion of renewable energy.
- Invest in entrepreneurial women throughout the developing world.

DOING BUSINESS IN THE NETHERLANDS: A GATEWAY FOR INDIAN ENTREPRENEURS

The Netherlands is one of the most attractive entry points for Indian entrepreneurs looking to expand into continental Europe. Its open economy, strategic location and English proficiency make it a natural hub for international business. Dutch companies, in particular, are known for their willingness to outsource— offering greater opportunities for collaboration than their German or French counterparts.

In recent years, Indian businesses have increased their presence in the Netherlands. As cultural barriers fade, local investments rise and employment grows, Indian firms are becoming key players in the Dutch business ecosystem.

Kooijman Autar Notaries: Your Trusted Partner in the Netherlands: Based in Rotterdam, Kooijman Autar Notaries is an innovative, full-service notary firm with roots dating back to 1869. Today, the firm consists of 9 notaries, 5 paralegals, and over 20 dedicated professionals, along with associated lawyers. Its mission is clear: 'To offer peace and security for the family, possessions and company of our clients.'

Operating nationally and internationally, the firm has built a loyal clientele of entrepreneurs, expats and high-net-worth individuals. Clients rely on Kooijman Autar for expert advice, cost efficiency and clear, actionable solutions.

Expertise across Legal and Business Sectors: Unlike common law notaries, Dutch civil law notaries are legal professionals with broad authority. Without a notarial deed, no real estate, registered ship or aircraft can legally change ownership in the

Netherlands. Kooijman Autar supports clients across a wide spectrum of services:

- **Family Law**: Advising on succession, inheritance and mediation, including digital estates.
- **Real Estate**: Supporting private, commercial and development projects with practical legal guidance.
- **Estate Planning**: Ensuring assets are protected, optimally distributed and tax-efficient.
- **Entrepreneurship**: Supporting start-ups and established businesses with structuring, share transfers, and mergers.
- **Business Transfers**: Assisting with family business succession, buy-ins and reorganizations.
- **Shipping & Transport**: Leveraging Rotterdam's strategic port location to serve logistics companies and individuals in maritime transactions.

Kooijman Autar's advisors are known for creative problem-solving and cross-disciplinary thinking. The firm works closely with tax experts and sector specialists to deliver integrated solutions.

International and Community-Minded: Kooijman Autar serves a growing expat and international client base, offering expertise in cross-border law and global estate matters. Clients include global IT firms, energy companies and logistics providers.

Beyond business, the firm actively supports the community. It serves as notary for social organizations and cultural institutions like the Erasmus Foundation, Museum Boijmans Van Beuningen, and the Giovanni van Bronckhorst Foundation, which promotes youth access to education and sports.

—Aniel Autar (CEO) and Aileen van Driel (Added Notary)

KOOIJMAN
AUTAR
NOTARIES | ADVISORS | MEDIATORS | LAWYERS

Part 4

Bold Choices

11

A Voyage into the Future

BBC Portable News Service
Your personalized news for 5 January 2050, 8.30 a.m.
News headlines:

Yesterday, Empress C xi II of China offered the prestigious membership of the CATA, the Chinese Atlantic Treaty Organization, to the European Union during a state dinner at Buckingham Palace. She did this in the presence of King William V and the European Union President David Beckham. She also announced that the introduction of gay marriage in China has significantly reduced the problems caused by the surplus of men. Since children can now be cloned, Chinese gay couples can meet the one-child policy of China. Chinese gay couples are, however, obligated to raise daughters, thus compensating for the shortage of women in China. The Empress thanked President Beckham, who had suggested this course of action, which had proved successful in various European regions since the end of last century, during his first state visit to China in 2026.

President Burna Boy of Nigeria starts his state visit to Colombia today. He is hosted in the presidential palace by Colombian president Shakira.

The European Union today set the price of a human life at €80,000. If a citizen spends more than this amount on healthcare annually, euthanasia becomes obligatory. People will receive a notification via mail that they have been removed from the digital population register; the letter will include a golden euthanasia pill that must be taken within 24 hours of receipt.

Tomorrow, the whole world will celebrate the Dog Festival. This originates from a centuries-old tradition in Nepal, where people honour their dogs on this special day. For the past five years, this has become a universal holiday, following a decision made by the World Government in 2045. Prime Minister Priyam Gandhi-Mody of India inaugurated this festival in Delhi this morning.

Yesterday, India installed the new nuclear Laika Power Station on Mars. It is named after the first dog who travelled in space. It will enforce space travel and space mining. Spaceships can also refuel there. Flying nuclear power plants elsewhere in space will encourage more space travel in future. Space has been divided among all the superpowers in the world to prevent war in space. Due to plenty of energy in space, manned rockets can now fly farther than ever before. Recently, an Indian rocket discovered a planet full of diamonds. Since space mining began there, every citizen can wear a big diamond on each finger and toe.

The population of Russia has been halved in the first half of this century, the Kremlin announced today. The Russian population is expected to diminish further. That's why Russia invites immigrants from populous countries to settle in Siberia.

Today the finals of Scoot-mobile dancing are being held in Washington. The events are being broadcast live and can be followed on mobile phones by the great-grandchildren of the participants, of whom the youngest is 99 and the oldest 152. President Elon Musk inaugurated this event last week.

From today it is official: there are more robots living in the world than people. For the first time, there are also fewer pigs than people in the world, the World Government announced this evening. Since 2008, doctors have shown that modified pig organs work perfectly in the human body, and an increasing number of infected human organs have been replaced by pig versions or artificially bred organs. People now live longer and healthier lives and health costs have been reduced by 50 per cent.

Personalized messages and advice

Our news service is synchronized to your financial, leisure and business diaries and thus we can offer you the following advice for today:

- You do not need to wear warm clothing for your 13.15 business lunch; you should, however, take an umbrella. Your lunch is scheduled with a person from Nigeria. He is from the city where a large university campus was built last week; you are advised to mention this to him. You can obtain more information about him via his avatar.
- Select code 9595 during your 16.00 hairdresser appointment. This code is for the trendiest hairstyle around at the moment—very suitable for men now that they no longer turn bald, especially for men in your age category (50+). This hairstyle can also withstand the heat of summer. Even when temperatures rise in the afternoon to 40°C, the air-conditioning in your hat will work perfectly, with your hair blowing seductively in the wind.
- Your investments have been automatically adjusted in line with developments in the US, India, China and Brazil.

'One generation plants the trees; another gets the shade.'

—Chinese proverb

The remarkable shifts that the world megatrends will cause, as described in this book, will influence all of us. Everyone who is alive now belongs to Generation T (technology), whether they are 8 or 80. Some trees were planted long ago, and we will feel their shade now. Think, for example, of the economic overhaul of India during the reign of the visionary Prime Minister Manmohan Singh (2004–2014), or the overhaul of China during the visionary leadership of Deng Xiaoping (1978–1989). Other trees have been planted more recently. Think of AI + QC + FR (Artificial Intelligence + Quantum Computing + Facial Recognition) software and Robotics.

We can all sense that an era is coming to an end. The current Age of Chaos marks the end of an old era and the start of a new one. So, what will the new era look like? 'The present is big with the future,' said Gottfried Leibniz. The future is now. We are currently witnessing the first contours of the most important trends that will radically change the world in the coming decades. There are already prototypes of several major technological developments that will arrive on the market within 10 years. For humanity, this will definitely be a century of transition. The West and the East will share power in this century, after centuries of Western global domination. The G20 of 20 major economies, including those of former poor nations such as Brazil, China and India, will rule the world economy. In the last half of the 20th century, we experienced great progress as humanity. For example, until the early 1970s, China was as poor as Somalia, but since the beginning of the 21st century, the country's economy ranks among the top three in the world. In the past 30 years in both China and India, a middle class of 500 million people in China and 432 million in India has emerged out of the underclasses—a major achievement indeed.

Technology changed the way we worked, lived and entertained ourselves in the 20th century. At present, the Technological Revolution is speeding up due to the combined rise of Quantum Computing, Artificial Intelligence, Robotics, Nanotechnology and Biotechnology.

In the year that this book is launched, Donald Trump began his second term as president of the superpower US. The authors believe that the 'Trumpification of the World', which he and his comrade Elon Musk have started, will have the following consequences:

1. Trump and Musk will wipe out the poisonous forces of Wokeism and Climatism from America and the Western world. We think that this is a good thing because woke activists and climatists have weakened the West over the past 40 years.

2. Trump is not known as a warmongering leader. He did not start a war during his first term. So he will end wars and try to prevent the eruption of new ones. We expect peace in Ukraine, Lebanon, Gaza and other regions. We also hope for a peace treaty between Israel and Saudi Arabia, along with the creation of a Palestinian state in Gaza. This new state could be expanded through land reclamation in the sea off the Gaza coast, with its capital named Trump-town. If two people are fighting over a cake, why not make the cake bigger?

3. Trumpism will lead to the redrawing of borders. The US bought Alaska from Russia in 1867 and

it wants to buy new lands again. This might set a trend all over the World. If the US could buy Alaska and maybe Greenland and Panama in future, why could others not follow this example? We suggest that India consider buying up land for its expanding population. Why not buy half of dirt-poor Afghanistan from the Taliban, thereby gaining safe passage into Central Asia and the New Silk Road? Why not buy half of Siberia from Russia and gain access to the valuable North Pole? Why not recover Pakistan-occupied Kashmir and China-occupied Kashmir, thus reuniting the Indian state? Why not buy Nepal, Bangladesh and Sri Lanka? Why not expand cities like Mumbai, Chennai and Kolkata through land reclamation as the Dutch did in Singapore and Dubai before? Why not repurchase the Pakistani part of Punjab and reunite this state? Pakistan definitely could use the money. In this way, by 2047, when India celebrates its 100th Independence Day, the country could be twice the size it was at the start of the Republic in 1947. Money makes the world go round, and in this century, demographics will do the same.

As mentioned before, the UN expects that by the end of this century, the world will be 700 per cent richer. We will have abundant intelligence. If we also have abundant energy sources, economic growth will speed up even faster. There is enough uranium and thorium to last for centuries. Nuclear fusion will break through soon enough. There is also enough oil, natural gas and coals. Solar energy is thriving. Geothermal energy is available everywhere. So, to reiterate: the Age of Plenty has finally arrived.

Hope During India's New Cycle

William Strauss and Neil Howe devised the Strauss–
Howe generational theory, which deals with a
recurring generation cycle in American and Western
history. The theory explains that historical events
are associated with recurring generational personas
(archetypes). Each of these archetypes unleashes a new
era (turning) that lasts around 21 years, during which
a new social, political and economic climate (mood)
exists. These turnings are part of a large 'saeculum'
cycle, representing a human lifespan of around 85
years, although some saecula have lasted longer.

The Strauss–Howe generational theory states that a
crisis recurs in American history after every saeculum,
followed by a period of recovery (high). During this
high, institutions and communitarian values are strong.
Succeeding generational archetypes ultimately emerge
and weaken these institutions in the name of autonomy
and individualism. This creates a tumultuous political
environment that ripens conditions for another crisis.

They laid the groundwork for their theory in
Generations: The History of America's Future, 1584
to 2069, which was published in 1991. Strauss and
Howe discuss the history of the US through a series
of generational biographies dating back to 1584. In
The Fourth Turning (1997), they expanded the theory
to describe the history of the US as a fourfold cycle
of generational types and recurring mood eras. This
included the Thirteen Colonies and their British
antecedents.

Strauss and Howe also examined generational
trends elsewhere in the world and identified similar

cycles in several developed countries. This proves that historical patterns emerge, and a country moves in 80-year cycles, divided into four 20-year periods (turnings).

India is now set to begin the first 20-year period of its second cycle following independence. Indian author Priyam Gandhi-Mody says, 'My best bet is that in this new cycle, a full reform of our bureaucracy will dominate, unshackling our economic inhibitions. Bureaucratic rot is the biggest and the most significant issue holding India back today.'

The authors agree with Gandhi-Mody's observation about India's bureaucratic rot. We hope India uses this new cycle to not only root out the rot but also modernize the mindset of its people.

After living in a poor, socialist country during the first cycle after independence, many Indians must now cast off old ideas and shift into superpower mode. They must also free themselves from a colonial heritage that introduced the Victorian anti-homosexuality laws or risk losing talented Indian homosexuals who will leave the country. Then, India may never get its own Alan Turing or other gay geniuses.

India should also use this new cycle to offer enough hopeful perspectives to surplus boys and protect its women from abuse, rape, murder and other forms of violence. Every Indian also expects better sanitation, of course.

'First buddy'

Elon Musk, who was born in South Africa in 1971 and became a tech oligarch after his migration to the US, is considered one of the smartest men in the world today. We both truly admire him. Musk is a bold entrepreneur who founded innovative companies such as SpaceX, which reshaped the world. His playful, provocative, creative and out-of-the-box thinking is an asset for Trump's second presidency. We are pretty sure that somewhere in India, a baby boy or girl will be born one day who will become the Indian Elon Musk. If Indian stakeholders create an environment that nurtures talented people, this Indian Musk can drive the country forward. South Africa was not able to nurture Musk's talent; America was. Today, Musk is not only the richest man in the world but also one of the most powerful, owing to his alliance with Trump. Trumpism and Muskism have a lot in common.

They generally share a great disdain for government, bureaucracy and the established media. The established Western media are only trusted by a minority of the population nowadays. Instead, people flock to X (previously Twitter), podcasts and other alternative media. Entrepreneur Ashutosh Garg, who founded two unicorns in India after starting his career at Google, created his podcast *The Brand Called You (TBCY)*. Within a few years, it has become one of the most successful podcasts in India because he fills a gap left open by the mainstream media. The market for alternative media will thus continue to grow, but established media could also diversify their businesses.

By scrapping laws and firing civil servants, Musk—never shy of setting ambitious goals—has promised $2 trillion in cuts to government bureaucracy. If he succeeds in cutting the millions of bullshit jobs, it'll serve as a good example for India. In our country, the Netherlands, with a population of 18 million, we have 1 million bullshit jobs done by people who just move air around. All over the world, 1 in 20 workers are in bullshit jobs, according to author David Graeber. It's a waste of human talent, especially in an ageing world.

Bullshit jobs

Author David Graeber, a specialist in bullshit jobs, was right to link people's attitudes towards their jobs to their psychological well-being. This is something that employers—and society as a whole—should take seriously. Graeber postulates the existence of meaningless jobs and analyses their harmful effects on society. He identifies five types of meaningless jobs, where workers pretend their role is not as pointless or harmful as they know it to be: flunkies, goons, duct tapers, box tickers and taskmasters. He argues that the association of labour with virtuous suffering is recent in human history.

Ageing is impacting most countries in the West, Japan, Korea and China. Migration and demographic warfare create regular power shifts in global politics. At the same time, despite or perhaps because of technology, spirituality is gaining ground. Currently, Silicon Valley is ranked the most religious and spiritual place on Earth.

Aliens and Religion

In this century we might discover life in space. What will happen to religion if we find life on other planets? What if God has designed all planets the same way? Will individual spirituality replace the world's major religions? Or will all religions merge into one new blend as the great Mughal emperor Akbar (1556–1605) once envisioned?

How will we define happiness in the future? What is the future of love? Many questions will ponder us during the next couple of years. Therefore politics, economy, technology, demographics, spirituality and futurology create a fascinating cocktail that decision-makers in the 21st century cannot live without.

Futurology

Futurology is exceptionally interdisciplinary and multidisciplinary. We can only recognize trends if we combine know-how from various disciplines and professions. As a futurologist, I pay particular attention to how countries, organizations, people and the world change, how resultant needs are thus shaped and how technological inventions transform people's lives.

This book describes, offering an international framework, the megatrends that will radically change life in the coming decades. Some people might find this book provocative. Others might find it inspiring and appreciate its unconventional approach. Contrary to many, we find this the most positive and inspiring period to live in. We believe that the future will be bright and that humanity can make life on Earth better than ever before.

This book is based on and inspired by various research programmes, books by several notable authors, lectures and other publications, discussions and interviews with about 250 people from several continents, brainstorming sessions, personal observations and interpretations, field studies, future scenarios of Shell, and sources from the CIA, IMD in Lausanne and many others.

The Future of the Past

There was a time when time itself didn't exist. Time must, after all, be related to a period and we can only define it if we have a sense of time—a sense developed through understanding days and nights and the division of days into hours, minutes and seconds. This only became possible when the Sun, the Earth and the other planets in our solar system came into being, about 13.7 billion years ago. Our current planetary system was formed with the Sun, the Moon and the various planets: Earth, Jupiter, Saturn, Mars, Pluto, Uranus, Neptune, Venus and Mercury. The entire assembly of planets developed its own circular dance, and time came into being. The Bible describes the phenomenon as: 'Darkness was upon the face of the Earth.' In 2008, the environment of the Big Bang was simulated in Switzerland in a fantastic experiment at a brand new laboratory. It caused great fear among some people: would the experiment not also create Black Holes that would swallow the Earth and humanity, reducing it to nothing? Luckily, that didn't happen. We will learn a lot of interesting things about how the Earth was formed from these types of experiments in the coming years. Imagine if we soon discover a second Earth somewhere in space with life on it! Would there be humans, humanoids or completely different beings?

Is Life All Just a Dream?

British astrophysicist Martin Rees says: 'Over a few decades, computers have evolved from being able to simulate only very simple patterns to being able to create virtual worlds with a lot of detail. If that trend were to continue, then we can imagine computers which will be able to simulate worlds perhaps as complicated as the one we think we're living in. This raises the philosophical question: could we ourselves be in such a simulation and could what we think is the universe be some sort of vault of heaven rather than the real thing? In a sense, we could ourselves be the creations within that simulation.' So what is really real?

The Eternal Struggle between the Sun and Saturn

Since the beginning of time, the Sun has stood for the 'good' in life and Saturn for the 'evil'. The struggle between the two heavenly bodies, between good and bad, has dominated the entire history of mankind and will continue to dominate the future. In various parts of the world and in various cultures, this struggle was symbolized. The Sun has always been a positive god symbol for mankind, from the moment human beings appeared on Earth. Saturn, on the other hand, has always been the symbol of death. Saturn makes everything on Earth finite; He is the God of Destruction or Death, often depicted as Father Time. It is because of Saturn that everything eventually dies. If we can defeat Him, then we as humans will finally win the battle between good and evil.

The Fall of Man

Another major influence in our lives is the Fall of Man, as it is told in the Bible. The snake in this famous story symbolizes the transition from paradise to an unruly period for mankind on Earth. According to esoteric teachings, this refers to a real change in the cosmos, leading to the separation of the Sun and Earth. At the time, a completely new element—procreation through sex—is thought to have emerged for mankind. As a result, our emotions became more complex: hunger and desire, dissatisfaction and frustration, worry and fear. In classical tradition, Lucifer could be seen as the embodiment of these emotions, just as Aphrodite and Venus represent love and beauty in Greek and Roman mythologies, respectively. We also publish this book in the Year of the Snake, according to Chinese and Japanese astrology.

Fire, Water and the First Life

In the beginning, the Earth was largely covered in water. It had, and still has, a fiery core, with different layers around it, filled with raw materials. The outer shell is the wettest, due to the oceans. The two poles keep the Earth in balance and have large concentrations of ice, which melt from time to time. This has happened a number of times throughout history and is happening again now. The Earth has only 2.5 per cent fresh water—the rest is all salty. The first life emerged on the Earth's moist surface with the arrival of microbes. These microscopically small creatures were made up of a single cell and were therefore called single-celled organisms. These creatures swam around and gradually evolved into other life forms, such as fish and water plants.

Congeal and Dry Up

Gradually, the Earth began to congeal and dry up. There were also volcanoes on the Earth's surface. The first continent, which we now call Pangaea, was formed as a result of various earthquakes, volcanic eruptions and other natural forces. The microbes that lived in the sea were washed ashore. The forces of nature broke up the supercontinent again, and the pieces started to drift, eventually forming the continents we know today: North America, South America, Europe, Asia, Africa, Antarctica and Australia. Later, further pieces broke off and drifted away, forming Sri Lanka and Madagascar. The continents now appear relatively stable in form, size and location; one can no longer imagine that they could break up again, start drifting or change shape in other ways. Neither can one imagine that new continents could be formed by the forces of nature, or that old ones could be entirely or partially devoured by the oceans.

Currently, there are fault lines in the Earth's crust,

such as in San Francisco and Ethiopia, where there is indeed a danger of land splitting off again. We are already witnessing a huge new rift in Africa, which is breaking the continent in two. It is awe-inspiring to witness the magnificent power of nature, something modern humans often forget. The Indian tribes in rural America and the African tribes who still live like their ancestors, are more aware of nature's grandeur. The Indian tribes now oppose the US's construction of wind energy parks at sea, as they disrupt the natural radar systems of whales, dolphins and other fish they consider sacred.

In the Netherlands, we see that windmills built on land cause stress for cows and other animals. Cows refuse to drink water, produce less milk, become sick and die prematurely. Our advice to India is: do not build windmills—neither on land nor at sea. Your holy cows will not survive them. Return to the ancient wisdom of nature. Your remarkable economic growth should not harm nature and humanity.

The Chinese, Japanese and Indians are among the few peoples on Earth who have lived on the same piece of land for millennia, while others are descendants of migrants. So clean air, blue skies and zero pollution are not only human rights but also a way to pay respect to nature and the land of your ancestors. Therefore, the Singaporization of the world is necessary, as we argue in this book. Waste management, water management and recycling practices are not just smart business—they are also a spiritual movement. Still, we advise against getting involved with Greenpeace and other Western NGOs, which, in our view, are criminal organizations. Greenpeace campaigned against modified rice, preferring millions of people to die of starvation instead. China developed its own modified rice with its own scientists, ended starvation and kicked out Greenpeace and similar organizations. All countries in BRICS and the Global South should follow suit.

Feeding one's own people is the top priority of every government. A new combination of Dutch and Indian agricultural food knowledge could turn India into a food superpower, enabling it to feed itself and also export food to other countries, as the Dutch do. We are now the second-largest food exporter in the world, but India can take either of the top two spots. India can learn from our mistakes too. There seems to be a correlation between cancer and certain processed foods. However, do not panic. The book *The Emperor of All Maladies: A Biography of Cancer* by Siddhartha Mukherjee is an elegant enquiry—both clinical and personal—into the long history of cancer, which, despite breakthroughs in treatment, still challenges medical science. Mukherjee argues that cancer existed in the time of the ancient Egyptians. It has always been among humanity and always will be. Yet we are what we eat. In recent times, there have been significant advancements in healthcare.

New medicines for cancer and other maladies are now being developed, even aboard spaceships. So India's investment in space might pay off in many ways.

Advice to young readers: become an astronaut, boys and girls! It is the occupation of the future!

From Amphibious Animals to People

Humans love water. About 55–60 per cent of our bodies are water. We are water animals; we love to shower, swim and bathe. Why? As already said, the first land animals were amphibious, capable of living both on land and in water. One of these creatures was apelike—the forefather of man and apes, called a *pre-hominid*. The first traces of pre-hominids date back to the Pleistocene period, in what is now

Africa. These pre-hominids, just like most plants, had both male and female sex organs. Each of them could fertilize themselves and reproduce—perhaps a bit similar to the hijra's biology today. Thus, the story of Adam, who created Eve from his rib, came about. However, Adam was not a man; he was a hermaphrodite who reproduced with himself to create Eve. In this sense, the Bible story is partially correct. Charles Darwin, who mapped out evolution, did not refute this story as he was deeply religious. Over time, most animals and humans evolved with separate sexes, and hermaphrodites were a thing of the past. While a few people are still born with both sexes, most humans have had separate sexes for over a thousand years. The earliest people were vegetarians; mankind started consuming meat much later. The earliest people couldn't speak either. Communication happened through gestures and throaty noises. It seems now we might be returning to that time and age.

For example, in Japan, there are already apps with earplugs that enable Japanese and foreigners to understand each other. The app translates any speech into the user's own language, making communication efficient. We see now that Indians in the diaspora no longer speak Hindi or other Indian languages. However, with the help of AI-powered apps and earplugs, they might be able to understand these languages again. In the Netherlands, most people of Indian origin (PIOs) do not speak Hindi. Some take Hindi lessons, but their busy lives prevent them from mastering it. Maybe AI will help us revive even dead languages such as Sanskrit and Latin, giving us better access to the wisdom in ancient texts and scriptures. An example of this is our friend, the Dutch food guru Rob Baan, and his company Koppert Cress. Rob discovered an edible plant species in medieval books that tastes like oysters. He started to look for this plant all over the world and found only the last specimen that still existed. Using modern technology, he cloned and reproduced this plant, growing it in his greenhouse now. His son, Stijn Baan, who is currently the CEO of this creative food company after his father retired, exports this vegetable all around the world. Now, even vegetarians can eat oysters, thanks to one man who was able to read old texts and grasp their knowledge and wisdom.

The Emotional Revolution and Our Reptilian Brain

The reptilian brain—the oldest of the three brain parts that humans have—controls the body's vital functions such as heart rate, breathing, body temperature and balance. Our reptilian brain includes the main structures found in a reptile's brain—the brainstem and the cerebellum. The limbic brain emerged in the earliest mammals. It can record memories of behaviours that produce agreeable and disagreeable experiences, so it is responsible for what we call emotions in human beings. The main components of the limbic brain are the hippocampus, the amygdala and the hypothalamus. This part of the brain is the seat of value judgements that we make, often unconsciously, which exert such a strong influence on our behaviours.

The neocortex first became prominent in primates and culminated as two large cerebral hemispheres in the human brain. These hemispheres play a dominant role and are responsible for the development of human language, abstract thought, imagination and consciousness. The neocortex is flexible and has almost infinite learning abilities. It is also what has enabled human cultures to evolve. These three parts of the brain do not operate independently; they have interconnected functions through which they influence one another. Now in the 21st century, we understand better how our brains work. The reptilian brain is most closely associated with body processing. Instinctive trauma responses, such as fight, flight, freeze, startle responses and crying out for help, are all examples of reptilian brain functions. Trauma is also stored in the reptilian brain.

In today's hi-tech world, it is necessary to understand the reptilian brain. We live in the time of an Emotional Revolution, which leads to the rise of Emocracy, where emotions are becoming more important every passing day. Many Asians don't discuss much about emotions, except maybe when they are intoxicated. However, pushing emotions aside in favour of work and career can prove to be dangerous. Psychiatrist Bram Bakker claims that most suicides in Europe today occur among heterosexual men in their 50s who have never discussed their emotions. During their 'penopause' (the male equivalent of menopause), the pent-up emotions of their past flood their reptile brain. If they cannot cope with these emotions, it leads to suicide. We need to prevent this from happening to future generations of men. Humanity needs men over 50 as much as women over 50.

12

The Future of Love

Sita and Francis are enjoying their tea. They are celebrating Sita's 86th birthday. This year, the retirement age in the UK has been raised to 95; 10 years ago, it was 85 and Sita had been expecting to retire early. Now, she is happy to continue working until she's 95. Francis, who is 97, sits at home most days, bored. His VirtualMe says that his life expectancy is 112 years, meaning he will have to manage his boredom for quite a while before entering Heaven. Last year, his wife bought him a soundproof Yamaha portable studio, expecting him to spend most of his days there. He can use his computer, play with his toy train and communicate with people around the world when he is locked up in there. His wife bought this soundproof studio because she concluded he was suffering from Retired Husband Syndrome. Since his retirement, Francis has started complaining about the quality of her curries, even though he used to eat them without issue. The Yamaha box, since its invention in Japan in 2025, has become a bestseller all over Britain. Francis has decided to coach young George, who is struggling with stress. The complete lack of privacy in this day and age makes it more and more difficult for George to see his 78-year-young girlfriend in private. His wife can track most of his movements, and while he enjoys working, overtime is no longer a good excuse because his wife's VirtualMe can trace him.

To solve the issue, Francis asked his web community if they knew of ways to deceive the VirtualMe avatar of George's jealous wife, so he could happily enjoy his extramarital affair. One member of his web community, the young Mr Grace—a sprightly 115-year-old—found an ingenious way to trick the hi-tech avatar. Thanks to him, George's stress has now been reduced to an all-time low. The two friends smile and enjoy the birds singing in the wind. Technology is fine, but nothing beats human naughtiness.

A day without love feels like a year of emptiness. As human beings, we need love. That's why we cherish our spouses, friends, family and pets. Yet, despite this fundamental need, many people live lives devoid of love.

We previously wrote a book titled *The Future of Love*, which was published in Dutch and Brazilian Portuguese. Perhaps one day it will be available in India. We expect that people will always seek love, although the way people experience love will change. In the past, you married at the age of 25 and, with life expectancy around 40, spent 15 years together. That was doable. But with longer lifespans, we expect fewer couples to love each other 'until death do us part'. In the Netherlands, for instance, one in three marriages ends in divorce. In France, many married individuals—both men and women—have extramarital affairs with the approval of their spouse, family and society.

Arranged Marriages and Love Marriages Evolve

The arranged marriage can work very well. The partners can gradually get to know each other, appreciate each other and love each other. We know many elderly couples, including both our grandparents, one an Indian couple in the diaspora in the Caribbean, the other a Jewish couple in Europe, who had great arranged marriages and were very happy with each other.

We still have arranged marriages everywhere in the world, for example amongst elites, but also in rural communities. In cities things have evolved. The love marriage is more popular these days. Yet arranged marriages can last longer than love marriages. So we expect that there will be a future for both arranged marriages and love marriages.

More or Less Platonic Marriages on the Rise

In Thailand we interviewed an elderly Buddhist monk about modern love. He remarked: 'You young people want all-in-one in love. Your lover must be handsome even if you are not, he must be financially able to support you and future kids, he must be a sex-bomb, he must be your best friend, he must go shopping with you, and-and-and. You are too demanding these days. And let's assume you find that perfect bride or groom and he/she dies or divorces you, then you lose your best friend, your fuckbuddy, your financial supporter, all in one at once. You should spread all these tasks and functions amongst several persons. That is much more stable. So do as we do in Thailand. We go for a platonic marriage. Only sex for procreation. You have fuckbuddies for the best Kamasutra-sex, you have friends for friendship and other psychological intimacy. This can be an arranged marriage or a platonic love marriage. If both partners don't have too high expectations from each other, the marriage is more solid. Management of expectations is key in the future of love.' Would this Thai concept work in India? We don't know, but we see it working amongst elites and royalty.

Asexuality is on the rise. There are a lot of people nowadays who don't need sex in their life. In the past this was the case with monks and nuns; nowadays we see a lot of people who feel that sex is overvalued and prefer to use their sexual energy for their work or hobby. Asexuals can stay single spinsters or they can choose a platonic marriage.

Marriage as a Way of Social Climbing

Social climbing has always been part of the landscape of love. In the past many poor, but beautiful people slept their way up. *Sleeping your way up* or *sleeping your way in.* is still happening today, although the term gold-digger is used frequently. British media call Meghan, Prince Harry's wife, a gold-digger. Spanish media call Queen Letizia a gold-digger. Yet these women slept their way up successfully. They must be doing something good, otherwise their men would not have fallen for them.

In the old days the pilot of a plane married a stewardess. A doctor married a nurse. A businessman married his secretary. And so on. This way of social climbing was accepted and it worked. Nowadays however we see that people marry someone of their own profession or social class. A male pilot marries a female pilot. A male doctor marries a female doctor. A businessman marries a businesswoman. So social climbing ends. This happens because many love relations start at the workplace and in tightly knit communities and groups of friends, the *framilies*, nowadays. Yet we believe that social climbing is here to stay as well.

Gen Z Boys Don't Want to Start a Family Anymore

In the West, we are seeing this trend among Generation Z boys, born between 1997 and 2012, who are increasingly opting out of romantic relationships. They are not falling in love anymore—not because they can't, but because they don't want to. Instead, they have a 'framily' (a self-chosen family of friends), 'frolleagues' (colleagues who have become their friends) and 'friends with benefits' or fuckbuddies. That is enough for them. Living without falling in love suits them.

For Gen Z girls, the story is different. They still desire love and want to settle down and start a family. In the Netherlands, we are now seeing more Gen Z girls marrying Millennial men. We expect this trend to grow.

But why do Gen Z boys prefer this lifestyle? We assume that there are several reasons for this, but this trend has not yet been researched. The reasons might be:

1. Many Gen Z boys grew up witnessing their parents' bitter divorces and custody battles. This makes them scared of marriage.
2. Casual sex is easily available in cities, so why trade sexual freedom for the risks of commitment? If you get milk for free why buy the cow?
3. They want to travel and party and are afraid that marriage and family life would pose a hindrance to this lifestyle.
4. The housing market is tough for youngsters nowadays. Moving in with a partner is a risk—if the relationship ends, where would they go?
5. According to CBS, the Dutch national statistics agency, more Gen Z boys prefer a bisexual lifestyle than a 100 per cent straight lifestyle. This could be an important factor.
6. Kids are expensive. In the Netherlands, raising a child till they turn 18 costs €2,00,000. While young women are willing to make this sacrifice, boys prefer to spend their money differently.

7. Above all, Gen Z boys prefer individual freedom to marriage, because they feel that this makes them happier. Perhaps they will settle down later in life—but for now, we don't know how this trend will evolve.

Of course many couples do still fall in love and stay happily together for decades, whether in arranged marriages or love marriages. We ourselves are an example of this—we were happily married for 25 years.

An Annual Marriage Evaluation

One key to our successful marriage was an annual evaluation—much like job performance reviews, but for our relationship. Every year, on 5 December, the Dutch national holiday *Sinterklaas*, we had a special dinner—either at home or in a restaurant—and openly discussed the past year in our marriage. What went well? What could be improved? What did we appreciate in each other?

In Dutch tradition, on *Sinterklaas*, people write funny poems that playfully critique their loved ones' habits—snoring, not flushing the toilet properly, shopping too much or communicating too harshly. Anything goes.

We took this spirit and made it into a tradition of our own. By doing this annually, we knew exactly how our partner felt, thus ensuring no pent-up emotions or lingering frustrations. We highly recommend this to other couples—it helped us stay happily married. For 25 years.

Note: Co-author Vinco David passed away from lung cancer in 2023. Among his family, he was the only one in a stable marriage—his parents, brother and sister all divorced. He wanted to break that cycle. That's why he came up with this brilliant idea.

Men Are the Weak Sex

Across the world, women live longer than men. In an ageing society, this means an increasing number of widows. But they can remarry or find new partners. So you can have more spouses in one life. We see many elderly people finding love again in their 70s, 80s or even 90s. At the same time, early deaths are becoming more common due to cancer and other diseases, leading to a rise in younger widows and widowers.

Note: Co-author Adjiedj became a widower twice—first at the age of 29, when his husband of eight years, Sjoerd, died of cancer, and again at 59. You can have two great loves in one life, dear readers.

An IBM director in the Netherlands once remarked that 50 is a dangerous age for men: 'I see so many of our IT guys work hard and play hard all their life, yet after reaching the age of 50, their body falls prone to cancer, heart attacks, brain haemorrhages and burnouts.'

So guys—live life to the max. It is over before you know it.

The 'Merry Widows'

An interesting trend has emerged in our country. Some women seeking a husband attend funerals of women around their age. They introduce themselves to the widower as an old friend of his wife, console him and—within two months—marry him.

Widowers don't want to stay alone, whereas widows often prefer their single life. In German, these women are called *Die Lustige Witwe*—The Merry Widow. They happily spend their inheritance and do everything they craved during their marriage but never got to do for whatever reason. They enjoy spending time with friends, children and grandchildren. That is enough for them. We now see that small groups of 3–4 widows rent or buy a house together and share their lives. Remember the American soap series *The Golden Girls* from the 1980s? That is now a reality for many merry widows.

Sugar Mommies, Cougars and Toy boys on the Rise

Elderly widows are increasingly seeking younger lovers—whether through casual arrangements, financial support or even marriage. In Nigeria, popular TV soaps often depict elderly widows renting young toy boys for sex; sometimes they even get married.

In Gambia, many elderly European widows actively seek toy boys, sometimes marrying them and making them their heirs. We once interviewed a 22-year-old Gambian groom who had married a 75-year-old Dutch woman. 'I close my eyes when we have sex and think about Monday morning's grocery list,' he had remarked.

Nevertheless, they both appeared happy and satisfied. The woman admitted that her children and grandchildren did not approve of her marriage, but she did not care. 'He keeps my creative juices flowing.'

The phenomenon isn't limited to women. Many elderly widowers import young brides from Thailand, Russia and other countries. They become their heirs as well. Beware: there is a lot of fraud going on in this industry. The Dutch ING Bank has a special helpdesk for customers at risk of falling victim to romance scams. In our ageing country where one in four adults is single, according to the CBS, scammers find ample opportunities to exploit the lonely and wealthy.

Meanwhile, in our country, several university students fund their education by working as escorts for widows and widowers. A friend of ours, an elderly lawyer, revealed that many young lawyers in his firm, both male and female, admitted financing their studies this way. Amusingly, some of their clients got a surprise when they saw them in court! Stories like this one are a running gag in cities like Amsterdam, where zillions of lawyers work or study. While no official research or reference confirms this as a widespread trend, it could certainly inspire a Bollywood movie script.

Falling in Love with an AI-avatar or a Robot

Since the 1970s, sex dolls have been popular among lonely singles in Japan and China. Today, advancements in robotics and AI have transformed these dolls into humanoid companions. Japanese and Chinese media report that some men even fall in love with their AI-powered sex dolls, which can now talk, walk and accompany them to theatres, restaurants, bars, even on shopping trips. For women, AI companions could also be a game-changer. If your husband refuses to go shopping with you, why not rent an AI robot who always agrees, carries your bags and never complains? In Japan, China, and South Korea, people are even forming romantic attachments to AI avatars. If it makes them happy, who are we to judge?

Blended Families: Divorced Men Remarry, Divorced Women Don't

Across Europe and America, divorced men seldom stay single for long—most remarry. Most elderly men don't like living alone. In contrast, the majority of divorced women choose not to remarry, though they may have lovers in LAT (living apart together) relationships. Even when their children encourage them to remarry, most women prefer their independence. With rising divorce rates, blended families have become the norm. A blended family consists of a couple and their children from current and previous relationships. While inheritance disputes often arise after a partner's death, these families generally function well when all members are alive and thriving.

Half of Americans Have No Close Friends

According to the US government, 50 per cent of Americans have no close friends. Many people exist only to work and pay their bills. Mass migration has left countless individuals navigating lonely lives far from home. Individualization is on the rise in India as well.

What does the future of love hold? Will lonely singles find each other, or will they turn to humanoid robots for companionship and maybe even marriage?

Sex in a Changing World: The Future of Intimacy

In Dutch talk shows, several women claim that the clitoral stimulator 'Satisfyer' is a better lover than men. Is this where intimacy is headed? Are we moving towards a sexless future, or simply a different kind of pleasure?

While some religious traditions strongly advocate suppressing sexual desire, others embrace it. The erotic sculptures of the Khajuraho temples (built between 950 and 1050 AD) in Madhya Pradesh in central India would be unthinkable in Christian churches. The *Vedas* acknowledge eroticism and view love as a connection between two souls, regardless of skin colour, gender or religion. So it can be concluded that the *Vedas* are neither against mixed marriages nor against LGBTQIA+ relationships, contrary to the beliefs of most modern Indians. Those who oppose these views likely haven't read the *Vedas*.

From the time the *Vedas* were written until the British colonization, India enjoyed significant sexual freedom, sexual liberty and sexual diversity. The Mughals also engaged in various sexual practices. Emperor Babur was openly gay (or bisexual), kept a male harem and wrote about all of this openly in his memoirs, the *Baburnama*. Although he first came to India to loot, later on he fell in love with the country and its culture. He turned Mughal India into a superpower on par with Imperial China. Mughal architecture, food, painting, poetry, music and all other art forms became a unique blend of Hindu and Islamic Central Asian styles. Babur's openness about his sexuality raises intriguing questions. Did his example encourage other men of his time to live authentically? We may never know—unless, of course, a brilliant inventor creates a time machine to transport us back to those days. But be warned: Babur was also a ruthless conqueror, responsible for the deaths of many Hindus. History is never as romantic as we imagine it.

13

A Government for the World

Sunita and her friends visit the reunion concert of Swedish pop group ABBA at Wembley Stadium. In the 1970s, ABBA was famous all over the world for their optimistic pop songs, such as 'Dancing Queen'. Later generations of musicians were heavily inspired by ABBA, as reflected in the musical *Mamma Mia*, which became widely popular around the beginning of the century.

Sunita does not have to queue for long. Security is tight, but nobody notices any of it. The new scans enable the security officers to see through the clothes of every visitor. There's a lot of naked skin on the security monitors—'a wet dream to work here on a day like this', Sunita muses as she flirts with the sexy security officer, who does not respond. 'Probably gay,' she shrugs.

Every time an ABBA song ends, one hears the buzz of wasps flying around, armed with cameras and sensors. Anybody carrying a bomb undetected by the body scans would be caught by this new generation of wasps, which are trained to smell explosives. They are now additional members of the security forces, patrolling every event these days. The ABBA concert is the main event this year. The world has waited for this reunion since the group broke up in the 1980s. Since the 2020s, fans have enjoyed ABBA concerts through avatars at London's ABBA Arena. However, experiencing the real thing is always best.

> Finally, it's happening. Sunita is utterly excited. Her watch shows that her temperature is high—almost feverish—and her pulse rate is elevated. She knows she needs to calm down and pops some designer drugs to level out her mood. Through her avatar, she connects with her mum, who is watching the concert via a camera projecting it on to the ceiling of her hospital room. At 68, her mum is preparing to give birth to the child of Sunita and her boyfriend Ping, having carried the pregnancy so Sunita can focus on her career and enjoy life without the inconvenience of being pregnant. The birth is scheduled for tomorrow. But today, she will watch the ABBA concert. Hurray! Isn't life wonderful? The ABBA members are all around the age of 125 now, but thanks to new vitamins and biotechnology, they can still sing and dance as they did when they were around 35!

After World War I, an attempt was already made to establish a body representing all the countries of the world. In 1920, it was called the League of Nations. It wasn't, however, fated to live very long and turned out to lack real power, particularly because large countries like the US didn't join. In 1945, another attempt was made: the United Nations was established. This was, at least, a more successful body than the League of Nations. The power of the UN has fluctuated over time, especially when looking back over the past 15 years. After the successful intervention by the UN forces during the First Gulf War (1990–1991), the UN was, in the words of Coolsaet, 'generally accepted as the heart of international peace and safety'. Only a few years later, during the ethnic conflicts in Yugoslavia and Rwanda, the UN lost much of its credibility. In 2003, its reputation reached the lowest point when the US invaded Iraq without a mandate from the UN Security Council. Other institutions of the UN, such as UNICEF, the World Health Organization and the World Bank—although the latter isn't technically part of the UN—are less affected by these fluctuations. In 2000, the UN Millennium Development Goals were formulated, based on six basic principles: freedom, equality, solidarity, tolerance, respect for nature and shared responsibility— principles echoing the ideals of the American Declaration of Independence and the French Revolution.

The Lessons Learnt

Studying the history of the world and humanity, as described in the preceding pages, reveals clear megatrends of the past. These trends may influence or even generate some of the megatrends of the future. History always repeats itself—just in a different way.

One of the lessons learnt is that climate change is nothing new; the climate has always changed in waves, just as it is doing now. Another lesson is the correlation between a surplus of boys of fighting age (15 to 35 years old) and the outbreak of wars. More on this theory will be explored later in this book.

We also learn that although humans have long tried to govern nature, nature is mightier than humankind and always strikes back. Periods of population growth are invariably followed by periods of population decline, which is likely to happen again.

Another key insight is that the world economy develops in waves, much like the seasons. Economic winters— recessions—cannot be prevented, nor can more severe ones— depressions. The current economic depression resembles that of 1870 more than the one in 1929, contrary to popular belief. Major depressions and crises in financial institutions tend to occur at the dawn of new technological eras.

Spirituality, too, is more important than it appears. Many economic waves seem to align with astrological cycles, which is why some European banks—particularly in Switzerland—employ financial astrologers.

With these megatrends and patterns of change in mind, we now move to the second part of this book, which explores the 12 megatrends that will shape our future. To map the world's future and develop the next supermodel for global economics and society, three scenarios must be formulated.

What will the future world economy look like? Is Anglo-Saxon neoliberal capitalism dead? If so, what will take its place in the 21st century? Is there such a thing as a crisis-proof economic model? Will there be a new economic order and will that still be global in an era of protectionism and rising economic nationalism?

We predict that globalization will evolve into slowbalization. China has invented 'Socialism with Chinese Characteristics'. Now, if India simply imitates Western capitalism, it will not make its citizens happy. As mentioned earlier, we propose that India develops a kind of capitalism with Indian characteristics, which we call Karma Capitalism or the Happynomy. This is a form of liberal capitalism that is beneficial for entrepreneurs, their employees, suppliers, customers and society as a whole. It not only makes people more prosperous and economically secure, but also makes them feel happy, safe and valued. Moreover, it provides personal freedom, allowing people to choose a lifestyle that truly brings them happiness. After all, we only live once. One might hope they can make amends in the next life if they are unhappy now, but what if they reincarnate as a chicken and end up as a restaurant dish? Karma Capitalism blends past, present and future in an ideal mix—a model that India can export to the populous countries in the Global South and to the Indian diaspora.

What should be the ideal relationship between the market and government? The British newspaper *The Economist* argues that the lack of real competition among large American companies is corrosive and hurts American innovation. India should encourage competition across all sectors of society to avoid the same economic and bureaucratic decay that has stifled the United States's progress.

Can the applicable paradigm—the belief that the free market creates balance and prosperity for everyone—be thrown into the bin? Then, what would the new paradigm be? Which region of our multipolar world has the most future-proof model?

Prominent experts in their respective fields from all over the world are mulling over new ideas and a clear vision of the future. Three economic models are now emerging from these contemplations. Kishore Mahbubani proclaims his belief in the Asian model. But is it really progressing? Brazilian economist Marcelo Neri praises the success story of his country, but Brazilians are leaving en masse and migrating to their old motherland, Portugal, and other countries, as they no longer believe in Brazil's future. Macroeconomist Willem Buiter of the London School of Economics sees the rise of the Singaporean model. Parag Khanna, the young geopolitical analyst, is putting his money on Europe. Amy Chua, globalization expert at Yale Law School, doesn't yet want to write off the US and remains critical of the alternative models. We will see. However, there is definitely enough food for thought.

Scenario 1. United World as 'Singapore-Plus'

In this model, democracy and autocracy merge into

technocracy. We also must be aware of the entry of enlightened despots onto the political stage. The world's leading powers would transform themselves, much like Singapore did. Singapore, which was a poor, marshy country until the 1960s, is now one of the world's richest nations. The economic model is capitalist, but the state plays an important role, particularly through state investment companies. This model is not very ideological; it is chiefly pragmatic, less religious and more spiritual. While norms and values are important, they are conventional. Diversity is a normal aspect of life, but firm action is taken against extremists. Law and order prevail, and the death penalty is common. Technology and science are given a free hand. Globalization perseveres and we make the best of climate change. The one-child policy is also implemented globally. Anger management is a cornerstone of the model: the class of losers and unemployed might not revolt against the established order. Those at the top integrate human and artificial intelligence. Luck is defined primarily in pragmatic terms.

Scenario 2. Back to the Middle Ages

In this scenario the current world order falls apart, as it did in 1870, when globalization was at its peak, as it is now again. Medieval times return, and the euro as a single currency implodes, as its predecessor, the Taler, did. Power blocs are dissolved, such as the EU. Its predecessor, the Austro-Hungarian Dual Monarchy, imploded too shortly after the start of the 20th century. The new world is more violent, extremists rise, and the combination of economic crisis, food crisis and climate crisis brings about the worst of humanity. We experience a major setback in science and chaos is the common value. In this new world order elites lose their status, and weak democracies coexist beside dictatorships.

Scenario 3. Back to the Middle
Ages and World War III

In this scenario, the current world order collapses, as it did in 1870, when the first wave of globalization peaked— just as it is now. Medieval times return, and the euro as a single currency implodes, like its predecessor, the silver thaler (which was also used in India), once did. Power blocs are dissolved, with the EU and NATO likely disbanding. The Austro-Hungarian Dual Monarchy—a predecessor to these organizations—also fell apart shortly after the turn of the 20th century. The new world order is more violent, with a rise of extremists. The combination of economic crisis, food crisis and climate crisis brings out the worst in humanity. We experience a major setback in science, and chaos prevails everywhere in society. In this new world order, elites lose their status and weak democracies coexist with dictatorships. Warmongers who believe that a nuclear world war can be won achieve their goal, and humanity ultimately dies due to their folly.

Becoming Antifragile

We personally hope that the first scenario becomes reality. However, when contemplating the scenarios, we also have to take wild cards or Black Swans into account—events that can radically change the future, just as a joker can change a game of cards. The current digital revolution will initially lead to mass unemployment, further giving rise to social unrest. Hence, we need to become 'antifragile' everywhere in the world, including in India.

This will create a market for extremism. Globalization will now take a temporary step backwards, but subsequently, it will regain momentum. Many problems cannot be resolved by a loose collection of nationalistic groups. We believe that globalization offers many benefits, even if only in terms of peace. Generally, economies that depend on one another are less likely to wage war. In world history, the longest periods of peace have occurred during times of reciprocal economic dependence between trading partners and different economies. However, globalization also has its disadvantages, which need to be addressed now. Many people feel out of place in a world that has become too vast. They fear that only one dominant culture will survive in the world, leaving no space for local identities. Therefore, our focus should be on glocalization or slowbalization. Major challenges, such as climate change, managing the Earth, energy and raw materials, require international cooperation. However, to bring about a sense of urgency in people, we should invest in storytelling. Stories resonate more with people than dry summaries of facts, figures, statistics and tables. The future is now!

Products and Services for the Elderly

Although the elderly are increasingly active and want to keep up with younger generations for much longer, they will still desire products tailored to their needs and limitations. Ageing will bring major changes to product and package design. The eyesight of older consumers demands clearer colour schemes. So we will see fewer pastel colours being used in the packaging for food and other supermarket items. Bottles, cans and food packages should be redesigned to allow people to open them with less muscle power. Already, there's a list of items that older consumers use to open packaging: pincers, screwdrivers and scissors. Teeth are no longer used to open packages containing snacks.

The elderly also have the time and the money to travel. India's rapidly growing tourism industry should adapt to the needs of elderly tourists, both domestic and foreign. Ageing is also creating lots of jobs abroad for young Indians. In Portugal, many young Indians and Nepalese work in the tourism and healthcare sectors. They send remittances back home or invest their savings to build homes in India, where they return after they have made enough money. Ageing Europe, Japan, China and Korea might need millions of young Indians to take over the jobs of their retired citizens. After all, not all jobs can be performed by robots.

Young Indians can also invent and manufacture helpful products for the elderly. For example, the ATTO is an Israeli-designed, Chinese-made foldable electric mobility scooter that enables elderly and disabled people to travel and move through museums, cities, shopping malls, temples and mosques. However, pavements should also be made accessible to this growing army of elderly citizens. In the past, older people stayed at home, but now they travel and lead a mobile lifestyle. Part-time living is also becoming common among them, where they spend part of the year in one place and the rest in another.

More Spiritual People

According to the most recent statistics, people are becoming increasingly spiritual. The number of adherents to major religions is growing relatively faster than the world population, while the number of non-religious people and atheists is stagnating. According to the UN the annual growth rate of non-religious people (0.8 per cent) and atheists (0.2 per cent) is far lower than the growth of the world population (1.2 per cent). Yet other sources claim that the number of non-religious people is actually increasing all over the world.

Although people say that they belong to a certain religious

movement, they experiment more often with spiritual and religious elements of other faiths and denominations as well. This aligns with the individualization trend in society. The automatic adoption of the belief of one's parents disappeared at the start of the 21st century, at least in large parts of the Western world. Religion is increasingly becoming a conscious and personal choice. The young do not only strive for a respectable image and lifestyle, but also choose a suitable moral attitude, a political viewpoint (or an opinion about politics) and a philosophical vision. If the call of the latter is not compelling enough, they simply explore bits and pieces of other religions. Such an extensive mix-and-match affair ultimately unites the varied religious elements. A statue of Mary in one corner of the living room doesn't need to be at odds with a Buddha or totem pole in another corner. Such individualization is also the result of pragmatism. Faith has to fit into the schedule of the busy world citizen. Religious practice has to compete with a busy job and an equally busy social and cultural life. You cannot focus on praying, meditation or yoga if your phone beeps all the time.

Again, people may consider themselves part of a religious movement, but this does not necessarily mean that they support every view of the movement or its leadership. For instance, many Catholics, straight and gay alike, despise the former pope's opinions on homosexuality. However, they still consider themselves Catholic. Religious leaders, therefore, should be aware that the broader democratization trend has also reached religious institutions. Authoritarian leaders who refuse to acknowledge people's desire for freedom in determining their own beliefs and defining their moral and ethical well-being will lose support. Take Iran, where the younger generation despises the current clergy and seeks a completely different version of Islam than that preached by the Iranian religious and political leaders. Next to the trend towards individualization, there is a simultaneous trend in the opposite direction—a shift towards group formation. We see, for example, a tendency among many young Hindus and Muslims to form their own identities based on the faith of their ancestors, often as a response to the worldwide tensions between religious groups. The future of religion will, in large part, depend on the balance between individualization and group formation. Perhaps Emperor Akbar's idea of a unified world religion will finally materialize.

Believing in 'Something'

All over the world, many people no longer believe in God but in 'something'. This is particularly true in northwest Europe and on the east and west coasts of the US. In large parts of the world, religion has never really left. Spirituality in many regions is, in fact, encapsulated in citizenship. If you trip over, strangers will help you back on your feet. Citizenship is spirituality, and you don't need a god for that. God is in the citizens and in the way we interact with one another. This shift has had consequences for formal religious structures and institutions.

Many churches in Europe have emptied over the last few decades; people in the US also attend church less often than they used to. In India, it's a similar case. More and more people visit temples, mosques or churches only during holidays. The democratization of religion means they can pray at home as well. However, many people don't pray anymore but meditate or organize their own rituals to connect with the spiritual world. In the West, they are called 'Christmas Christians'. Maybe the Indian equivalents could be 'Diwali Hindus' or 'Eid Muslims'.

In the coming years, religion will be expressed more explicitly. We will see elements of various religions more emphatically on our streets. Headscarves and burqas will face competition from crosses, bindis, yarmulkes, magical gemstones, pentagrams and more. The Buddha also gels well with our modern lifestyle. We see his statues everywhere—in restaurants, garden centres, interior design shops and so on. The reason the Buddha is so appealing to the general public is, first and foremost, his appearance. People enjoy looking at his serene face. It brings them inner peace and offers respite from the rat race. The Buddha is immensely popular because he has a high tactile quotient. The tealights and cheerful colours of Tibetan Buddhism feature well in lifestyle magazines, as does the sober, minimalist design associated with Japanese Zen Buddhism. In New York, there is now a community of Buddhist Jews. We are going to see more such combinations emerge. Several Indian gurus have given spiritual guidance to many foreigners over the past 40–50 years. Today, wiser Indians can find ways to create and market spiritual guidance in this hi-tech, fast-moving world. A modern, well-connected human being has to process the same amount of information every three months that their grandparents processed in a lifetime. That's indeed a lot to deal with. As a result, most burnouts in the West today are occurring among Generation Z. Yoga, meditation, better sleep and an information diet might help mitigate this issue. Perhaps a new Indian guru will find a way to deal with this era of loneliness. Many Indian migrants abroad are lonely—and they are not alone in this. People drown in work and often forget to live. Many souls die as early as 20, but the physical body is buried or cremated at 70. There is thus definitely a market for a new Bhagwan!

Creolization Everywhere

With increasing migration and globalization, we are witnessing a worldwide pluralization of the religious landscape. In colonial times, Christianity was spread across the globe by fervent missionaries. Since the migration of people from former colonies and economic migrants heading to Europe and America, religions such as Buddhism, Hinduism, Sikhism and Islam are no longer considered exotic. These religions are becoming deeply embedded in Western religious life and are now accessible to people who traditionally did not belong to these religious movements. In practice, globalization doesn't always mean that one religion is completely replaced by another, as happened during the era of the Silk Road. Different religions, including Hinduism, Buddhism, Islam and Zoroastrianism, travelled far and wide along the Silk Road, which allowed people to trade one religion for another. Now, they blend all religious principles. We therefore call this the Age of Créolization. This concept is derived from the French word *Créole*, which was the name given to describe the hybrid French-mixed cultures and peoples that evolved in the French colonies. Today, Créolization is happening everywhere.

It is evident when Indians marry non-Indians, when Indian musical instruments are combined with Western ones (as the Beatles did), when Indian-origin artists like Freddie Mercury of Queen conquer the world, or when Indo-Western fashion garners worldwide appreciation, as it did with the works of the late Indian designer Rohit Bal.

The Contact between Various Religions Ensures Mutual Influence and Adaptation

The branch of Buddhism practised in the Western world is a decidedly Western form of this teaching, but at the same time, we see that many Buddhist notions have seeped into the religious consciousness of Christians. Finally, there is a noticeable tendency across all religions towards religious hybrids, ecumenical movements and worldwide ethical standards, even though individual contradictions and 'schisms' may initially prevail.

Incidentally, hybrid forms of religion have been common for a long time in China and Japan. People in these countries traditionally do not have an 'either-or' attitude towards religion, but rather an 'and-and' attitude. It is often said that the Japanese 'are born Shinto, married as Christians and buried as Buddhists', which can be taken quite literally. Marriage ceremonies generally follow Christian traditions while burial rituals are Buddhist. Only 30 per cent of the Japanese population considers themselves belonging to a specific denomination, although participation in certain Buddhist and Shinto rituals is extremely high. The custom of visiting the graves of ancestors on certain days is honoured by 90 per cent of all Japanese, and three-quarters have a Buddhist or Shinto altar in their houses. The fact that so few Japanese consider themselves members of a specific denomination is rooted in their experience with these religions. Buddhism is often associated with the lucrative funeral industry, Shinto with the military state, and the new religious movements have become suspect following the 1995 Tokyo subway sarin attack by the Aum Shinrikyo sect.

I Don't Believe in God Anymore, but I Do Miss Him

More people than ever are creating their own mini-faiths, often blending traditional religious elements, scientific information and mysticism. The way we regard new technology also has something sacred about it, even religious. A young scientist in Silicon Valley recently said to me: 'I don't believe in God, but I do miss Him. Who is going to tell me how far science can go? Within five years, the computer will be as smart as a human being. In 2085, the first robot will win the Nobel Prize. Will they still listen to us, or will we end up as slaves to our own technology?'

As mentioned, many believe in 'something' between Heaven and Hell. This 'something' can be a god, but it could also be something spiritual. In countries such as China, the fall of communism has made way for religion. The way Christians respond to this shift can have significant political implications. Christian missionaries have set their sights on this densely populated area, particularly following their success in South Korea and South Vietnam, where large parts of the population have converted to Christianity in recent decades. In 2008, the Chinese government announced that a majority of Chinese identify as religious again. But what kind of religiosity does the government mean? We think the Chinese are exploring their old spiritual roots and returning to the values of Confucius—the spiritual founder of the Chinese nation.

New Mythos

Religious symbols, such as a cross on a chain around the neck, are reappearing in public, even within atheist or agnostic circles. Every person has a need for both logos (for rational matters, such as science, technology and the economy) and mythos (for inspiration, religion and spirituality). Non-religious people can find their mythos in art, nature, sex or other spiritual sources. The elites in the West flirt with Buddhism: one will find statues of the Buddha in many wealthy households. At the same time, it is traditionally true that in times of great technological and scientific progress, there is an automatic resurgence of religion. The very moment people start doing things they once thought were governed by God—flying in an aeroplane or travelling to the moon—they begin to wonder if there is more between Heaven and Earth. Now that we are increasingly successful in tampering with our bodies and lives, and with all sorts of artificial procedures that can enhance our physique and extend our life expectancy, we start asking ourselves where life emerged from and what happens when it ends. It is certainly true that we can now postpone the end. Once we become older, when will the moment come when we do not die anymore? With the gifts of medical science and genetic technology, when can we replace, renew or give new impulses to parts of our bodies so that we live longer? If we automate death out of our lives, is there still a God? If women can soon have children without male intervention, what will the consequences be for the balance between the sexes? People are seeking answers to these questions in religion.

Believing in Spirits

However, a greater belief in spirits goes deeper. It is also an answer to the continuing desire (even among non-believers) for spirituality and a certain contact or communication with 'the other side'. This explains the increase in mediums, fortune tellers and spiritual leaders. Fortune telling is becoming modernized, where one can have their horoscope drawn by computer. Talking to trees, mice and the like is not favoured by the younger generations, who find it all too airy-fairy. However, Eastern healing methods such as acupuncture, shiatsu and acupressure have a growing following. The use of new mind-altering substances is also on the rise and will become a permanent part of our lifestyle in the future. Traditionally, the West has had an alcohol culture; migration has brought the West into contact with people from drug cultures. In the West, people drink a beer or a glass of wine with friends and discuss business over meals where the wine flows. Hence, alcohol is the lubricant of bonding. In other cultures, drugs are the lubricant. In Yemen, people chew on *khat* with their friends and business acquaintances; in Arabic countries, they share a water pipe; in ancient China, opium was consumed. The indigenous people of South America used drugs obtained from a variety of plants to contact the spirit world. Brazilian religious cults, such as Candomblé and Umbanda—a blend of Catholicism and rituals from Indian and African religions—which are now growing worldwide, also make use of drugs. At the start of the church service, people drink a cup of a bitter, hallucinatory herbal mixture, and then the rhythmic mass gets underway.

Drugs and Spirituality

We live in an age when alcohol and drug cultures are mingling and the use of new artificial drugs such as ecstasy is growing. A comparison with the ancient Greek and West Indian cultures, where drugs were used to induce a trance and connect with the world of spirits and gods, is not out of place.

Perhaps in the new, more spiritual world, we shall need a new mind-enhancing drug mix suited to the current age, its population and trends. Maybe it will be a new artificial drug with an alcohol flavour?

Today, the number of atheists, nihilists and agnostics is decreasing. This group of non-believers can, without losing face, embrace Buddhism or the new multi-religions like Brazilian Candomblé and Umbanda. Christianity is making a comeback among the youth in the West, Africa and Asia, although in different forms and variations. At the same time, Catholicism is losing ground in South America, while Europe increasingly admires Evangelicals.

Towards a New Orthodoxy

In the early 21st century, we are confronted with a revival of orthodoxy. This revival can be attributed, on one hand, to the increasing polarization on the political-religious world stage, and on the other, as a reaction to the uncertainty that modern life in a 'risk society' brings with it. This is certainly true in 'secular' Europe. Even though a decreasing number of Europeans are members of a church, the traditional religious forms will not simply disappear in 21st-century Europe. In the United States, Christian fundamentalism has been an important force for much longer, and with the emergence of Islam in Western Europe, this trend will also appear in Europe. One advantage that the old churches have is their extensive management infrastructure, recognizable icons and authentic authority. In this age of storytelling and renewed interest in history, old religious stories can be effectively retold, particularly if new media are used for this purpose. The moderate Christian denominations (such as the liberal Protestants) will become smaller or even disappear in the coming years, while the more conservative and orthodox sects will gain ground. The appeal of conservative churches lies in their total dedication, irrefutable belief and a unique lifestyle, as described by Dean Kelley in his book *Why Conservative Churches are Growing*, which deals with the American situation.

The growth of religious conservatism can be partly explained as a populist revolt against the power of a secular elite (particularly baby boomers), who still have the reins firmly in their hands in Europe due to their high level of education. A similar tendency towards orthodoxy can be seen in the Islamic world. Here, it is primarily the confrontation with modernity that drives people towards the certainties of traditional belief systems. Brazil also has its Evangelical orthodox churches. For example, the Assemblies of God had a membership of 8.4 million in the 2000 census, which is about 4.5 per cent of the total population. The Assemblies of God is a response to a less appealing Catholic Church and includes some pre-Christian, Afro-Brazilian elements that are absent in Catholicism.

Converts and New Religions

The number of converts will grow in various directions: Muslims who become Catholics, Protestants who become Hindus, Catholics who become Muslims and Christians who become Buddhists. Humanism will only have a future if it no longer labels itself—as it does now—as an alternative to religion. It has to coexist with religion, and only then will it have a future market. Eras such as the current one, marked by rapid scientific and technological change, are times that often witness the emergence of new religions. The Sikh religion in India arose in such a period, and so did Buddhism. It is quite possible that a new religion may now appear, attracting a large number of followers.

This could be a sect (as yet obscure) in California that suddenly breaks through in the West, similar to what happened with the Bhagwan cult on a limited scale. It could also be a new politician or pop star who suddenly achieves prophetic or almost divine status—much like Donald Trump in the US, Xi Jinping in China and Narendra Modi in India.

In Conclusion: For Everyone a God

With the increasing speed of life and the development of technology, everyone will seek their own way to find a counterbalance in life—whether by returning to orthodox beliefs or by creating a new blend of everything and in between.

14

Towards the Economy of Happiness

It's early Monday morning. Deng and Ram log in for the virtual meeting with other members of their team, who are joining from several places around the world. Everyone just stays at home around their big dinner table, and suddenly through a three-dimensional projection, they see the 3D images of their colleagues appearing around the table. Whoever is still a bit sleepy (because of the time difference) is dressed by the computer in a suit and tie. Everybody can look each other in the eye as if they were physically sitting together at the same table. They don't really have to travel anymore to meet other people for work.

Virtual meetings arose as one of the solutions to reduce energy use, decrease pollution and prevent global warming—a trend that emerged at the beginning of the century. They meet, exchange views and ideas for about an hour and make decisions for their company for the coming week. Afterwards, everybody says goodbye, logs off and starts working on their individual tasks. Jim remembers that there was a time and age when they had to physically meet all colleagues. People voluntarily travelled for hours and endured traffic jams, delayed flights, overcrowded trains and other inconveniences, in order to reach work. Now everything has changed. The low-energy economy of the 2020s stimulates people to travel less, and if they do, they use cars that are no longer fuelled by oil or gas. People are enjoying this shift. Solar energy and nuclear energy, in particular, have made life more secure and peaceful in Europe than ever before. Although they have not really stopped global warming, everybody feels good about their new lifestyle and the fact that they do not have to sponsor terrorism anymore. Through their VirtualMes, they are recommended to book a holiday trip to the Emirates, where a wonderful new art exhibition will be launched and where the beaches lure them. Why not? They have earned enough CO_2-emission bonus points to deserve this trip. Go east, my friends, go east!

Abraham Maslow revolutionized psychology in 1943 by elevating the discipline to a new and far deeper understanding of what it means to be human. Instead of trying to make sense of the insanity of broken minds, he explored the sanity that made people exemplary. One of the findings from Maslow's studies was that there were layers of human needs. If basic needs are not met, there is a tendency to ignore higher needs. Maslow's Hierarchy of Needs is often portrayed as a pyramid.

Maslow's Hierarchy of Needs:

1. Self-Actualization Needs (full potential, spirituality).
2. Self-Esteem Needs (self-respect, personal worth, autonomy).
3. Love and Belonging Needs (love, friendship, comradeship).
4. Safety Needs (security; protection from harm).
5. Physiological Needs (food, sleep, stimulation, activity).

Welfare Systems

Many countries have some kind of welfare system. This meant that until the 1990s, many governments, particularly in Northern Europe, increasingly transferred activities from the private sector to the public sector. The welfare state enjoyed a golden era. Childcare, which had been traditionally handled by parents, became a task of the government. The same happened with the care of the elderly: grandmothers were put into state-run elderly people's or nursing homes, no longer cared for by their families. State involvement is now becoming a thing of the past. Governments are withdrawing from these areas—largely due to financial reasons—and the welfare state is being shrunk. A trend can be discerned, which moves away from governmental involvement towards collective opinion-forming, signalling the end of the welfare state. Today, we see governments returning to the economic stage and investing largely in banks to save the economic system. In the meantime, there is also a noticeable individualization taking place. Young people, in particular, are clearly showing that they want to carve their own ways, no longer allowing themselves to be influenced by the spirit of the times. Instead, they are making their own choices. They value being individuals more than belonging to a group, although they prefer to maintain family relationships. Young people serve as a good measure of how individualization is proceeding.

New Citizenship

Family will play an increasingly important role, while the government will move further into the background (arguably, it will be forced to do so). This will give society a totally different look. A new form of collectivism will arise, partly fuelled by successive technological developments.

Thanks to interactive media, we should collectively keep abreast of global events and form our own opinions. For society, this means that power is now shared among various organizations. This is not a pleasant prospect for the social elite. As self-organization becomes more important, the power of the elite will diminish. This new society is characterized by Harlan Cleveland, the American political scientist and public executive, as the 'nobody-in-charge' society. The internet and the international monetary market are prime examples of this trend. With each new generation of information technology (that will happen every two to three years), our society will become less centrally managed. The reason for this is that the products that people buy and exchange will become increasingly 'virtual'. When a physical product is purchased, there is a change in ownership. However, if an idea, a vision or an opinion is sold, both the original and new owners possess it. Cleveland argues: 'If it's a thing, it's exchanged; if it's information, it's shared.' The transformation we are currently experiencing is due to the fact that the most important source of assistance—the Internet—is shared by billions of people.

Ideal Image is No Longer Realistic

The ideal image of an independent person with a protected private life, unique thoughts, knowledge and opinions is no longer realistic. George Orwell saw this as a threat to the individual. Susan Greenfield, an English scientist with a particular interest in the workings of the mind, argues that the human mind is the personification of a person's experiences. She asserts that the more experiences a person gains and gives personal meaning to, the higher their status and importance. She adds that information technology has an unprecedented influence on our experiences, enabling people to shape their minds as they see fit.

This leads to a collective ego. Terrorism, whether caused by the Nazis or Al Qaeda, is not the terror of people who do not know what they are doing, but of people with a strong group mentality and a clear set of values. The cause of World War II is often attributed to the fact that, after World War I, the German people were unable to exist as private individuals—a condition that was cleverly exploited. The communists, too, believe in the supreme power of the collective. In the 20th century, the private ego defeated the collective ego, but in the 21st century, the reverse will be true. In their essay *Globalization: blessing or curse?* the Dutch authors couple this phenomenon with globalization. Initially only associated with multinationals such as Coca-Cola and McDonald's, globalization now also refers to the way we define citizenship. Ultimately, the latter is a consequence of the former. Smit comments: 'People witnessed a government that was constantly retreating, that handed over many tasks and responsibilities to private enterprises and thus ultimately became employed by private businesses. The citizens, on the other hand, had elected that government in a democratic manner and now saw their position as citizens transformed into one of consumers; then they became, through a non-democratic position in corporate life, the producers of the products and services for private enterprises. In addition, necessary steps were taken to transfer healthcare and pensions to the private sector, which resulted in a further depreciation of the role of government, while the citizens were given greater responsibility for their health and pension provisions.'

Citizens: Investors in Themselves

Thus, citizens have become investors in themselves in the long run. An awareness has been created that citizens are now producers, consumers and investors. As a result, the idea of citizenship has changed, and it's no surprise that there are hardly any organizations capable of representing this new citizenship in an effective manner. Citizens are, according to Smit, eagerly searching for ways to oppose the private sector and government, as they have lost faith in these institutions due to pay-rise restrictions and the 'grab everything you can' culture. There is also a growing lack of interest in politics. Who should we vote for? Who can we trust? Who will stand up for the rights of the citizens? Smit believes that citizens will have to join forces to combat the effects of globalization.

If I connect this opinion to the ones mentioned earlier, I can conclude that technology will play an important role in the process. Smit quotes the Italian philosopher Gianni Vattimo: 'The new popular culture of the mass media has not led to increased transparency, either in the political or economic sense; it has led largely to greater chaos and disorder... It is precisely chaos that offers the best chances for renewal and change.' Few would dispute that citizens collectively can achieve a lot. The fact that this process has been underway for some time is evident in the impotence of politics, as we shall discuss later. Citizens have lost faith in old politicians, who are now being replaced by 'political pop stars'. The citizen is thus gradually taking the lead.

Soft Power

The British could build their empire by making their language so appealing and easy to learn that it became widely spoken, connecting people from all over the world. The US also used its soft power to establish dominance. Hollywood films, American music, jeans, caps and other articles of American fashion conquered the world. Meditation and yoga are further examples of soft power.

The superpowers of the future will need to use their soft power to become more popular and be loved globally. India, for instance, can use Bollywood and Indo-Western fashion styles.

Thanks to these developments, we now see the growth of 'soft power'. Soft power is the ability to influence others by gaining respect for one's aims and methods so that voluntary participation replaces the use of force. The term is attributed to the American political analyst Joseph Nye, who defines it as 'the ability of a country to persuade other nations to participate in its aims without applying any force'. Soft power is not limited to nation-states. Many non-governmental organizations (NGOs) exercise this power. It is further stimulated by the rapid growth of the internet, resulting in the emergence of online political platforms.

People thus use the internet for social aims, and the web has become a political platform. The networks that arise share a common cultural identity, religious beliefs, political views, corporate ethics or social values. Many of these networks will remain small, while others will grow into large organizations with considerable economic and political power. In the future, these networks will become more important than geographical networks.

The power of the bloggers is interesting in this context. The internet is increasingly becoming a part of the regular world, providing access to vast information. Opinion formers will often be more influenced by bloggers than ever before. Bloggers are individuals who provide commentary on national and global events through their weblogs. They do not have any media backing and may not come from a journalism background, which allows them to operate freely and independently. The opinions of the bloggers are valued and widely accessible. As a result, they have become a challenging force—a flea on the hide of the existing authoritative media.

The phenomenon of soft power will be strengthened by the way work is organized. The traditional office, now 150 years old, has had its best time. It is expected that very soon, a third of the workforce will work from home. An increasing number of people work as freelancers—independent entrepreneurs—and will not be dependent on a company for their identity and career. The number of managers will likely decrease by 90 per cent in the next 10 years. This development is partly due to the fact that many employees are now extensions of computer-managed production systems. Robots and other machines are changing the nature of work. Already 35 per cent of telephone contacts with call centres are handled automatically. Many jobs will disappear, but new ones will emerge. Machines have to be installed and programmed, until these 'second order' jobs are also automated. This will result in a 'black box' economy, in which a considerable portion of work is automated, and people will need to adapt if they wish to continue working. The most stable sector now is the care industry. After the industrial and information economies, we are now entering the 'care' economy. People are prepared to pay for interpersonal care, making medical care, education and personal services the most important job generators for the future.

Back to the Shareholder Democracy

The traditional left–right division in politics will be replaced by a conflict between 'old' and 'new' politics. Influential people who remain distant and infused with corporate thinking will be replaced by icons chosen by the citizens themselves. This will result in a transition from corporate democracy to shareholder democracy.

The Rise of Political Pop Stars

In all democracies, many voters no longer identify with traditional party politics. Citizens recognize problems and expect politicians to provide solutions, as they believe they are not capable of doing so themselves. However, they have often been disappointed.

Now that citizens believe traditional politicians are incapable of addressing important issues, there is a healthy market for 'one-issue parties' in several countries. These are new political parties that focus on a single issue, have charismatic leaders in charge and profile themselves extensively in the media. There's a growing sense of alienation that leads to a rising demand for new heroes, new gods, idols—figures who are frequently created but have increasingly short shelf lives. They are people who have become folk heroes in ways different from those of traditional politicians and are now venturing into politics. The one-issue politicians of the future will position themselves with strong personal profiles. People who are already well-known through television will enter politics, and the personality cult surrounding tomorrow's politicians will become more prominent than it is today. If this trend continues, countries will see more coalitions between 'old' and 'new' parties. The new political pop stars will combine left-wing and right-wing issues successfully. The traditional left–right debate has become completely meaningless. Voters are better attracted to political pop stars who can appeal to both sides by addressing a mix of left and right issues in the elections. This is already evident in various countries. Donald Trump turned the Republican Party from a white, elitist–capitalist party into a blue-collar, multicultural workers' party. In many countries of the Global South, Generation Z votes for new political pop stars whom they trust more than the regular politicians. In Africa, the same is happening in countries like Nigeria and Senegal. The youth demands their future now (education, job security, homes, etc.) and refuses to wait. The CIA warns of the Z-Bellion—the rebellion of Generation Z against the current economic and political establishments in democracies around the world.

'The personal in politics' will be the motto of future politics. In the past, the private lives of politicians used to be irrelevant. Journalists knew that John F. Kennedy had affairs but did not write about it—it was considered improper. However, the private lives of politicians will become more important than ever as part of their appeal to voters. Politicians who go off the tracks and admit their failures will become popular, just like the former US president Bill Clinton, who was threatened with impeachment but held on to his position thanks to his popularity with the public.

Social Debate

Social debate about important matters takes on new forms under the political pop stars. The gulf between politics and citizens is narrowed. New networks of people and organizations, seeking to reach agreements on various issues, arise in different places and forms. An example of this new form is the '21st Century Town Meeting' developed by AmericaSpeaks—an institution that organizes various debates in the United States. This model became widely known during the discussions on the redevelopment of Lower Manhattan following the attack on the World Trade Center on 11 September 2001. The climax of the debate was held in a conference centre in New York, where 4,500 people participated. During the meeting, the Lower Manhattan Development Corporation and the Port Authority presented six plans for the redevelopment of the area. The meeting ended with a declaration rejecting all six proposals. At the same time, the developer was given accurate feedback concerning the requirements for the new buildings. Thus the rebuilding of the Twin Towers got underway after the foundation stone was laid in July 2004.

An attractive option is to combine public actions, as described here, with the suggestion made by Jean-François Rischard of the World Bank to create global issues networks (GINs). A network composed of governments, companies, private organizations and action groups should be formed to tackle major global problems. These groups would lay down standards and norms, such as for a responsible attitude towards the environment. Those who do not comply with these standards would be publicly humiliated by the media. Rischard argues that while reaching agreements and ratifying international treaties often take years, if not decades, such networks could operate much more quickly. Furthermore, citizens would identify more easily with these networks, which focus on a concrete problem than with a world government or other abstract bureaucratic institutions. It is an idealistic and somewhat haphazard plan, which Rischard admits, but he also believes the time is ripe for it. He states: 'Deep down, people feel that the way in which the world is developing has enormously positive sides, but also terribly negative ones.'

Knowledge about how to organize such debates is growing. Larry Susskind, professor at MIT and frequent author, emphasizes that such participatory processes do not necessarily need to result in any unanimity about the outcome. As an authority in the field of 'consensus building', he highlights that consensus should be seen as agreement on a proposal that may not be the best option for everybody, but can be supported by as many people as possible. This allows people from different backgrounds and with different motives to participate in the debate. Collective opinion forming has a future. Wim Smit also couples this with globalization: 'Thanks to globalization, almost everything is open to borderless debate.'

No Welfare State: Family Life or Framily Life and Frolleagues Take Over Social Security

In the 21st century, the citizen is in the lead. As a result, family life will take on a new guise. An important change is the introduction of the 'rush-hour family', which primarily comprises children and their elderly parents. This concept also includes taking care of childless aunts or elderly uncles whose children have emigrated abroad. We also see the rise of the *framily*—a self-created family of friends—and *frolleagues*—colleagues who become close friends. The rush-hour family will become the cornerstone of society. Their lifestyle and the way they organize their days will be different from that of 'normal' families. So, what will change? During the week, life will be organized as efficiently as possible. Technology and all sorts of convenience products will be used extensively so that the many activities—the rush hour—can be managed. For example, during the week, there will seldom be time to cook elaborate meals. So ready-made meals from the supermarket, easily prepared food or takeaways (which are rapidly proliferating in large cities) will be used frequently.

The nature of takeaways will also evolve. There will be kilo restaurants—a sort of takeaway where the food is prepared in large dishes and customers fill a plastic dish, paying per kilo. Whether they take a kilo of potatoes, pasta or rice mixed with sauce, the price per kilo remains the same. Such restaurants already exist in Brazil and New York, but now, thanks to ethnic entrepreneurship in large cities, they are making their appearance in Europe. They are a godsend for rush-hour families: fast, cheap and healthy. The wok restaurant also satisfies this need.

In contrast, weekends will become an oasis of peace and hospitality. Elaborate meals will be on the menu for the rush-hour family and their friends. Slow cooking will be the norm. People will cocoon, garden, spend time in the open air and also take part in the nightlife of the cities. In short, weekends will become mini-holidays. The strict division between work and holiday will thus blur. As more people from the higher social classes own two houses, which allow them to experience two lifestyles simultaneously in the new experience economy, they will be able to spend their relaxed weekends either in their countryside home or in their city apartment. This will mean that people take fewer traditional holidays as the energy and impulses that people get from a vacation will be integrated into their daily lives.

A Call to Ethics

In this new era, when there are not only global possibilities but also threats coming from everywhere—German sociologist Ulrich Beck refers to this as the 'risk society'—we hear a worldwide call for more ethics.

With increasing globalization, there is a danger that people with evil intentions can find refuge in places where laws or their enforcement are lacking. Think, for example, of the dumping of toxic waste, expired medications in Africa or child labour in South Asia. The development of new technologies raises different ethical issues, such as those about stem cell research. If we don't address these concerns, we will wind up with an immoral kind of 'Wild West' hurting everyone in the process. But which authority can or wants to take on such a heavy moral responsibility?

New World Values

Not only will values and standards become more important in the future, but Nout Wellink, former president of the Dutch Central Bank (De Nederlandsche Bank), also asks us to consider the changing values and standards in these times of economic and political power shifts. He points out that: 'In China, the government has a much more prominent position than it does here. The government reaches into the private life of the average Chinese—something we would not accept in the West. On the contrary, we want to reduce the role of government even more. China also has a completely different idea about democracy and the notion of human rights.'

The fact that Wellink is right is confirmed by this quote from the *China Daily*, defending the country against criticism of its human rights and Olympics: 'We (the Chinese) have implemented the biggest human right there is: we are now able to feed 1.3 billion citizens.'

To some extent, we must agree. The World Bank estimates

that between 1990 and 2024, at least 400 million Chinese have been lifted from poverty. Since Deng Xiaoping's economic reforms began around 1978, extreme poverty has disappeared and the average Chinese enjoys an acceptable living standard.

With that comes a certain level of security and peace— no small feat! The same happened in India, thanks to the liberalization of the economy by the visionary leader Manmohan Singh.

In the past century, the Western world has indulged in the arrogance of thinking that it is ahead of the rest of the world. It believed it could export democracy, Western values and culture to all corners of the world.

However, with the increasing power of autocratic countries like China, the West may need to compromise somewhat on its seemingly obvious values and standards. China is a giant—one that, in the foreseeable future, will most likely own one-third of the world economy through its visionary investments in the Global South and New Silk Road. This giant is thus not prepared to simply trade its values and standards for Western ones.

Anything in this respect that applies to China also goes for countries like Russia and oil-rich countries like the UAE in the Middle East. A major acceleration in the transfer of wealth over the past five years has shifted trillions of petrodollars from oil consumers to producers, altering the world's balance of power. Western ideas about civil society, the environment and women's rights may well be replaced by new sets of values.

We also see this shift in the business world today. In the sale of luxury carmaker Aston Martin by Ford, Sharia-compliant structures were followed as required by Kuwaiti investors.

A Re-evaluation of Democracy

Democracy is the political system at the heart of Western culture. However, fewer and fewer people in the West are willing to fight for the values of democracy. Meanwhile, in countries that are new to democracy, there are growing doubts about the benefits of this political system.

In Russia, many people value stability more than democracy. With today's global competitiveness, many companies are all too willing to *kowtow* to authoritarian regimes to gain new business. Paying lip service to values such as human rights is considered bothersome and counterproductive.

An Indian Minister—normally proud to live in the 'world's biggest democracy'—once lamented that he sometimes wished for the kind of fast, uncomplicated decision-making processes the Chinese have.

In a democracy like the Philippines, rising food prices (dictated by global markets), incompetent governments and rampant corruption have made a farce of the institutions that allegedly serve the people. On the other hand, great progress has been made using the Chinese model. Its increasingly open economic system and closed political one seem attractive to many Third World countries. Personal happiness is not defined in terms of free elections, a free press or freedom of assembly; it is defined in terms of opportunities for economic advancement and stability.

According to recent polls taken by social scientists at the World Values Survey, people in Moldova, a poor but formally democratic country, are among the least happy in the world. On the other hand, the inhabitants of the People's Republic of China, a one-party state, are among the most optimistic. Maybe the West should get used to the idea that not everybody in the world believes democracy is the best political system.

The question for the West in coming years will not be which countries will open up to or adopt the Western model of parliamentary government. There is no question that many things can be done more easily in an authoritarian system. 'Who wouldn't prefer to do business in a country that doesn't have free labour unions? Who would pass up the chance to reconstruct entire cities without the public getting to have its say?' asks prominent author Ian Buruma, who advises against preaching purism in matters of democracy.

A New World

With the rise of private wealth, we foresee an increase in public poverty. The internet makes us all free citizens in a 'nobody-in-charge society'. Through the internet, everyone can participate in policymaking, which diminishes the power of the elite, as they are no longer the ones who 'know it all'. One-issue parties and the personal lives of politicians will become more important. Western countries will increasingly have to share their values with emerging powers like China, Brazil, India, Russia and the Middle East. Western ideals may soon be replaced by new sets of Eastern values. Even democracy, long considered the best form of government, will face scrutiny.

Never Enough Time

In this era when people never seem to have enough time, dealing with new techniques, worldwide competition and ageing, they place an ever-greater emphasis on health and wellness. Citizens are becoming more vocal and demand greater control over their own bodies. Healthcare and wellness must therefore be increasingly tailored to individual needs. New medical developments and large integrated relaxation centres offer these possibilities.

Wellness

The word 'wellness' is already used in German and other languages. It covers a mix of welfare, well-being, personal care, relaxation and loss of haste, and is virtually always coupled with water. Wellness centres are typically located in spas and health centres and include services such as water-based treatments in swimming pools, mud baths, physiotherapy, fitness, saunas, solaria, detoxification and other therapies. 'Relaxation' is the key. Wellness, in its strictest sense, is a way of managing stress. It has become one of the main pillars of life in the 21st century.

Seniors, in particular, with plenty of spare time and money, seek to live with minimum stress and maximum relaxation. So spas, thermal baths and other public facilities for wellness have a bright future in this market.

People will integrate wellness into their daily lives, with luxury bathrooms featuring all sorts of amenities to help them relax, such as baths, bubble baths, massaging shower heads, mini-saunas and solaria. In addition, they will regularly visit masseurs, physiotherapists (either specialized or general), beauty specialists and tanning studios. The modern sedentary lifestyle leads to weight gain, so more people want to exercise to stay fit. Children today are heavier than in the past due to the time they spend sitting in front of computers and television instead of running around and playing.

More sport and exercise will be essential to the wellness trend, even though plastic surgeons will frequently be consulted for weight reduction. Liposuction, liposculpture and other forms of fat removal by medical specialists will become common treatments for excess fat.

At the same time, people will seek greater contact with nature. We have lost this due to the hi-tech influences in our lives. People will garden more and visit natural sites. Eco-tourism is in, with people taking more walks through forests and along beaches. Nature reserves in the countryside, woods, lakes and beaches will have good times ahead, as long as they are made accessible for future generations.

Synchronicity

Synchronicity is an explanatory principle founded by Swiss psychiatrist Carl Jung (1875–1961). According to him, synchronicity explains 'meaningful coincidences', such as a beetle flying into his room while a patient was describing a dream about a scarab. He noted that the scarab is an Egyptian symbol of rebirth. Therefore, the precise moment of the beetle in the room and the scarab in the dream indicated a transcendental meaning—the patient needed to be liberated from her excessive rationalism. His notion of synchronicity is based on an acausal principle that links similar events by their meaningful coincidence in time, rather than through a sequential relationship. He claimed that there is a synchronicity between the mind and the phenomenal world of perception.

Jung coined the word to describe what he called 'temporally coincident occurrences of acausal events'. He variously described synchronicity as an 'acausal connecting principle', 'meaningful coincidence' and 'acausal parallelism'. He introduced the concept as early as the 1920s but only elaborated on it in 1951. It was a principle that Jung felt provided conclusive evidence for his ideas of archetypes and the collective unconscious. He saw it as a governing dynamic that underlies the whole of human experience and history—social, emotional, psychological and spiritual. Events that appear to be coincidental at first but are later found to be causally related are termed 'incoincident'. Jung believed that many experiences, which are coincidences in terms of causality, suggest the manifestation of parallel events or circumstances in terms of meaning, reflecting this governing dynamic.

At the beginning of the 21st century, his theory is more popular than ever. Bestselling books like *The Secret* are rooted in the principle of synchronicity.

Age of Aquarius

One of these days, the Age of Aquarius is supposed to begin, signalling the end of the current Age of Pisces. As mentioned earlier, astrology is more popular than ever, and millions of people are studying and anticipating this new age. Whether you believe in it or not is not really relevant. What is important is that so many people believe in this, which might make them, in terms of the theory of synchronicity, act differently than they did before. The estimated start date is believed to be sometime around the millennium, but its exact date is contested among astrologers, astronomers, theologians and others. However, millions claim that the effects of the Age of Aquarius are already being felt.

I can sense that an era has come to an end. The main issues of today and tomorrow—finance, energy, food, water, overpopulation and climate change—will need to be addressed in bold, new ways if humanity is to make this century the one that truly matters—the one in which we can either achieve what is necessary or perish and celebrate this as our last century. As optimists by nature, the authors passionately believe that we can tackle all these major challenges and harmonize the material and spiritual worlds.

Renewal

As mentioned, the new world order, with its 12 pillars of power, will definitely need new approaches to global governance and creativity. The impotent United Nations urgently needs to be replaced by a true World Government. The transition of power must be reflected in international institutions, and the evil aspects of human nature, such as greed, must be managed. If not, we'll experience many more crises than the current one in the international financial industry. Although states seem to be more popular now, this is only temporary. In the end, new ways of modern governance need to be designed—ways that align with people who are smart, who can share know-how and experiences both in real life and through the web. Renewal is not only a matter of economics or politics; it is also a matter of spirituality.

The key phrase for Aquarius is 'I Know', but that knowledge is not righteous, superior or exclusionary. It's a sort of wisdom that draws people together, for Aquarians are, above all else, social beings. They crave interaction with large groups of people, thriving in humanitarian and social causes, and in any situation where collective thought, innovation and cooperation are required. They tend to be eccentric and disdainful of tradition and, while they love magic and believe in the esoteric arts, they prefer to discover knowledge through scientific experimentation and exploration.

Technology is like a hobby for the 'water bearer'. Aquarians stockpile all the new gadgets on the market and are at ease in front of a computer or connected to a cell phone. Sure, they're trendy—they need to be at the forefront, in the midst of social action and up on the latest fads—but they also truly love other people and believe strongly in the independent spirit.

Aquarians are thus sociable, open-minded, innovative, eschewing tradition, scientific and technologically driven. If we extract these qualities from the individual and apply them to the world, we can see what the Aquarian Age is all about. We will loosen the ties of tradition and forge ahead in a cooperative effort to improve human relations and our relationship with the world around us. We will be respectful but also playfully, intelligently rebellious. We will admire and encourage individuality and embrace differences rather than fear them.

There's no way to know where the Age of Aquarius will lead us. Who knows what the world will be like in the year 4000? As science proves that we are all one race—that regardless of our colour or origin, we are all essentially the same beneath our skin—we will grow, change and learn to adapt to one another's cultural and individual differences. We have an opportunity to apply the most positive qualities of Aquarius—intellectual openness, humanitarianism and compassion for the environment—to making our world a more considerate, benevolent and tolerant place.

Finally Solving Major Political Problems

If the new age is as predicted by astrologers, this must be the time to finally resolve festering political issues in a bold, creative way. Quantum computing and AI will enable us to do this.

If states are eroding and becoming less important, as tribes of individuals form new coalitions and are happy with societies of their own making, why should we bother about the creation of an independent state for Tibetans, Kurds, Basques, Palestinians or other tribes who crave for their own state but don't have one? Maybe we should allow them to experiment with their own state. Later, when they are ready, they can decide whether to retain the state or dissolve it, just as others are moving away from conventional state concepts.

Reality Check

'Listen now to a further point: no moral thing has a beginning, nor does it end in death and obliteration. There is only a mixing and then a separating of what was mixed, but by mortal men these processes are named *beginnings*.'

The Greek philosopher Empedocles wrote these words a long time ago (BC 492–432) during the Age of Pisces. In BC 500, when the West (Europe) was not yet Christian and the Middle East was not yet Islamic, there was a certain tension between the two entities. As time passed, the concept of the 'East' changed occasionally for Westerners. During the Cold War (1945–1989), Russia was the 'Evil East'. However, in that period, the West did not really consider the Middle East, which had traditionally been viewed as the Evil East. Still, for the majority of history, tensions existed between the East and the West. Can we really change this now? Yes, we can.

Not Always Tensions between the East and the West

Such tensions were not always present. There were periods of cooperation and mutual positive influence—times when the Orient was held in high esteem by the West, and Western culture, science and societies were considerably influenced by the East. Think of the period between the end of the 19th century and the first quarter of the 20th century: Art Nouveau and later Art Deco were strongly inspired by the Middle East. There have been other such periods, even in pre-Christian and pre-Islamic times. The Macedonian king Alexander the Great adopted much from the Orient in his time. In those times, the East also cherished and preserved the Greek remains, monuments and knowledge (including mathematics) for the world, especially after the decline of the Greek civilization. I call these the 'mixing periods'. These periods of positive mutual images and influence in history are always interspersed by periods of mutual rejection, which resulted in wars and demonizing each other. I call these the 'division periods'. Both have their function—both are 'new beginnings', as defined by Empedocles.

Vertical Farms in Cities and a New Future for Farmers

During World War II, American soldiers in North Africa, who were fighting the Nazis there, needed fresh food daily. Shipping food from America to North Africa was dangerous, so the American army developed hydroponic food farming. Hydroponics is the technique of growing plants using a water-based nutrient solution rather than soil, and it can include an aggregate substrate or growing media such as vermiculite, coconut coir or perlite. Hydroponic production systems are now used by small farmers, hobbyists and commercial enterprises.

In Sweden, a huge vertical farm operating on hydroponics shows what the future of farming might look like. In India, half the food produced by farmers does not survive transportation to the cities. We interviewed hydroponics experts who suggest that a vertical farm with 100 floors, requiring only 100 × 100 metres of land, could provide enough vegetables daily for one million people. For example, in a city like Mumbai, with its current 21 million residents, 21 of these vertical farms, spread all over the city with short distribution channels and high-tech logistics, could supply the entire city with enough fresh vegetables every day. Such a vertical farm could be operated by a cooperative of farmers. What to do with the farmland that becomes available? Farmers could grow rice, potatoes, onions, wheat and other crops that cannot thrive in hydroponics. They might also build homes for youngsters on this land and sell them, or sell the land to industrial companies so that new factories could be built there.

Management of Anger

Not everybody can be a winner in the future. The technological revolution will rob many people of their jobs. Recently, I interviewed some postmen who were laid off. One of them was 62; he had been a postman all his life, delivering letters, postcards and small packages to people's homes. Now, he has lost his job because people prefer emails. He is angry and says: 'Because of you people and this damned technology, I am now out of my job.' There are many more like him.

How will we deal with the pent-up anger of people like this postman? The German philosopher Peter Sloterdijk argues that managing anger will be one of the major challenges of the future. I agree with him, and I'd like to add that managing boredom will be crucial as well. What should we do with all these people who are simply bored? Sloterdijk expresses his hope for a 'peaceful utilization of monotheistic energies'. He says: 'The greatest achievement of institutionalized Christianity is, to extend the metaphor, that it has given rise to a highly developed reactor technology. What in naïve hearts might easily spark combustive mania can, through ascetic and meditative practices and learnable forms of spiritual inquiry, be contained within a workable format.'

In Conclusion: The Future Is Now

The world has always been something of a salad bowl. Thanks to relocations and a continuing flow of migration, people in more regions are now accustomed to the presence of those from other nationalities, religions and ethnicities. It has not always turned out well; several ethnic wars have flared up in the Balkans, and in Northern Ireland, conflicts between Catholics and Protestants continue. In the Middle East, tensions between various tribes are part of everyday life. Despite this, we are entering a new age in history—one where a new global culture may emerge. The new world will have its winners and losers, just as the old world did.

A mix of private citizens taking the lead and public institutions will design the new forms of governance needed in the new world. There is a lot to be positive about but also a lot to worry about. Yet, nobody ever got anywhere with pessimism. So the best way to create new governance and manage anger is to do so with optimism.

A FISH NAMED FRED: BRINGING COLOUR AND JOY TO THE WORLD

A fish named Fred is on a mission to make the world a happier and more colourful place!

We have a strong following, especially among men who want to make a statement with their fashion choices. We've become a go-to brand for those who value individuality and self-expression— who want to stand out from the crowd. Whether you're looking for a new shirt, a pair of trousers or a unique accessory, *A fish named Fred* has something for every style-conscious man. 'Be proud, stand out!'

Who Is *A Fish Named Fred*?

Founded in 2011 by Rob Schalker and Martin van den Nouwland, *A fish named Fred* brings joy and vibrancy to the world. We specialize in unique men's clothing and accessories featuring bold designs, bright colours and playful textures. Our pieces are perfect for those who want to express themselves and stand out.

We are known for our distinctive design aesthetic and high quality. We use only the finest cotton and linen to ensure comfort and durability—our customers return season after season for long-lasting style. Each collection is inspired by a central theme, ranging from wild to practical, abstract to concrete. Fred and his team draw inspiration from nature, culture, art, history and technology, carefully selecting fabrics, colours, patterns and textures that bring the concept to life. Our shirts are made of

97 per cent Better Cotton, while blazers vary in fabric depending on the style.

The Creative Process

Each collection begins with a brainstorming session to come up with a compelling theme. This theme serves as the thread that ties the entire collection together. From there, we design custom prints and choose fabrics that match the aesthetic while ensuring quality and comfort. Every detail is considered.

The final step in bringing the collection to life is the photoshoot—where all elements come together into one cohesive, eye-catching brand story. It's a creative journey that results in a vibrant and memorable collection.

Collaborations and Patterns

Every season, *A fish named Fred* seeks out original collaborations to create unique, surprising items that enhance the collection's theme. These partnerships result in standout pieces that add even more fun and personality to our line. At the heart of every Fred product is a love of insane patterns. While they may look wild, each one is thoughtfully connected to the theme of the collection. This creative madness is part of what gives Fred its unique charm—and why our fans keep coming back.

—Rob Schalker
CEO, A fish named Fred

Part 5

Some Ideas for the Future

15

New Artificial Islands for Mumbai

Mumbai has a long history of land reclamation. In the past, almost all shallow parts of the sea surrounding Mumbai have been used to expand the city. However, with the continuously growing population, we think Mumbai should explore further land reclamation. Adding artificial islands to the city in the same way Dubai did may not be feasible, but there are other possibilities. According to Shell, gigantic offshore oil drilling rigs are now being constructed in the sea, with their foundations at 2,000 metres below sea level. Shell also operates floating oil drilling rigs. The sea surrounding Mumbai is about 500 metres deep. So if the foundation technology of oil drilling rigs could be used, Mumbai could potentially add artificial islands to the city. Building artificial islands in the deep sea is naturally more expensive than in shallow waters, so a feasibility study is needed. Artificial islands should be Monsoon-proof. Taiwan and Japan show how to build Monsoon- and typhoon-proof islands.

We are storytellers and men of ideas, and everything grand begins with an idea. We give you some food for thought in this final part of the book.

Flower Islands for Mumbai?

One of your authors, Vinco David, was the project leader for the Dutch credit insurance company Atradius for the creation of Dubai's Palm Islands from 2001 to 2007. Dutch companies Van Oord and Boskalis built the island, and Atradius insured it. Vinco's well-documented experience is valuable for India. We, the Dutch, are well-known for our expertise in land reclamation and the marine industry. We have done it in our own country—I live in the city of Almere, which was built on land reclaimed from the sea. We have also done it in Singapore and Dubai. So, why not in India? Mumbai is growing rapidly. Why don't we create a string of artificial islands in the sea off Mumbai? Indians love flowers and offer them to the gods, so we came up with the idea of Flower Islands, shaped like a bouquet of flowers. Think of Lotus Island, Sunflower Island, Tulip Island, Rose Island, Dahlia Island and many more. Mumbai can follow the Dutch experience in land reclamation to gain plenty of extra land for its growing population. The Flower Islands could also become a major tourist attraction.

I had so much fun working on the creation of Palm Islands in Dubai. It's energizing to be part of something so grand. I also previously shared the idea of creating food islands in the sea off the coasts of other Indian cities, such as my beloved Chennai and Kochi. We could name these islands Pineapple Island, Corn Island, Mango Island, Pork Island and more.

Twin Cities Mumbai–Dubai as the Financial Capital of the Global South

The authors welcome the idea of the UAE connecting Dubai and Mumbai with a superfast train, to be built in a tunnel beneath the seabed of the Arabian Sea. This would allow the two financial hubs to merge. The twin cities of Mumbai and Dubai should combine their city marketing strategies and brand themselves as the financial capital of the Global South. They could do so by persuading more tourists who visit Dubai to also include Mumbai in their travel itinerary. The hotel and tourism industry in Mumbai would become prosperous in this way.

Mumbai has a long history of land reclamation, and nearly all shallow coastal areas have already been utilized. But there is another option. Oil companies like Shell and Exxon build heavy oil platforms in the sea. They are either floating or rest on pillars extending up to 2,000 metres. A combination of pillars with floating structures is also used. We think that a feasibility study should be conducted in order to find out the possibility of building artificial islands off the coast of Mumbai using offshore engineering techniques. If it is feasible, then let's go for it!

The artificial islands for Mumbai are only one of the many bold ideas in this book. It took the Dutch only six years to build Palm Islands in Dubai. We could easily do the same in Mumbai, although this will take longer to ensure they are monsoon-proof. If construction were to start in 2026, the new islands could be inaugurated in the 2030s. This would give a boost of positive energy not only to Mumbai and Maharashtra, but to all of India. On one of these islands, we propose building an enormous iconic statue, about the size of New York's Statue of Liberty. This could become the symbol of Mumbai—a key feature of its city marketing.

Revived One of the Seven Wonders of the World: the Colossus of Rhodes

In our opinion, Mumbai needs a huge statue of about 150 metres in height to become its landmark. We could try to start from scratch, but why not use a bold idea that was never realized before? Ari A. Palla is an architect who led an international team of architects, engineers and economists to design a modern Colossus of Rhodes. The proposed colossus—although not a direct copy of the original—would be a 150-metre-tall museum and cultural centre, housing archaeological findings. The team's goal was to create a structure that would evoke the same emotions as the original 2,200-year-old statue. They planned to use solar panels to power the structure. The team included professionals from Greece, Spain, Italy and the United Kingdom. The design is brilliant, yet it was never built due to lack of funds. Why not purchase the design from this team, give it an Indian touch and build it on the new artificial islands in Mumbai?

Never-Built Top Designer Buildings

Many famous architects have designed stunning buildings that were never built for one reason or another. The famous Catalan architect Antoni Gaudí, who built the tourist magnet Sagrada Família, also designed a hotel for New York that was never constructed. India could buy this design and build the hotel on one of the new islands in Mumbai. It would definitely become a major attraction for the city.

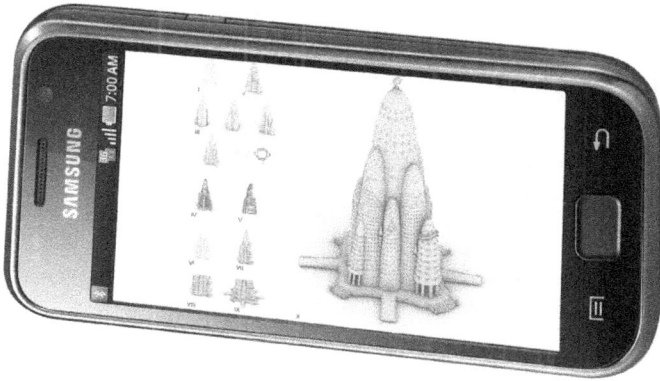

In the competition to build the UN Peace Palace in The Hague, many renowned architects submitted their design ideas. Only one won, but the runner-up was an Art Deco palace that was much more to our liking. Why not buy this particular design and build it on one of the new islands? It could become the second Taj hotel, as it exudes a similar ambience to the Taj Mahal Palace. Otherwise, the Oberoi or another hotel chain might want to use it as their property. Perhaps it could even serve as the new city hall of Mumbai, a museum or an apartment building.

In the competition for the design of the Eiffel Tower in Paris, many designers sent their ideas to the jury. Several great designs did not win, but we love them and believe they could easily be built on the new islands in Mumbai.

In the Soviet Union, many grand buildings were designed but never constructed. The stunning design by Boris Iofan in 1931 for the Palace of the Soviets was never realized. Why not build it now on one of the new islands in Mumbai?

How different Chicago's skyline would have looked if Santiago Calatrava's 2005 design had been built. Standing at 444 metres, this slender, twisted steel and glass tower, called the Chicago Spire, would have had a whole lot of style. The massive structure, covering 9,20,000 square feet, was planned to feature residential apartments, retail space and a five-star hotel, with each floor rotating 2° around a central core, turning 270° degrees through the height of the building. Now, it could be built on one of Mumbai's new islands.

The Badshahi Masjid (Emperor's Mosque) is a 17th-century mosque in Lahore, carved with sandstone and marble. Commissioned by Mughal emperor Aurangzeb in 1671, the mosque was completed two years later in 1673. At the time of its opening, the Badshahi Mosque was the world's largest mosque, reflecting the power and wealth of the Mughal Empire. We propose building a replica of this iconic mosque on the new islands in Mumbai. It is an integral part of both India's and Pakistan's history. India lost Lahore, including the original mosque, during the bloody Partition, but a replica on one of the new islands in Mumbai might serve as a soothing reminder. We predict that the mosque's stunning beauty would make it an attractive landmark. If Mumbai does not want it, the mosque could also be rebuilt in Agra.

The British architect Lutyens, who designed and built the beautiful New Delhi, also planned a cathedral that was never built. Now, Mumbai can finally build it on one of the new islands.

We propose that one of the islands be named the 'Island of the Gods'. The skyline should include the following:

- A stunning Hindu temple, in the style of the famous Meenakshi Amman Temple in Madurai
- The cathedral of Lutyens
- A Mughal-style mosque
- A Bahá'í temple
- A Buddhist temple
- A Sikh temple, in the style of the Golden Temple in Amritsar.
- A replica of the demolished Jewish temple in Jerusalem, Israel.

The image of these grand places of worship, standing peacefully side by side and surrounded by beautiful parks, will be shared by billions all over the world. It will symbolize the religious harmony that modern India strives for.

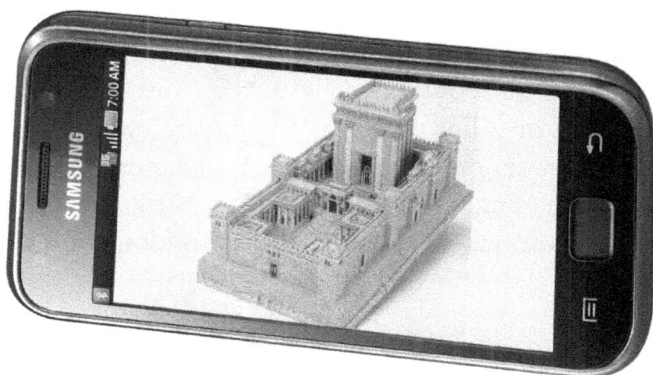

On our proposed Pork Island, we suggest building an enormous statue of Miss Piggy in Bollywood colours. In our home, we have a similar Dutch-Indian glass statue, created by a modern artist. Everybody loves it.

German architect Albert Speer designed the 'Volkshalle', which was never built. It could now be constructed on one of the new Mumbai islands as a theatre. Speer was a great architect, though his affiliation with the Nazis tainted his name. Both Nazi architecture and Mussolini-era architecture in Italy were impressive, and we think that they deserve a new chance. For instance, the railway station in Milan—a classic example of Mussolini-era architecture—is one of the most photographed buildings in the city today.

Many famous buildings have been destroyed by fire, earthquakes or other reasons. Why not rebuild the best of these lost jewels on the new artificial islands of Mumbai? Imagine the Singer Building in New York, which could become a luxurious hotel or apartment building for Mumbai.

Other fascinating structures that could be rebuilt on these islands include the Wabash Terminal in Pittsburgh, the Crystal Palace in London, the Second Imperial Hotel by architect Frank Lloyd Wright in Tokyo, the Federal Coffee Palace in Melbourne and the New Elbe Bridge in Germany. Sheikh Mohammed bin Rashid Al Maktoum of Dubai was incredibly visionary when he conceived the idea of artificial islands at the beginning of his rule, when most of Dubai was still desert. Many people at the time thought that he had lost his mind. He asked the Dutch to help him turn his dream into reality, and today, he is widely praised as a great leader. We sincerely hope that Maharashtra's current governor, the honourable Mr C.P. Radhakrishnan, who was appointed in 2024, will embrace this idea during his first five-year term so that it can be realized in his second term, should he be re-elected. In doing so, he might become an early reincarnation of the visionary sheikh of Dubai. Of course, the project would be expensive, but we believe this would be a solid investment for pension funds, institutional investors, banks, real estate developers and other stakeholders in India and the Netherlands. Don't forget: the future belongs to those who prepare for it today.

Babies in Artificial Wombs

Science communicator Hashem Al-Ghaili predicts that soon, babies could be conceived in ways other than the natural biological process. For example, women would be able to produce sperm cells from their skin cells, allowing two women to conceive a baby without men. Another possibility is babies growing in artificial wombs. As men would also be able to create egg cells from their skin cells, two men could conceive a baby without women. This revolution in conception and the growth of babies in artificial wombs could help end the current ageing process in Russia, China, Japan, South Korea and Europe. Millions of new babies could help balance the ageing and shrinking populations in these regions. However, one question remains: who will raise these babies? That is not answered yet.

Spreading Tourism and Preventing Overtourism

Overtourism is a severe problem in Europe. The renowned Louvre Museum in Paris welcomed 8.7 million tourists in 2024, even though it was originally designed to accommodate only 4 million visitors per year. The Louvre is expected to welcome 12 million visitors annually after the major renovation, which is scheduled to be completed by 2031. This indicates a 30 per cent increase from the museum's current annual attendance. It's only one example of the impact overtourism can have on top attractions.

India definitely has the potential to become one of the most attractive tourist destinations in the future. At present, most foreign tourists focus on the Golden Triangle of Delhi, Agra and Jaipur. However, the scorching heat combined with air pollution in the summer months is a major disadvantage.

India could create a second Golden Triangle for tourists in the South, for example, between Chennai, Hampi and Hyderabad. Hampi could be rebuilt and restored to its former glory, earning the same status as the Taj Mahal in the tourism industry. Hyderabad and its surroundings are also full of architectural wonders.

A third Golden Triangle for tourists could be formed between Kolkata, Bhubaneshwar and the tea plantations around Patna.

A fourth Golden Triangle could be between Mumbai, Kochi (and the rest of Kerala) and Mysore.

If the Indian tourist industry prepares for the distribution of tourists across these four Golden Triangles, it can prevent overtourism.

Relocating the United Nations Headquarters from New York to Mumbai

After the end of World War II, the newly established United Nations made a real estate deal with the US to establish its headquarters in New York. However, the buildings of the UN headquarters are too large, outdated and unsuitable for modern times, when working from home (WFH), hybrid working and remote working have become the new normal. The UN and the US are now considering relocating the current headquarters. Some sources name Dubai or Singapore as potential alternatives, but why can't Mumbai make a bid?

Rebuilding Dwarka

The ancient Indian city of Dwarka is known in Hindu culture as the great and beautiful city of Krishna. Hindu writings state that when Krishna left the Earth to join the spiritual world, the age of Kali began, and Dwarka, along with its inhabitants, was submerged by the Arabian Sea. It is considered a holy pilgrimage site in Hinduism and is mentioned in the epic *Mahabharata*.

Archaeologists believe they have found evidence of the city's existence off the coast of modern-day Dwarka and are looking for the foundations of the city walls. Archaeological evidence from the site confirms the existence of a city-state. Dwarka in Sanskrit meant 'Gateway to Heaven'. This beautiful city is said to have housed 9,000 palaces constructed with crystal and silver and decorated with emeralds. The city was connected by roads and had marketplaces, temples, huge assembly halls, gardens and lakes.

Many artefacts and structures found at the site suggest that the city of Dwarka may have existed around 9,000 years ago, after which the city was rebuilt at least seven times. The archaeologists believe that the city was submerged sometime around BC 2,000 due to heavy flooding over a period of time. This date coincides with the end of the Dvapara Yuga and the death of Krishna, as described in the ancient texts like the *Mahabharata, Harivamsa, Matsya Purana* and *Vayu Purana*. Other scriptures, such as the *Shrimad Bhagavad Gita, Skand Purana* and *Vishnu Purana* also talk about the beautiful city of Dwarka, which existed during Lord Krishna's time and was a place of great significance. Several pieces of evidence and excavations suggest that various civilizations flourished in the area, dating back to BC 15 century.

With the help of AI, we can now have a better idea of what Dwarka looked like during the time when the Vedas were written. We are deeply impressed by the look of this mythical city and believe that people should have the opportunity to explore its palaces again in the 21st century—this time, through replicas to be built on the new artificial islands in Mumbai.

Co-author Vinco David was at the time working for the Dutch credit insurer Atradius. After learning of this city of Krishna, he personally intervened to end this harbour project. Atradius refused credit insurance, and without credit insurance, such a project was no longer feasible.

Expanding megacities through land reclamation is not only an option for Indian coastal cities like Mumbai, but also for rapidly growing African coastal cities, such as Lagos in Nigeria.

THE NLR: TOWARDS THE END OF LEPROSY

Leprosy still exists today, impacting the most marginalized communities. Every two minutes, someone is diagnosed, often facing stigma, social isolation and lost opportunities. Disabilities caused by leprosy fuel discrimination, primarily due to a lack of awareness. Yet, this is entirely preventable.

Leprosy is curable. It can even be prevented. With warmth and respect, we can support those affected. With knowledge and collaboration, we can eradicate it within a generation—our generation. After centuries, we are on the brink of eliminating leprosy. Join us in achieving this goal.

Who We Are

For over 50 years, NLR has been a driving force in leprosy prevention, leading research and implementing innovative solutions. We are committed to stopping leprosy transmission by 2040. Major breakthroughs in preventive treatment bring hope that this goal is within reach. Ending leprosy means future generations will no longer suffer as their ancestors did.

Working alongside partners in Mozambique, India, Indonesia, Nepal, Brazil, and beyond, NLR is part of international networks such as the Global Partnership for Zero Leprosy and the International Federation of Anti-Leprosy Associations (ILEP). Together, we are making significant strides towards a leprosy-free world.

Making a Difference in India

NLR India, based in New Delhi, is an ISO 9001:2015 certified non-profit, non-religious, and non-governmental organization dedicated to supporting persons affected by leprosy, Neglected Tropical Diseases (NTDs) and Persons With Disabilities (PWDs). Since 1999, NLR India has been a key player in the National

Leprosy Eradication Programme (NLEP), working towards Zero Transmission, Zero Disability and Zero Exclusion.

NLR India focuses on Health, Education, Livelihood, Empowerment, and Research to create sustainable change.

For more information, visit nlrindia.org

Making a Difference in Nigeria

From 1978 to 2017, NLR operated in Nigeria, later transitioning into the independent Leprosy and TB Relief Initiative Nigeria (LTR). LTR remains committed to leprosy and tuberculosis control, partnering with NLR to work towards a leprosy-free world.

Through the Ready4PEP project, we are implementing SDR-PEP, a preventive treatment to stop leprosy transmission in Nigeria. By focusing on active case finding, geographic mapping, capacity building for health workers, and medication distribution, we aim to interrupt the spread of leprosy.

In collaboration with the Nigerian government and key partners, we are integrating SDR-PEP into national leprosy control programmes, improving care and reducing transmission.

For more information, visit ltrnigeria.org

Together, we will continue until **No Leprosy Remains**.

—**Stephen Labib**
International Communications Advisor & Brand Manager

16

New Artificial Islands in the Sea off the Coast of Lagos, Nigeria

Lagos, like Mumbai, was founded on islands. Over the centuries, the city has expanded to its current size of 17 million residents, with an area of 1,170 sq km. It is one of the most densely populated cities in the world. The population of Lagos is projected to be over 40 million by 2050, making it the sixth-largest city in the world. In order to prepare for this growth, we propose two grand ideas. The first is a typical Dutch one, since both of us are Dutch.

We propose that Van Oord and Boskalis, backed by the credit insurer Atradius, build 12 new Palm-like islands off the coast of Lagos. This would allow the city to expand into the sea. These new artificial islands can be used to make the city more attractive to tourists. With tourism booming in the 21st century, Nigeria has the potential to become a prime tourist destination. Following the example of Dubai, these islands could create artificial beaches for resorts, hotels and restaurants. Additionally, the islands could feature attractive museums, theatres, cinemas, operas and similar venues for musicals, ballet, modern dance shows and cabaret. Replicas of ancient palaces, such as those from Edo, could also be built. Nollywood, Nigeria's movie industry, could be concentrated on one of these new islands.

Senegal's capital Dakar has a giant statue built by North Korea, which functions as the iconic landmark of this vibrant city. Lagos too needs something similar. Therefore, we propose that a grand statue be erected on one of these islands, designed by one of Nigeria's greatest artists, such as Yinka Shonibare, whose artwork we greatly admire. His installation *The Last Supper Exploded* at the Lisser Art Museum (LAM) in the famous flower garden of Keukenhof in the Netherlands attracts huge crowds. With such an iconic, huge statue—maybe almost the size of the Statue of Liberty—Lagos could further establish itself as the cultural capital of Africa.

A Corridor from Lagos to Ibadan

Here is our second idea: we propose the creation of a 130-kilometre-long corridor between Lagos and Ibadan. The current Expressway 1 could become a huge 10-lane highway, combined with a train track for superfast trains, which would cover the distance between Lagos city centre and Ibadan city centre in just 20 minutes.

Along this corridor, 20 new satellite cities could be built, each housing one million Nigerians. India has done the same along a corridor between Mumbai and Delhi. With superfast trains and small electric drone-like planes, people within the corridor and Lagos could travel between the cities. The current slums in Lagos could also be demolished and replaced with affordable housing for the poor. Similarly, in the satellite cities along the corridor, affordable housing could be implemented, along with many new factories to create employment opportunities. This way, the city would not only grow in terms of quantity but also in quality.

The quality of life in Greater Lagos should improve for all its citizens as well as for tourists and expats. The city should be green, with plenty of trees, lanes, parks and plants. Green buildings should become the new standard in every megacity. With Dutch expertise, Lagos could take the lead in this megatrend for Africa.

Religion in Africa in the 21st century

Today, Africa is one of the most religious continents on Earth. This has both advantages and disadvantages. On the positive side, belief in God or gods who look after people provides hope, courage and comfort in times of illness, setbacks, death and grief. However, the ongoing conflict between Christianity and Islam in Africa is risky and has negative consequences. The Islamic fundamentalists of Iran are financing Islamist uprisings, terrorism, massacres and civil wars across Africa. The terrorists of Islamic State have strong bases in Somalia, Mali and Congo. They have created a bloody civil war in northern Nigeria, which has lasted for many years with no resolution in sight.

Christianity in Africa, on the other hand, is now dominated by extremely conservative, hate-spreading American evangelicals. In their megachurches spread all over the continent, they preach hatred towards homosexual Africans, who fear for their lives in countries like Uganda. They also face aggression in countries such as Nigeria, despite Nollywood's promotion of diversity and tolerance in its movies and TV series nowadays. The evangelicals' hatred towards homosexuals in these countries stands in sharp contrast to the tolerant environment in South Africa, where Nelson Mandela's government introduced same-sex marriage after the end of Apartheid.

#Forwardism for Afr ca

We are no longer living in a *Time of Change* but in a *Change of Time*.

- Due to AI-driven education, every African child could soon have Einstein as their teacher.
- Africa has the youngest population of any continent.
- Finally, Africa can use its huge demographic dividend in an ageing world.
- The BRICS countries are leading the Global South towards new prosperity.
- India's airline IndiGo could create a budget airline for entire Africa: AfriGo.
- With airships, more efficient mining would be feasible even in the most remote areas.
- All wars would eventually end at the negotiating table.
- A tunnel on the seabed between Nigeria and Brazil would connect these two giants. With a superfast train in this tunnel, one would be able to travel between Lagos and Rio de Janeiro in just a few hours.
- The twin cities of Lagos and Rio de Janeiro could become the pleasure capitals of the world. In these lively beach cities, there would be a creative blending of Carnaval, Nollywood, art, fashion, literature, music, samba, Burna Boy and jollof.
- China and India could build millions of factories across Africa.
- If Nigeria were to rebuild Benin City—the kingdom of the ancient Edo—it could eventually become the 'Taj Mahal of Nigeria'. This would boost Nigeria's tourism and enhance the country's image on the

global stage. As a result, better-paying jobs would be created for aspiring young Africans.
- A new Silk Road would connect EurAfrica with EurAsia.
- Electric planes would further develop into flying buses and flying taxis, connecting every village in Africa.
- Elon Musk's SpaceX could provide all of Africa with superfast 6G internet. Remote working can become accessible to every African. Work from home on the global labour market could become a reality.
- With the help of artificial intelligence, Africa could finally free itself from bureaucratic rot and outdated Victorian laws. Sexual freedom for every African would become the new normal.

Africa could thus enter the Economy of Happiness: the Happynomy.

Marriage of Seven Years

Until the 19th century, the average human lifespan was around 40 years. If someone met the love of their life at the age of 25, they'd be together for a maximum of 15 years. That seems doable. But soon, we will live to be 100 and one could live with the same spouse for 75 years. On top of that, their mother-in-law could also reach 100! The concept of marriage was conceived in a radically different time and age. We think that it will change tremendously in the 21st century. Many couples stay happily together until their death, but many others divorce or have affairs, with or without their spouse's knowledge. This can work for some, not for everyone. Open marriages can work as well, as we often see in France, where women's liberation started right after the end of World War I. Many young men had died, so one man could have affairs with several women at the same time. Society accepted this. This might happen again in Ukraine and Russia after the Ukraine war ends.

Towards Self-Actualization

Self-actualization is at the top of Maslow's hierarchy of needs. This need refers to the desire to reach our full potential. According to Maslow, it can only be fulfilled once all the other needs have been met. In our opinion, this need is about knowing yourself, your place, your identity and how to feel happy, thankful and content. It aligns with the Economy of Happiness or Happynomy.

Diversity Rules

'Being diverse is not optional; it is what we must be.' In 2012, Lloyd Blankfein, the then-chairman and CEO of Goldman Sachs, embodied this principle when he became the Human Rights Campaign's first national corporate spokesperson for same-sex marriage, placing him among the first Fortune 500 CEOs to publicly support this issue. The Jewish, straight banker Blankfein was not into 'pinkwashing'. He is a man who puts his money where his mouth is.

'I'm Lloyd Blankfein...and I support marriage equality.' These were the words used by him in a video spot produced by the Human Rights Campaign, a national organization that advocates equal rights for gays, lesbians, bisexuals and transgender people in the US. Apart from that, Blankfein also personally lobbied for marriage equality with the then-US president Barack Obama and members of the Parliament. Goldman Sachs and its rivals heavily recruit gay and lesbian applicants, and in cities like New York and London, there are even interbank mixers where young male traders with similar tastes can drink together.

Compared to other elite fields, such as politics and law, finance has adapted in ways we shouldn't underestimate. So it's not really surprising that the CEO of Goldman, which had already endorsed the eternally stalled Employment Non-Discrimination Act, has supported gay rights. The financial industry in Europe is similarly very gay-friendly.

One of the reasons for this is practical. Gay men and lesbian women are either single or have one partner and no kids; they are the so-called 'DINK-ies' (Double Incomes, No Kids). Without such responsibilities, they are much more flexible to travel and pursue careers. They also bring their own humour and creativity to the workplace, which is very beneficial. Moreover, they teach banks and insurance companies how to change their marketing strategies to appeal more to economically important consumer groups, such as gays and lesbians. Co-author Vinco David, openly gay since he was 18, made a successful career in the global credit insurance industry. His sexual identity enabled him to travel more often than his colleagues, who had wives and children to care for at home. We thus hope for the 'Blankfeinization' of Indian bankers and other business leaders. Diversity is good business, dear readers.

Windians

Indian culture is appealing to many white people, leading to a growing trend of 'Windians'—Westerners who embrace Indian traditions, attire and customs. Even Queen Máxima of the Netherlands loves to wear Indian-inspired dresses. In Britain, the Netherlands, and beyond, white individuals who marry Indians often adopt elements of Indian culture, especially during wedding celebrations.

In India, too, mixed-cultural weddings are on the rise. Many Indian brides and grooms with foreign partners choose to have both a Western-style wedding abroad and a traditional Indian ceremony at home. More often than not, the white partner enthusiastically dons Indian attire for the occasion.

Beyond weddings, Indian cuisine continues to gain popularity worldwide, particularly in the UK, where it has long been a staple. So we expect more Windians in the future. They are good ambassadors for India.

Dancing with Change and Fluidity

Our friend, thinker, author and former Dutch police commissioner Hans Schönfeld advocates that we humans must learn to dance with change and fluidity, as the world will continue to become more fluid every passing day.

At the end of his remarkable career, Hans Schönfeld reflects in his book, *Dancing with Change & Fluidity, From Organization to Organizing,* on a theme that is more relevant than ever: fluidity. This concept, which stands for the blurring of boundaries, has significant implications for both individuals and organizations. Boundaries that were once fixed—whether social, organizational, biological or technological—are becoming increasingly fluid, leading to far-reaching consequences.

Schönfeld bridges the gap between theory and practice, making fluidity both recognizable and manageable. How can leaders respond to this dynamic? What skills are essential in a world of constant change? Schönfeld provides practical tools and concludes with 10 commandments for leaders, encouraging them to embrace fluidity rather than resist it.

This book is an indispensable guide for anyone who wants to learn, adapt and keep pace with the times. Whether you are an experienced leader or a newcomer to change, this book offers valuable insights and inspiration. Some ideas in this book are a bit wild. The author predicts that in the future, each one of us can live half their life as a man and the other half as a woman and vice versa. We will see.

Towards Woven Cities

In the past, cities were woven and interwoven. Everything— homes, shops, workshops, food stores, bakeries, farms, government offices, banks and more—was all interwoven with one another. Many buildings served multiple functions simultaneously. Later on, modern city planning completely changed the concept of the 'woven city'. We witnessed the rise of shopping malls, financial districts, government districts and housing districts— all separated from one another. However, in the 24-hour city, where there is a significant level of activity and accessibility to services like restaurants, shops, transport and entertainment available around the clock, everything operates 'all day and night'. This city model is often associated with a vibrant nightlife and diverse economic activity across different time zones.

The 15-minute city (FMC), or 15mC, is the urban planning concept where most daily necessities and services—such as work, shopping, education, healthcare and leisure—can be easily accessed by a 15-minute walk, bike ride or public transport from any point in the city. This approach aims to reduce car dependency, promote healthy and sustainable living and improve the well-being and quality of life for city dwellers.

Implementing the 15-minute city concept requires a multidisciplinary approach, involving transport planning, urban design and policymaking to create well-designed public spaces, pedestrian-friendly streets and mixed-use developments. This change in lifestyle may include remote working, which reduces daily commuting and is supported by the widespread availability of information and communication technology. The concept has been described as a 'return to a local way of life'.

As people spend more time working from home or near their homes, the demand for large central office spaces decreases, while the need for flexible, local co-working spaces increases. The 15-minute city concept suggests a shift towards a decentralized network of workspaces within residential neighbourhoods, reducing the need for long commutes and promoting work-life balance.

With the rise of the 24-hour city and 15-minute city concepts, the woven city of the past returns, albeit in a different form. The city of the future will be an interwoven city.

Cricket Tourism, Football Tourism and Olympics Tourism

Cricket is extremely popular throughout the British Commonwealth, with many people travelling to see live matches. Cricket tourism will therefore become a rapidly growing economic pillar in India. If people want to see live cricket championship games, they will likely combine this with leisure activities such as shopping, visiting museums and more.

The FIFA World Cup is a major sports event. Qatar successfully used the 2022 FIFA World Cup to market itself to the world, and now everybody knows about Qatar. Saudi Arabia will host the FIFA World Cup in 2034 and use it as a tool to revitalize the country's image.

Similarly, China used the Beijing 2008 Summer Olympics to introduce itself to the world as a new superpower. Maybe, one day, India might host one of these global events. However, it's important to note that such a venture is incredibly costly.

Death Isn't Something that's Only Felt by Humans—It's Universal

Hashem Al-Ghaili writes: 'When a crow spots another dead crow, it calls out to alert others, and soon a whole group gathers around the deceased. They'll hang out, cawing and trying to figure out what happened. It's like they're trying to learn from the unfortunate event and avoid the same fate. Scientists have been studying this crow behaviour, and they've found that crows are actually quite good at recognizing danger. In one experiment, researchers had people wear masks and carry around dead crows. The crows quickly learnt to associate those masks with danger and would scold the masked individuals even weeks later. They even figured out how to use drones to study this behaviour! It turns out that seeing a dead crow really gets a crow's brain working. Brain imaging studies have shown that it activates the parts of their brains responsible for complex decision-making. So, while we don't know exactly what they're thinking, we know they're definitely thinking hard. This crow behaviour has also sparked some interesting questions about how humans deal with death. Crows are social creatures like us, and they live in communities where they interact with each other regularly. Some scientists believe that studying crow behaviour could give us clues about how our own death rituals evolved. Crows are incredibly smart birds. They can solve problems, remember faces and even hold grudges. They've been observed bending wires to make tools, and they can even learn to communicate with humans using simple symbols.'

Using AI, we can already understand the language of chickens and learn from them. Perhaps, in the future, AI will help us understand the languages of crows, dogs, elephants and other animals. Maybe it will lead us to treat them better.

50 Million Young Indians Could Migrate Legally to Southern Europe

Not all young Indians will choose to stay in India. For decades, many have dreamed of migrating to America—legally or illegally—often risking their lives along the dangerous Panama route and paying exorbitant sums to human traffickers. However, with President Donald Trump deporting illegal immigrants back to India, a new and far more promising alternative has emerged.

Southern Europe is ageing faster than the rest of the continent. Rural areas in Italy, Spain, Portugal, and France are now largely abandoned, with only a few elderly residents remaining as younger generations migrate to the cities. As a result, these countries are offering a remarkable opportunity: in many villages, you can buy a house with land for as little as €1.

Granted, these houses have been unoccupied for years and require renovation. Plumbing and electrical systems may be outdated, but with countless YouTube tutorials and online courses, learning to fix them is within reach. Imagine a group of young Indians coming together to buy and restore an entire village, creating a new life in the picturesque European countryside.

If you work remotely in IT, editing, or other digital fields, you can settle in these areas while enjoying a lower cost of living. Alternatively, you can grow your own vegetables, start a family or earn extra income by renting out rooms on Airbnb—a lucrative option given Southern Europe's ever-thriving tourism industry.

For those seeking employment, the region has countless job vacancies in tourism and healthcare. There is a constant demand for nurses, doctors, paramedics, chefs, waiters, bartenders, bus drivers, and tour guides. Portugal, in particular, has simplified its immigration process for Indians and Nepalis, making it easy to live and work there legally. After just five years, you can obtain Portuguese citizenship.

During our recent trip to Portugal's Algarve region, we witnessed first-hand the Indianization and Nepalization of the country's tourism industry—all done legally, without the risks of human trafficking. Young Indians have a golden opportunity to work, save money, and either return home financially secure or settle in Southern Europe long-term.

Of course, learning the local language is essential, but Indians are naturally multilingual. With AI-powered language learning tools and free online courses in Italian, Portuguese, French or Spanish, adapting to a new country has never been easier.

Time Travel Turns into Reality

The use of the 'communicator' in science fiction TV series such as *Star Trek* in the 1970s inspired the development of the mobile phone. The first flying car was also seen in science fiction movies. Time travel is another concept introduced by the writers of science fiction books and films. We remember from our youth the famous Belgian series *Suske en Wiske*, featuring Professor Barabas, who created a 'Time Machine' that allowed people to travel back in time. We loved it! The first two parts of the American movie *Back to the Future* were also impressive.

But what if these fantasies could be turned into reality? What if technology could enable us to travel back in time? Maybe to the time of our parents' youth? To the time of ancient Egypt during the reign of the pharaohs, over 5,000 years ago? Or to the time of ancient Indian cities like Dwarka, which existed around 9,000 years ago?

Scientist Hashem Al-Ghaili writes: 'While time travel

has long been considered science fiction, physicists Ben Tippett from the University of British Columbia and David Tsang from the University of Maryland have proven it could be mathematically possible. Using Einstein's General Relativity, the duo developed a theoretical model for a time machine they call the TARDIS, short for Traversable Acausal Retrograde Domain in Space-time (yes, it's a play on *Doctor Who*). Their concept suggests that time, like space, can curve under the influence of massive objects, creating a circular path that allows passengers to move forwards and backwards in time. However, the leap from theory to reality faces significant hurdles. Tippett and Tsang's TARDIS requires "exotic matter"—a hypothetical material capable of bending space-time in unprecedented ways—which has yet to be discovered. Some researchers also argue that time travel may never be possible due to the intimate connection between time and energy or the notion that the future doesn't yet exist. While a physical time machine remains out of reach, Tippett believes exploring the nature of space-time is vital, stating, "Studying space-time is both fascinating and problematic". Whether or not we ever traverse time, the pursuit of understanding continues to expand the boundaries of human knowledge.'

So let's keep exploring, and maybe one day we can find out for ourselves what it was like to live thousands of years ago.

We are pretty sure that humanity will discover soon enough that we are not the only ones in the universe. Aliens will either become our friends or foes, sooner or later. Maybe they are already among us but we cannot see them yet. Not believing in aliens is like taking a spoonful of water from the ocean and saying, 'There are no whales in the ocean because there are none in my spoon'.

As Danish philosopher Søren Kierkegaard once remarked: 'Life can only be understood backwards, but it must be lived forwards.' So live forward, dear readers, and enjoy your life. It will be over before you know it.

Bibliography

1. Arntz, M., T. Gregory and U. Zierahn, 'The Risk of Automation for Jobs in OECD Countries: A Comparative Analysis', *OECD Social, Employment and Migration Working Papers*, No. 189, OECD Publishing, Paris, 2018.
2. Autor, D.H., 'Polanyi's Paradox and the Shape of Employment Growth', *NBER Working Paper*, No. 20485, September 2014.
3. Bakas, A., *Plenty. Megatrends water, energie, grondstoffen en duurzaamheid*, Scriptum, Schiedam, 2013.
4. Bakas, A., *The State of Tomorrow*, Dexter, Amsterdam, 2013.
5. Bakas, A., *Megatrends Werk*, Bakas Books, Amsterdam, 2014.
6. Bakas, A., *Capitalism and Slowbalization. The Market, the State and the Crowd in the 21st Century*, Bakas Books, Amsterdam, 2015.
7. Ball, P., 'Reproduction revolution: how our skin cells might be turned into sperm and eggs', *The Observer*, 14 October 2018.
8. Barber, G., 'San Francisco could be the first to ban facial recognition tech', *Wired*, 31 January 2019.
9. Berg, A., et al., 'Should We Fear the Robot Revolution (The Correct Answer Is Yes)', *IMF Working Paper*, WP18/116, IMF, New York, 2018.
10. Brynjolfsson, E., and A. McAfee *Race against the machine. How the digital revolution is accelerating innovation, driving productivity, and irreversibly transforming employment and the economy*, ebook, Digital Frontier Press, Lexington, 2011.
11. Brynjolfsson, E., and A. McAfee, *The second machine age. Work, progress and prosperity in a time of brilliant technologies*, W.W. Norton & Company, New York, 2014.
12. Dekker, F., A. Salomons and J. van der Waal, 'Fear of Robots at Work: The Role of Economic Self-Interest', in: *Socio-Economic Review*, 15–3, pp. 539–562, 2017.
13. De Wachter, D., *Borderline Times. Het einde van de normaliteit*, Lannoo Campus, Leuven, 2012.

14. Dimension Data, *The Digital Workplace Report: Transforming Your Business. Understanding the Trends that Are Driving the Workplace Evolution*, Dimension Data, Johannesburg, 2017.

15. Dolgin, E., 'Making Babies: How to create human embryos with no egg or sperm', *The New Scientist*, 11 April 2018.

16. Durden, T., 'The Wealth of the 12 Richest Davos Billionaires Has Increased by $175 Billion in Ten Years', www.zerohedge.com, 1 January 2019.

17. Durden, T., 'China responds to George Soros', www.zerohedge.com, 27 January 2019.

18. Fergusson, M., 'In Solitude What Happiness?', *The Economist*, February–March 2018.

19. Freedland, J., 'The Road to Somewhere by David Goodhart—A Liberal's Rightwing Turn on Migration', *The Guardian,* 22 March 2017.

20. Frey, C.B. and M.A. Osborne, *The Future of Employment: How Susceptible Are Jobs to Computerisation*, Oxford University, Oxford, 2013.

21. Gilovich, T., et al., 'A Wonderful Life: Experiential Consumption and the Pursuit of Happiness', in: *Journal of Consumer Psychology*, 25, 1, pp. 152–165, January 2015.

22. Goldman, D. P., *How Civilizations Die (And Why Islam Is Dying Too)*, Regnery Publishing, Washington, 2011.

23. Gordon, L., 'Feeding the Ten Billion', *Project Syndicate*, 1 February 2019.

24. Greenhill, K.M., *Weapons of Mass Migration: Forced Displacement, Coercion, and Foreign Policy*, Cornell University Press, Ithaca, 2011.

25. Guilluy, C., *No Society. La fin de la classe moyenne occidentale*, Flammarion, Paris, 2018.

26. Harari, Y. N., *Sapiens: A Brief History of Humankind*, Harvill Secker, London, 2014.

27. Harari, Y.N., *Homo Deus: A Brief History of Tomorrow*, Harvill Secker, London, 2016.

28. Heinsohn, G., *Söhne und Weltmacht. Terror im Aufstieg und Fall der Nationen*, Orell Füssli Verlag, Zürich, 2003.

29. Helliwell, J., et al., *World Happiness Report 2017*, SDSN, New York, 2017.

30. Keynes, J.M., 'Economic Possibilities for our Grandchildren', *Essays in Persuasion*, pp. 321–332, Palgrave Macmillan, London, 2010.

31. Khanna, P., *The Future Is Asian: Commerce, Conflict, and Culture in the Twenty-First Century*, Simon and Schuster, 2019.
32. Klinenberg, E., *Going Solo. The Extraordinary Rise and Surprising Appeal of Living Alone*, The Penguin Press, New York, 2012.
33. McKinsey & Company, *Shaping the Future of Work in Europe's Digital Front-Runners. Digitally-Enabled Automation and Artificial Intelligence*, McKinsey & Company, 2017.
34. Mishra, P., *The Age of Anger. A History of the Present*, Farrar, Straus and Giroux, New York, 2017.
35. Moïsi, D., *The Geopolitics of Emotion: How Cultures of Fear, Humiliation, and Hope Are Reshaping the World*, Anchor Books, New York, 2010.
36. Molteni, M., 'The World Might Actually Run Out of People', *Wired*, 4 February 2019.
37. Murray, D., *The Strange Death of Europe: Immigration, Identity, Islam*, Bloomsbury Publishing, London, 2017.
38. Nedelkoska, L. and G. Quintini, *Automation, Skills Use and Training*, OECD, Paris, 2018.
39. Paul, M., *Don't Fear the Robots. Why Automation Doesn't Mean the End of Work*, Roosevelt Institute, New York, 2018.
40. Pfeffer, J., *Dying for a Paycheck. How Modern Management Harms Employee Health and Company Performance*, HarperCollins, New York, 2018.
41. Pinker, S., *Enlightenment Now. The Case for Reason, Science, Humanism and Progress*, Viking Press, New York, 2018.
42. PWC, *Workforce of the Future. The Competing Forces Shaping 2030*, PWC, 2017.
43. Rahim, S., 'Interview: Pankaj Mishra—The inner turmoil that fuels terrorism', *Prospect*, 7 February 2017.
44. Ridley, M., 'My life as a climate lukewarmer', www.rationaloptimist.com, 20 January 2015.
45 Schönfeld, J. J. (Hans), *Dancing with Change and Fluidity: From Organization to Organizing*, Inspinity, Amsterdam, 2025.
46. Taleb, N.N., *The Black Swan. The Impact of the Highly Improbable*, Random House, New York, 2007.
47. Taleb, N.N., *Skin in the Game. Hidden Asymmetries in Daily Life*, Random House, New York, 2018.
48. Twenge, J.M., *iGen: Why Today's Super-Connected Kids Are Growing Up Less Rebellious, More Tolerant, Less Happy—and Completely Unprepared for Adulthood—and What That Means for the Rest of Us*, Atria Books, New York, 2017.

49. Ward, G., 'Reflective Leaders Needed in the Age of Rage', INSEAD Knowledge, reprinted at www.kdvi.com, August 2016.
50. Watts, E.J., 'Mortal Republic: How Rome Fell into Tyranny', New York Journal of Books, www.nyjournalofbooks.com.
51. World Economic Forum, *The Future of Jobs Report 2018*, WEF, Geneva, 2018.
52. World Health Organization, *Depression and Other Common Mental Disorders. Global Health Estimates,* WHO, New York, 2017.